GUERRILLA WARFARE

The Stackpole Military History Series

THE AMERICAN CIVIL WAR

Cavalry Raids of the Civil War
Ghost, Thunderbolt, and Wizard
Pickett's Charge
Witness to Gettysburg

WORLD WAR II

Armor Battles of the Waffen-SS, 1943–45
Army of the West
Australian Commandos
The B-24 in China
Backwater War
The Battle of Sicily
Beyond the Beachhead
The Brandenburger Commandos
The Brigade
Bringing the Thunder
Coast Watching in World War II
Colossal Cracks
A Dangerous Assignment
D-Day to Berlin
Dive Bomber!
A Drop Too Many
Eagles of the Third Reich
Exit Rommel
Fist from the Sky
Flying American Combat Aircraft of
    World War II
Forging the Thunderbolt
Fortress France
The German Defeat in the East, 1944–45
German Order of Battle, Vol. 1
German Order of Battle, Vol. 2
German Order of Battle, Vol. 3
The Germans in Normandy
Germany's Panzer Arm in World War II
GI Ingenuity
The Great Ships
Grenadiers
Infantry Aces
Iron Arm
Iron Knights
Kampfgruppe Peiper at the Battle of
    the Bulge
Kursk
Luftwaffe Aces
Massacre at Tobruk

Mechanized Juggernaut or Military
    Anachronism?
Messerschmitts over Sicily
Michael Wittmann, Vol. 1
Michael Wittmann, Vol. 2
Mountain Warriors
The Nazi Rocketeers
On the Canal
Operation Mercury
Packs On!
Panzer Aces
Panzer Aces II
Panzer Commanders of the Western Front
The Panzer Legions
Panzers in Winter
The Path to Blitzkrieg
Retreat to the Reich
Rommel's Desert Commanders
Rommel's Desert War
The Savage Sky
A Soldier in the Cockpit
Soviet Blitzkrieg
Stalin's Keys to Victory
Surviving Bataan and Beyond
T-34 in Action
Tigers in the Mud
The 12th SS, Vol. 1
The 12th SS, Vol. 2
The War against Rommel's Supply Lines
War in the Aegean

THE COLD WAR / VIETNAM

Cyclops in the Jungle
Flying American Combat Aircraft:
    The Cold War
Here There Are Tigers
Land with No Sun
Street without Joy
Through the Valley

WARS OF THE MIDDLE EAST

Never-Ending Conflict

GENERAL MILITARY HISTORY

Carriers in Combat
Desert Battles
Guerrilla Warfare

GUERRILLA WARFARE

Irregular Warfare in the Twentieth Century

William Weir

STACKPOLE
BOOKS

Copyright © 2008 by William Weir

Published in paperback in 2008 by
STACKPOLE BOOKS
5067 Ritter Road
Mechanicsburg, PA 17055
www.stackpolebooks.com

Cover design by Tracy Patterson
Image of medal provided by the U.S. Army Heritage and Education Center

Printed in the United States of America

10 9 8 7 6 5 4 3 2 1

FIRST EDITION

ISBN 0-8117-3497-8 (Stackpole paperback)
ISBN 978-0-8117-3497-4 (Stackpole paperback)

The Library of Congress Cataloging-in-Publication Data:

Weir, William, 1928–
  Guerrilla warfare / William Weir.
    p. cm.
  Includes bibliographical references and index.
  ISBN 978-0-8117-3497-4
  1. Guerrilla warfare—History—20th century. 2. Military history,
  Modern—20th century. I. Title.
  U240.W38 2008
  355.02'180904—dc22

                                                              2008002323

Table of Contents

This one is for William.

Introduction

Much of the writing on guerrilla warfare is done by regular military officers. The reason, of course, is that regulars, like guerrillas, are primarily concerned with warfare. The trouble with that is that the regular and the guerrilla approach war from entirely different directions.

Regulars seem never to have lost the medieval idea that war is some kind of a game, although a bloody one. There are supposed to be rules about what combatants can do and not do. They must wear uniforms and must not only represent a nation-state, they must belong to an organization with hierarchical structure. During a guerrilla war, there are always complaints from regulars about the "unfairness" of fighting against an enemy who wears no uniform and blends into the civilian population. Presumably, it would be only fair if that enemy, armed with homemade bombs and mortars, low-power rifles and pistols, would "stand up and fight like men" against troops with tanks, machine guns, artillery, helicopter gunships, and fighter-bombers equipped with guided bombs and rockets.

Guerrillas typically see war as an effort to get rid of an unwelcome occupier, an effort that has only one rule—win. Guerrillas are almost always natives of the area, because they simply can't function without the support of the population where they are operating. Because they can't match the firepower—and usually, the training—of regulars, guerrillas avoid stand-up, knock-down battles. They hit the enemy where he is not prepared, and then they disappear. The ability to disappear is their main strength. They may do that by mingling with the civilian population, or they may be mobile enough to lose pursuers in miles of open space or in the depths of jungles. The last two alternatives have become increasingly limited as aerial surveillance becomes more effective, but irregular warriors are still using them.

Modern technology—satellites, drones, night-vision glasses, and precision-guided munitions, among other things—might be expected to make guerrilla warfare less effective. It apparently has not. The twentieth century produced as many guerrilla campaigns as any other hundred-year period, and a lot more than most. Most of the wars in the twentieth century were fought by irregulars, and almost all had an irregular component.

There are reasons for that. During the last century, nationalism spread all around the world, and weapons and communications equipment of unprecedented power became available to ordinary citizens. Further, many of those ordinary citizens no longer "knew their place." They refused to blindly follow traditional leaders, although they often followed nontraditional leaders like clerics who had previously stayed out of politics.

This is a good place to explain what we mean by guerrilla warfare. It's not terrorism. According to *Webster's Encyclopedic Unabridged Dictionary of the English Language* (New York: Gramercy Books, 1989), a terrorist is "1. a person who uses or favors terrorizing methods; 2. (formerly) a member of a political group in Russia aiming at the demoralization of the government by terror; 3. an agent or partisan of the revolutionary tribunal during the Reign of Terror in France." Before the government decided that everyone fighting us in Iraq is a terrorist, a terrorist was commonly thought to be someone who tried to kill a large number of people in a spectacular way to draw attention to a cause. Timothy McVeigh, who blew up the federal building in Oklahoma City, was a terrorist. The 9/11 hijackers were terrorists. So were the IRA (Irish Republican Army) and ETA (Basque Separatist Organization) operatives who bombed innocent civilians. But that statement demands qualification.

The line between terrorists and guerrillas is blurry. Soldiers, both regular and irregular, commit acts of terrorism. The carpet bombing of cities during World War II was the most egregious practice of terrorism since Tamerlane had built his pyramids of skulls. But those airmen fought enemy airmen and braved antiaircraft fire while slaughtering civilians. And, of course, nations are never called terrorists. Only outlaws are. Many of the IRA men who set off bombs in England also fought British soldiers in Northern Ireland. Bombing civilians was a sideline for them. And, like all acts of terrorism (including carpet bombing) that sideline was an ineffective way of winning a war. The Algerian War of 1954 to 1962 was filled with terrorism of the worst kind, perpetrated by both the Algerians and the French. And as we'll see, the French terrorism, which dwarfed that of the Algerians, was totally counterproductive. But all these soldiers, Allies, Germans, Irish, British, French and Algerians, regulars and irregulars, were also fighting armed enemies. This book is about irregular soldiers who fight other soldiers, regular or irregular.

Incidentally, although it proclaims that it is fighting the "Global War on Terror," the U.S. government has never been interested in Irish or Basque terrorists. Nor in Japanese or Latin American terrorists, either. It certainly does not consider all Muslims to be terrorists. Chechens are Muslims, and some of them are terrorists. But Chechen Muslims are Russia's problem, not ours. Unless you consider the guerrillas we're fighting in Iraq to be terrorists, the U.S. government appears to have done less to fight terrorism than the British, the Spanish, or the Pakistanis.

Knowledge of guerrilla warfare—when it is effective and when it is not—is particularly important for Americans. The United States, by spending more on its military than most of the rest of the world combined, should be able to overwhelm any possible enemy in regular warfare. For some time into the future, it seems likely that the only wars we'll be fighting will be guerrilla wars.

And aside from understanding strategy and tactics, the study of guerrilla warfare is worthwhile because much of the world we live in was shaped by guerrilla warfare. The Russian Revolution, which began as a guerrilla affair, upset much of Europe. The Poles and the Finns took the opportunity to free themselves from Russian domination. Many German veterans became Bolsheviks and fought the right-wing *Freikorps*, which also sent some of its irregular troops to the Baltic to help the Estonians, Latvians, and Lithuanians break away from Russia. Czech and Slovak POWs in Russia formed a national army before they had a nation. The Czech Legion fought its way across Siberia to China—the longest fighting march since the time of Genghis Khan. Out of all this chaos, a crop of dictators emerged, the most important—and most evil—being Adolf Hitler and Joseph Stalin.

Another European dictator, Spain's Francisco Franco, rose to power because of the Rif War, a surprising demonstration of guerrilla strength in Morocco. That war was also a kind of wake-up call to Muslims in North Africa and the Middle East.

In Ireland, the Black and Tan War and the Civil War, during the same period as the Rif War, also had effects worldwide. The Irish showed how a small, weak nation could use low-intensity guerrilla warfare and high-intensity propaganda to win independence from a large, powerful nation. Their example inspired both Ho Chi Minh and the Algerian rebels.

A third, barely noticed, guerrilla war in a global backwater had effects we feel today. When Abdul Aziz ibn Sa'ud took the holy cities of Mecca and Medina from T. E. Lawrence's ally, King Hussein, he launched the puritanical Wahhabi sect on its campaign for spiritual conquest of the Muslim world.

Mao Zedong began his "protracted war" before the Japanese invaded China and continued it until after World War II. It resulted not only in Communist China, one of the emerging superpowers (with India) of the future, but also in a theory of guerrilla war followed around the world, notably by Fidel Castro and Vo Nguyen Giap.

Giap led his troops to victory over the French in Indochina, which became Vietnam, Cambodia, and Laos. The Vietnamese victory precipitated the Algerian War, which resulted in, among other things, a new French constitution. More important, it resulted in the Vietnam War, the longest-lasting

U.S. war and the first American defeat in history. Muslim puritanism, which could be traced back to ibn Sa'ud's campaigns, led to the Soviet Union's invasion of Afghanistan. That war led to the demise of the Soviet Union, the end of the Cold War, a vast increase in the heroin trade, a new civil war in Algeria, the creation of al Qaeda, and the current involvement of the United States in Afghanistan and Iraq.

PART I

Rehearsals for the Big Show

CHAPTER 1

Invisible Enemies:
The Boer War, 1899–1902

The Afrikaans-speaking Transvaal Republic won its virtual independence from Britain after the battle of Majuba Hill in 1881, a stunning military upset in which a bunch of farmers defeated some of the most experienced soldiers in the world. The Boers (Dutch for farmers), as the British called them, were innocent of drill and had no uniforms and almost no discipline, but they were expert marksmen and hunters who knew all about taking cover and concealment. And they had breech-loading rifles that let them use those skills on the battlefield.

But the Transvaal could not long continue the somewhat anarchic and financially irresponsible ways that caused British interference in the first place.

Then gold was discovered in Witwatersrand.

That changed everything in South Africa. The Transvaal was no longer an impoverished republic, and it was no longer isolated from the world. Thousands of gold-seekers from Europe and the Americas flooded into "the Rand." The shiny yellow metal also attracted the "gold bugs"—European, chiefly British, millionaires who bought up as much of the gold-bearing land as they could.

The most famous gold bug was Cecil Rhodes, a man with two main objectives in life—power for himself and the expansion of the British Empire. Which of these two was his prime interest is anybody's guess. Rhodes had come to South Africa from England to farm, but he became a diamond miner when the diamond rush to Kimberley began. He made a fortune, and eventually got a charter from Queen Victoria to form the British South Africa Company. The company's modest goal was to turn all of Africa below the Sahara into a British possession. The Germans, Portuguese, French, and Belgians blocked that ambition, but Rhodes's company did defeat the Matabeles, a nation with close ties to the Zulus, and took over a vast territory that became known as Rhodesia.

Rhodes saw the newly rich Transvaal as a prime target, and he saw a method to take that over. The foreign miners in the republic were the key.

To the native Afrikaners they were *uitlanders* who threatened to dominate the *volk*. So the volk made it difficult for them to get the vote. The uitlanders were unhappy, and Rhodes had journalists and other agents agitating for them to revolt. To trigger the revolt, he had one of his followers, Dr. Leander Starr Jameson, lead a party of Rhodesian Police (actually Rhodes's private army) into the Transvaal on December 29, 1895.

In spite of Majuba Hill, Rhodes greatly underestimated the military power of the Afrikaner republic. Jameson and his troops were quickly rounded up and lodged in jail.[1] But Jameson's raid enormously exacerbated tensions between the Transvaal and Britain.

The British high commissioner for Cape Colony, Sir Alfred Milner, shared Rhodes's ambition to Anglicize as much of Africa as possible. He particularly wanted to incorporate the two Afrikaner republics, the Transvaal and the Orange Free State, into a union of South Africa. The British colonial office wanted that, too, but they wanted it done without starting a war. So Milner, pressuring President Paul Kruger of the Transvaal to adopt a more liberal policy toward the uitlanders, became so unreasonable Kruger was convinced that the British meant to move into his country again. He decided on a preemptive war. Afrikaner troops would move into British territory, Cape Colony and Natal, and seize defensive positions. That, of course, was what Milner wanted. He could claim that the Boers started the war.

In many ways, the Transvaal was better prepared for war than it was in 1881. It had an agreement with the Orange Free State that both republics would fight together in the event of a conflict with Britain.

The armies of both republics were still composed of militia commandos. Whenever danger threatened, all the men between sixteen and sixty would gather to form a "commando" and elect officers. Each man would bring his own rifle, ammunition, and horses. The leader of a commando, a "commandant," commanded anywhere from 200 to 1,000 men. Smaller units, called "field cornetcies," could have between 150 to 200 men and were led by "field cornets." They were broken up into the smallest units, led by "corporals." Other soldiers were simply "burghers," or citizens. If a burgher didn't like an officer in what would normally be his unit, he was free to join another unit. If, during a battle, he thought he could do more good elsewhere, he was free to go there. The members of a commando had no discipline at all by European or American standards, and they received no pay. If a major war loomed, a number of commandos would join together under a "commandant general."

The Transvaal had made some improvements since the last clash with the British. It now had a small regular artillery force. The troops were better armed, too. The government had purchased artillery from Germany and France, including some of the latest products of France's Creusot factory.[2] It had also bought a large quantity of 7mm Mauser Model 1893 magazine rifles—the world's best military rifle at that time—and issued them to the commandos. Instead of a hodgepodge of privately owned rifles, almost all the troops had a standard rifle using the same ammunition. The Mauser cartridge was vastly superior in range and penetration to the old black powder cartridges the Transvaalers used at Majuba Hill.

The Transvaalers also obtained a few specimens of one ultramodern weapon, the Maxim one-pounder. This had been developed at the request of the British navy for an automatic cannon that battleships could use to defend against torpedo boats—small, fast steam launches armed with torpedoes. Maxim built a huge machine gun that could fire 37mm shells. The navy decided not to buy it, but the French did and used it in their colonial campaigns, where it acquired the nickname "pom-pom."[3] The performance of the pom-pom impressed the Afrikaners. The Boers were to use it as an antiartillery weapon. The exploding shells made it easy to see where they landed. When they were landing near an enemy gun, the Afrikaners would load the pom-pom with a twenty-five-round belt and cut loose. After the war started, the British army also adopted the pom-pom.

The Afrikaner commandos invaded Cape Colony from both the Transvaal and the Orange Free State. The Transvaalers also crossed the Drakensberg mountain range and the border of Natal, a relatively small colony on the southeast tip of Africa. The first collision of the British and the Boers was at Dundee, a small town in Natal. Gen. Penn Symons, commander of the Dundee garrison, attacked the Transvaalers directly with his infantry while he sent his cavalry on a wide sweep to take them in the rear. The cavalry ran right into the main body of Afrikaner riflemen, who emptied many of the saddles, surrounded the British, and captured the survivors. The infantry, in relatively close order, advanced on where they believed the Transvaal trenches to be. Because the Afrikaners were using repeating rifles with smokeless powder, their enemies seldom saw them. The British pushed on in spite of terrible losses. When they got too close for the Afrikaners' comfort, the burghers slipped back to the horses they had hidden in a draw, mounted, and rode to another ridge.

The tactics of the Afrikaners greatly resembled those of the American guerrillas during the Revolutionary War in the South. Like the Americans, they were all mounted riflemen, which made them far more mobile than the British forces, which included both infantry and cavalry. The big difference was that the South Africans had a far better weapon. The Mauser rifle was sighted for two thousand yards, considerably more than a mile. And it was reasonably accurate at that range. Its penetration was remarkable. During the Cuban revolt that preceded the Spanish-American War, a Spanish soldier fired a 7mm Mauser at an American filibuster, Frederick N. Funston, who later became an American general. (See Chapter 2.) The bullet passed entirely through Funston from side to side, hit a tree he was standing beside, passed completely through the tree, and killed a man standing on the other side of it. The Mauser was also fast. Loading a five-round clip took only a second or two, and a good rifleman could fire thirty aimed shots a minute. The British, of course, also had repeating rifles using smokeless powder. Their Lee Enfield and Lee Metford rifles had ten-round magazines that were loaded with two five-round clips. That made them marginally faster than the Mausers, but they were also somewhat less accurate.

The biggest British handicap was that, as in the first Boer War, their officers didn't know how to get the most from the weapons their troops had. Their troops still often fired volleys on command, instead of picking individual targets and firing when the sights were lined up. British infantry tactics had been copied from those of the German Army, which, after the Franco-Prussian War, had been considered the ne plus ultra of military forces.[4] An American military attaché, after observing German maneuvers in 1893, wrote:

> They evidently intend to handle their infantry in close lines in the next war. The average German private is not a person to be turned loose in a skirmish line and left to a certain degree to his own devices. . . . They prefer to lose men than to lose control of the officers over them.[5]

Richard Meinertzhagen, a British regular who served in both the Boer War and World War I, described how the infantry were taught to attack in 1899:

> Today we were taught how to assault an enemy position. The battalion moved forward in tight little bunches of about twenty men each, marvelous targets for modern riflemen and machine gunners, but the drill was splendid, shoulder to shoulder and perfect line. We should have been annihilated long before we reached the assaulting line.[6]

The British advanced under fire in two or three lines, with officers blowing whistles to signal troops when to fall prone and when to get up and run until they heard the next whistle. What the enemy saw was a mass of platoons leapfrogging each other until they were close enough to use their bayonets.

They seldom got close enough to use their bayonets. Close quarters fighting had never been a favorite Afrikaner way of war. They frequently opened fire from a mile away. Although Boer troops were probably the most accurate military marksmen of their time, there were many misses. But the Mausers laid down such a heavy volume of fire that musketry at this extreme range was quite effective.

The British claimed a victory at Dundee because they had captured a hill, but their losses were many times greater than their enemies'. Among the dead was General Symons. And the Boers didn't go away. They stayed on a nearby mountain and bombarded the British with their new long-range Creusot cannon, a 155mm piece nicknamed "Long Tom."

Another battle took place near another Natal town called Elandslaagte. This time, when the Afrikaners mounted up to move to another line, the British lancers and dragoons charged them. The Transvaalers tried to surrender and waved white flags, but the lancers didn't stop. In his great history, *The Boer War,* Thomas Pakenham attempted to explain this action. "The charge of two hundred horsemen galloping across a plain is designed to be an irresistible force. It does not stop simply because the enemy would like to surrender."[7]

But when that "irresistible force" rides through its enemy, turns around, and spears more men, some of them wounded and lying on the ground, then repeats this action a *third* time, it cannot be blamed on the impossibility of stopping at the sight of a white flag.

The British claimed another victory, and the claim, if not the tactics, was justified. But over at Dundee, Long Tom continued to drop shells into the British position. The British fell back to Ladysmith, which the Boers promptly besieged.

They also besieged the two Cape Colony towns, Mafeking and Kimberley, that were just over the borders of the Afrikaner republics. That there were any Afrikaners around Mafeking, an isolated hamlet in the dry, sandy wastelands of northern Cape Colony, was due to a British stroke of strategy that worked in an unexpected way. When the war began, there were fewer than 7,000 British troops in Cape Colony and only 3,000 in Natal. The armies of the two Afrikaner republics totaled well over 35,000, and Gen. Piet Cronje had 7,700 on the northern and northwestern borders of Cape Colony. If Cronje hadn't stopped to lay siege to Mafeking, he could have swept down the thinly populated northern Cape Colony, taken Cape Town, and probably incited the colony's majority Afrikaner population to revolt. The possibility of such an Afrikaner revolt in the colony gave High Commissioner Milner sleepless nights all through the war. And in the early stages of the conflict, it was even a probability—if the Boers had a general with more initiative than Cronje.

The commander of the Mafeking garrison was Col. Robert Baden-Powell, nicknamed "B-P," who was later to found the Boy Scouts. B-P was a versatile type, a conventional cavalry officer who excelled in the British-Indian sport of pigsticking, but was also an actor, an artist, a singer, and a military eccentric with a passion for scouting and small unit tactics that his contemporaries found (unfortunately for them) laughable. As Pakenham put it, "B-P would have made an ideal headmaster in a Victorian adventure story. A ripper when the going was good, but an alarming man to have as your enemy."[8]

When the war was about to begin, British authorities thought this unconventional colonel would be the ideal leader of a Jameson-style raid into the Transvaal. B-P was to recruit two regiments of irregular cavalry from British colonials in Rhodesia and Bechuanaland, establish a base at Mafeking, which had been Jameson's base, and attack the Transvaal. (The authorities apparently didn't remember what happened to Jameson and his raiders.) The plan was idiotic. If carried out, it would have been a disaster. But it never had a chance to be carried out. The Boers moved too quickly. Mafeking was surrounded. Cronje's men settled down around the town, and they lost the best chance they ever had for winning the war before the British could mobilize their forces in the home islands and the distant dominions.

The siege did not upset British plans. Milner anticipated it and Baden-Powell enthusiastically accepted it, using his raw irregulars to lure the Boers toward Mafeking. Because Mafeking had been the Jameson raiders' jumping-off point, its capture was a point of honor for the Transvaalers. And as it was on the Transvaal frontier in the extreme north of Cape Colony, cut off from Cape Town by the Kalahari Desert, it was also the most vulnerable town in Cape Colony. Mafeking was bait to distract Cronje and his 7,700 burghers. Cronje swallowed the bait and besieged B-P and his 700 irregulars. After the first two months of the siege, he detached 1,500 men to continue the siege under an even more slothful leader, Commandant Gen. J. P. Snyman, and moved south. But by that time the British reinforcements had arrived, and the chance of taking Cape Town had vanished.

B-P kept the Boers off balance by raiding their positions and firing at them with his ridiculous artillery, which included an antique muzzle loader. He also earned the reputation among the Afrikaners as a war criminal. He had done the unthinkable in South Africa. He had armed the natives in Mafeking. In a message to B-P on October 29, 1899, Cronje wrote "[Y]ou have committed an enormous act of wickedness . . . reconsider the matter, even if it cost you the loss of Mafeking . . . disarm your blacks and thereby act the part of a white man in a white man's war."[9]

The second siege on the western front, at Kimberley, was much less of an advantage for the British. Kimberley was a town that had been snatched from the Orange Free State and incorporated into Cape Colony after diamonds were discovered. It was also the headquarters of Cecil Rhodes's De Beers company, which had a virtual monopoly on the world's diamonds. Rhodes had dashed into Kimberley as the war was beginning, probably hoping to enter the Orange Free State at the head of a conquering British army. Instead, he was besieged. British regulars were a minority of Kimberley's defenders. Most of them were De Beers employees. For that reason, even more than Rhodes's enormous wealth, the voice of the gold-and-diamond magnate was heard loud and clear in London. When he threatened to surrender Kimberley unless aid was sent, the British authorities knew he could do it. The British plan, when they eventually concentrated an overwhelming army in South Africa, had been to strike from Cape Colony directly at Bloemfontein, the Orange Free State capital. But because of Rhodes, they had to first divert their attack to Kimberley.

Meanwhile, in Natal, Gen. Sir Redvers Buller was trying to break the siege of Ladysmith. The going was slow, because the terrain was ideal for the Boers' offensive-defensive strategy—seize a defensible position and wait for the enemy to come to you. Richard Harding Davis, an American war correspondent who covered the war from both sides, wrote that the Natal hills did not form a lineal range:

> They hide each other, or disguise each other. They can be enfiladed by the other, and not one gives up the secret of its strategic value until its crest has been carried by the bayonet. To add to this confusion, the river Tugela has selected the hills around Ladysmith as occupying the country through which it will endeavor to throw off its pursuers. It darts through them as though striving to escape, it doubles on its tracks, it sinks out of sight between them, and in the open plain it rises to the dignity of water-falls. It . . . twists and turns so frequently that when one says he has crossed the Tugela, he means he has crossed it once at a drift [a ford], once at the wrecked railroad bridge, and once over a pontoon. And then he is not sure that he is not still on the same side from which he started.[10]

Buller had been made commander in chief of British forces in South Africa just before the Boers locked up the sizable British garrison of Ladysmith, commanded by Sir George White. The day before Buller landed at Cape Town, Piet Joubert outmaneuvered White at the battle of Ladysmith and drove him into the town, while a column White had detached from his main force, under Lt. Col. R. F. C. Carleton, was forced to surrender. Total British casualties were 1,272.

Buller was still waiting for the rest of his troops who were en route from England, when Commandant Gen. Louis Botha led a raid deep into Natal, in the course of which he wrecked a British armored train and captured a socially prominent war correspondent named Winston Churchill. At this point, Joubert, Botha's nominal superior, lost his nerve. "Slim Piet" ("slim" means wily or shrewd in Afrikaans) was no longer the man he was at Majuba Hill. The sixty-eight-year-old commander in chief panicked at the thought of being so deep in British territory, urged an immediate retreat and telegraphed Kruger pleading for him to make peace. Kruger immediately wired Joubert to return home and told Botha to fortify the line of the Tugela River.

When Buller got his reinforcements, he split them into two parts, one to advance from Cape Colony in the west, and one to push up through Natal and relieve Ladysmith. He commanded the eastern column and gave the western to Lt. Gen. Lord Paul Methuen. Methuen won two minor victories against the Boers on the way to Kimberley at the cost of twice as many casualties as the Afrikaners suffered. The Transvaal and Free State burghers used their usual tactics—cutting down their attackers from long range and then retreating to another line. The British moved north and crossed the Modder River, suffering 460 casualties to the Boers' 80.

Eleven days later, Methuen resumed his attack. Koos De la Rey, commanding the Orange Free State troops under Cronje, had an idea. The British artillery had given the Boers trouble when they occupied hilltops. They used shrapnel shells, which explode above an enemy position and shower the troops in that position with lead balls—each shell, in effect, a short, flying gun firing grapeshot.[11] De la Rey dug and camouflaged trenches at the *foot* of Magersfontein Hill. In front of the trenches, he placed barbed wire. The British attack resulted in 902 casualties on the British side and 236 on the Boer. The Boers stayed in their trenches.

The same week, on the eastern front, Buller attacked the Tugela line. Botha had built his trenches the same way De la Rey had. He also built dummy trenches on the hilltops to attract British fire. The attack, near the town of Colenso, had the same result as all the other frontal attacks against invisible, entrenched riflemen with modern weapons. British casualties came to 1,138 plus the loss of ten field guns. They retreated seven miles to the town of Frere, the nearest water supply. The Afrikaners made no attempt to pursue them. Their defensive tactics were working well.

News of Buller's defeat at Colenso, Methuen's at Magersfontein, and another reverse in Cape Colony when Lt. Gen. Sir William Gatacre got lost, blundered into the Boers, and lost 696 men, arrived in England the same week. In Britain, it was called Black Week. Buller was replaced as commander in chief by Frederick Sleigh Roberts, nicknamed "Lord Bobs," leader of one of two feuding factions of the British Army. Roberts led a clique of officers, most whom had served with him in India. His rival was Garnet Wolseley, whose clique were veterans of African service. Buller was the number-one man after Wolseley in the "Wolseley Ring." Roberts was a popular hero in Britain because of his successes on the Indian-Afghan frontier. For his chief of staff, he chose another popular hero, Horatio Herbert Kitchener, who made his reputation in the Sudan. Along with his new position, Roberts got thousands of new soldiers, including contingents from Australia, Canada, and New Zealand. Before long, he would be leading the largest army Britain *ever fielded in all history* up to this time. Buller would continue to command the column in Natal, but Roberts would command all of South Africa and take personal command in the west.

Theoretically, the two Boer republics had around 40,000 men under arms. Actually, according to Byron Farwell in *Queen Victoria's Little Wars*, they probably never had more than 30,000 men in the field at any time.[12] The Boer militia resembled the American militia in the Revolution: when the spirit moved them, they would go home and return to the front later. The British would eventually send nearly half a million men to South Africa— about *ten times* the number of *all* men of military age in both Boer republics.

Roberts and Kitchener simply swept over the Afrikaners. Cronje, hardly the brightest star in the Afrikaner military firmament, got himself surrounded. He literally circled his wagons, as if the enemy was a mob of spear-wielding Bantu instead of a huge modern army with artillery.

British column including an observation balloon moves toward Pretoria as Lord Roberts's column advances. Roberts learned that capturing territory does not end a guerrilla war. LIBRARY OF CONGRESS

Finally, the reality of the situation dawned on Cronje. He and his 4,000 men surrendered.

Roberts pushed on to Kimberley. He had troubles, but they weren't caused by Afrikaners. The British armies in South Africa had always used regimental transport—the movement of supplies had always been under the control of individual regiments. "Bobs" and Kitchener (known as "K of K" for Kitchener of Khartoum, his most famous victory) decided that system was wasteful and uneconomical, so they consolidated the transport.[13] The result was an unholy mess, which resulted, among other things, in the loss of 3,000 oxen and 200 wagons loaded with food and medical supplies—about a third of all Roberts's transport. The animals and their cargo were captured by Christiaan De Wet, the Boers' greatest guerrilla leader. Later, eager to relieve Kimberley and to relieve himself of a great pain named Cecil Rhodes, Roberts sent his cavalry too quickly and with too few supplies across a waterless waste to the besieged town. As a result he lost a large portion of his horses. And as a result of that, at Poplar Grove, he lost the chance to capture the presidents of both the Transvaal and the Orange Free State.

On the eastern front, Buller continued trying to break through the Afrikaner ring around Ladysmith. At a hill called Spion Kop, the British almost exactly duplicated their action at Majuba Hill. They occupied a hilltop but brought up no artillery. The Boers attacked, and after a bloody fight at close quarters, the British withdrew. The Boers had also decided to withdraw, but the British did it first. Buller was learning, though. As Pakenham points out, the typical battle up to that time was a one-day affair, and a play with three acts. First, the artillery bombarded the enemy, then the infantry attacked, finally—assuming the infantry was successful—the cavalry pursued the beaten enemy.[14] Buller saw that modern warfare, with repeating rifles, machine guns, high-explosive shells, modern shrapnel, barbed wire, and complicated trench lines, demanded a new approach. He instituted "creeping barrages" with artillery bombardments going on as the infantry advanced, moving just ahead of the foot soldiers. Battles consisted of large numbers of small engagements going on simultaneously and spread over several days. Buller was pioneering tactics that would become standard fourteen years later in World War I.

And they worked. British troops entered Ladysmith February 28, 1900.

Roberts had no trouble reaching Bloemfontein, the Free State capital, March 13. He proclaimed amnesty for all Afrikaners under arms except their leaders. He believed the war was almost over. Two months later, the British announced that the Orange Free State was now the Orange River Colony.

All was not well in the new colony. A typhoid epidemic struck Bloemfontein and laid up hundreds of soldiers, most of whom died, in spite of the efforts of volunteer physicians, including Dr. Arthur Conan Doyle. One reason for the devastation was the sad state of Roberts's transport, which could not bring enough medical supplies or even fresh water. The general limited his troops to a ration of half a canteen a day. Many of them quenched their thirst with the waters of the polluted Modder (Afrikaans for muddy) River.

Roberts was disappointed that so few burghers turned in their rifles for his promised amnesty. He believed that the capture of an enemy capital meant the end of a war. The Boers thought otherwise. They were still in the field, and still besieging Mafeking. When a British column broke that siege, London greeted the news with a hysterical celebration. Baden-Powell, who had commanded the garrison during the 217-day siege, was canonized as a hero and a military genius.

He was neither, of course. But in reaction, later historians painted him as a dilettante clown and the siege as a sort of bucolic interlude with cricket matches, theatricals, and polo. As Byron Farwell put it, "For Baden-Powell, it [the siege] was something of a lark. He employed his energies less in fighting the Boers than in arranging amusements. . . . It was a delightful siege, marred only by a handful of casualties."[15] The "handful" of casualties—163 out of a garrison of 700—was *ten times* the casualty rate at Ladysmith.[16] Beneath his playboy exterior, B-P was a hard, ruthless soldier who played to win and made up the rules of the game as he went along. With raids and dummy fortifications he bluffed the Boers into thinking the town was too strong to storm. In spite of arming black troops, he was no civil libertarian two generations ahead of his time. During the siege, he repeatedly cut the rations of blacks in Mafeking, finally expelling all who were not natives of the town. Earlier, during the Matabele War, he was accused of murdering an African chief, but the investigation was aborted for political reasons. Baden-Powell was no lightweight. He was basically another Kitchener, but a Kitchener with brains and a sense of humor.

The two British forces, those of Roberts and Buller, invaded the Transvaal and linked up. Kruger went into exile, and many members of the commandos decided the fight was over.

But many did not.

President Marthinus (or Martinus) Steyn of the Orange Free State did not go into exile. He stayed with the army of his country's best general, Christiaan De Wet. Buller had finally beaten Louis Botha, but the Boer general refused to give up. Neither did his right-hand man, Jan Christian (or Christiaan) Smuts. From semiguerrillas, these diehards became pure guerrillas. They no longer tried to hold territory. They roamed over the veld, attacking British convoys and outposts. De Wet, De la Rey, and Smuts, all at one time or another invaded Cape Colony. But it was too late to incite the Cape Afrikaners to rebel. Two years before, when they outnumbered the British, they probably could have done it. Now South Africa was full of British soldiers—

more than the combined populations of the two Afrikaner republics. The dullest Cape Afrikaner could see that a rebellion was hopeless.

The British conducted "drives" as if they were hunting pheasants, instead of peasants, but the "bags" were disappointing. At the rate they captured enemy guerrillas, the war could have continued for a generation. So Roberts sent out his troops to drive off the livestock, burn the crops—and burn the homes—of families of men on commando. He reasoned that the burghers would come in to protect their families. A few did, but only a few. Then Roberts went home and accepted a peerage, leaving the mess to Kitchener.

Kitchener tried to achieve peace by giving the "bitter-enders" liberal terms while he conducted the war with even more drastic measures. He recommended to London that the Afrikaners be promised self-government and that nothing be done to interfere with their culture except lessening the oppression of blacks in their territories. Milner, who wanted an all English-speaking South Africa governed directly from London, was not happy with Kitchener's proposal, but London agreed with the general. Kitchener, like Baden-Powell, was no humanitarian, but if liberalism would end the war, he'd be liberal. Meanwhile, he'd just as readily take the opposite extreme.

Kitchener contacted the Boer leaders through various intermediaries. In 1901 he sent to Botha in Middleburg a ten-point proposal that had been approved by London:

1. Amnesty for all bona fide acts of war (with disenfranchisement for colonial rebels).
2. All prisoners of war to be brought home.
3. The two new colonies to be given self-government "as soon as circumstances permit."
4. Both English and Afrikaans be used in schools and courts.
5. Property of the Dutch Reformed Church to be respected.
6. Legal debts of the state, even if contracted during time of war, to be paid, with a limit of one million pounds.
7. Farmers to be compensated for horses lost during the war.
8. There would be no war indemnity for farmers.
9. Certain burghers to be licensed to keep rifles.
10. "As regards the extension of the franchise to Kaffirs in the Transvaal and the Orange River Colony, it is not the intention of His Majesty's Government to give such a franchise before a representative government is granted to those colonies." [17]

The Boer leaders looked over the proposal and began negotiations.

While the guerrilla war and the peace negotiations were going on, Kitchener was showing his hard side. He had decided to go Roberts one better. In addition to taking the cattle of the Boer bitter-enders, he would also take their families. He adopted a measure—concentration camps—that had been introduced in Cuba just a few years earlier by Gen. Valeriano Weyler y Nicolau, a Spanish viceroy known to the Cubans as "the Butcher." K of K, sometimes now called K of Chaos, built concentration camps and loaded them with Afrikaner women and children. Black servants and farmhands on the Boer farms ended up in concentration camps of their own. Rations were poor and scanty. There was no shelter in some "camps." Even blankets were in short supply. Sanitation was worse than primitive. Medical help was almost nonexistent. Kitchener didn't care. His only concern was ending the war. People were dying like flies in the camps. They died of malnutrition, typhoid, dysentery, and even measles. Twenty thousand Afrikaner women and children and 12,000 blacks died in those concentration camps. That didn't bother K of K.

It did bother anyone else who heard of the situation. It especially bothered an Englishwoman named Emily Hobhouse. She managed to tour the camps. Then she went back to England and reported to the leader of the Liberal Party, Sir Henry Campbell-Bannerman. He was aghast at what he heard: "The wholesale burning of farms . . . the deportations . . . the burnt-out population brought in by hundreds in convoys . . . deprived of clothes . . . the semi-starvation in the camps . . . the fever-stricken children lying . . . upon the earth . . . the appalling mortality."[18]

The government transferred responsibility for the camps from Kitchener to Milner. The death rate began dropping immediately. But by that time, the war actually was ending.

The end had been hastened by another innovation by Kitchener. For some time, the British had been protecting the railroads from Boer commandos by stringing barbed wire fences parallel to the tracks and building blockhouses at intervals within rifle range of each other. Kitchener expanded this wire and blockhouse construction to divide the open veld into districts and conduct sweeps through those districts. Blockhouse construction was simple. The walls were two corrugated iron circles filled with stones. Loopholes were built into the walls and the whole roofed with more iron. The Boer guerrillas had no artillery, and the iron-and-gravel walls were bulletproof. Old cans on the wire rattled when someone moved it, as they would while attempting to cut it. In the blackest night, guards in the blockhouses could resist an attack merely by firing along the wire. To help man the blockhouses, Kitchener took a page from Baden-Powell's book and armed 5,000 black Africans.

But the biggest inducement for the Boer bitter-enders to end the war was that they could get no food or horses except what they captured from the British.

Kitchener had finally found an effective counterguerrilla strategy, even if it could only be effective if the counterguerrillas had the imbalance Kitchener enjoyed—the resources of the entire British Empire against two small, isolated, and thinly populated states.

In 1902, after Britain specifically promised that the "Kaffirs" would not get the franchise until it was granted to them by the legislatures of the Transvaal and the Orange River Colony—in effect, never—the Boer leaders signed the peace. De Wet signed most reluctantly in spite of the promise.

In 1908, the Union of South Africa was created. It included both of the former republics as well as Natal and Cape Colony. The whole territory was dominated by Afrikaners. When World War I broke out, De Wet and some other bitter-enders rose in revolt. They were quickly defeated by commandos of burghers loyal to the new dominion. Most Afrikaners saw no reason to revolt. They already had more than they had before the war.

CHAPTER 2

Civilizing with a Krag:
Philippine Wars, 1899–1913

Damn, damn, damn the Filipino—
Pock-marked, khakiak *ladron!*
Underneath the starry flag,
We'll civilize him with a Krag,
And then go back to our beloved home.

Fred Funston heard that informal marching song everywhere. Some Americans back home may have heard it too, but while they may have guessed that *khakiak* referred to the complexion of the natives of America's newest colony, they probably didn't know that *ladrón* is Spanish for thief or bandit, and they may not have understood the implications of "civilize him with a Krag." The brand-new U.S. service rifle was the Krag-Jorgensen.

In spite of the tough talk that had earned him the hatred of American anti-imperialists, Brig. Gen. Frederick N. Funston knew that defining the Krag as a tool of civilization was no more true than, as Gen. Philip Sheridan put it: "The only good Indian is a dead Indian." True, when he first returned from the Philippines with a Medal of Honor, the nation's highest honor, and a promotion to brigadier general of volunteers, Funston said things like "exterminating the Goo-Goos" had been his job and that Emilio Aguinaldo, who claimed to be president of the Philippines, was "a cold-blooded murderer."

But the fact is that Funston couldn't resist shocking reporters with outrageous statements after he'd had a couple of drinks. His old college chum, William Allen White, the famous editor of the Emporia (KS) *Gazette,* said, "Funston, who was rising in the army, was still talking too much. Kellogg and I guessed why: Funston, who was still 'Timmy' to us, [his college nickname] still could not carry his liquor. Roosevelt [President Theodore] sent me to Timmy to tell him to quit talking or the President would have to rebuke him publicly. When I told him my message, Timmy looked at me and grinned: 'Oh, Billy, look not upon the gin ricky when it is red, and giveth color to the cup, for it playeth hell and repeat with poor Timmy.'"[1]

16

Funston's utterances were not the only reason anti-imperialists like Mark Twain despised him. He personified the war, because he was the war's greatest hero. As commander of a Kansas volunteer regiment, he had led the way in the drive against the Philippine Army of President Emilio Aguinaldo. His regiment, the 20th Kansas Volunteer Infantry, held the center of the American line, astride the railroad from Manila to the Lingayen Gulf on the main island of Luzon. Always a maverick, Funston modified infantry tactics to fit the situation. The enemy troops were poorly armed and terrible marksmen, but they built formidable field fortifications and were skilled at cover and concealment, brave and deadly at close quarters. His own soldiers were civilians—farmers, cowboys, teamsters, and railroaders. Most of them were used to guns, but not adept at long-range fire. And they did not adapt well to excessive regimentation. So instead of advancing by rushes and firing volleys on command, Funston had his men walk up to the line, firing at will when they saw a target until they were close enough to charge with bayonets. And so, during the American advance, the 20th Kansas was always the most advanced regiment.

At one point the Kansans captured several disassembled locomotives. Headquarters wanted the engine parts towed back to Manila for assembly. But one of Funston's men repaired locomotives in civilian life. Under his direction, the troops assembled the engines on the spot and created "Freddy's Fast Express," locomotives pushing armored cars bristling with machine guns and light artillery pieces. The Filipinos had destroyed all the railroad bridges and set up defensive positions on the opposite shore of each river the railroad crossed. The "FFE" provided the firepower to drive the enemy out of most of their trenches. But not all of them. Funston personally led the assaults, crawling over the twisted girders of blasted bridges and even swimming across rivers. After successful crossings, engineers repaired the bridges.

At one river, the Rio Grande de Pampanga, the largest in Luzon, Philippine general Antonio Luna built his most elaborate fortifications where the bridge once led to the town of Calumpit. "Calumpit will be the sepulcher of the Americans," he boasted. But Funston, leading both the 20th Kansas and the 1st Montana, crossed the river, drove away Luna's troops, and opened the way for Gen. Arthur (Douglas's father) MacArthur's division. Funston got the Medal of Honor and a promotion to brigadier general. He became a hero to the public.

But he was not a hero to many in the regular army. Funston, they said, was not really a soldier. He had joined the army near the top. He came in as a colonel of volunteers. In those days, when the tiny, Indian-fighting army had to fight a major war, the president called on the state governors to contribute volunteer regiments. Volunteers, the professional soldiers held, were not really soldiers. Further, Funston became a colonel not because he had any regular military experience, but because he had been a guerrilla in a foreign army.

As a young man looking for adventure, Funston had taught himself, with the aid of an arms merchant, how to assemble and fire a Hotchkiss twelve-pounder. He then traveled with the gun to Cuba, which was in revolt against Spain. He became a colonel and chief of artillery for the rebel army before he was seriously wounded and had to return to the States. His lectures about the situation in Cuba brought him a measure of fame. So when, in 1898, the United States declared war on Spain, the governor of Kansas appointed his state's leading living war hero, Funston, a colonel of the militia and commander of a volunteer regiment.

Funston's critics were even less happy about him when the 20th Kansas and 1st Montana were demobilized, but Funston was asked to stay on as a volunteer brigadier general and return to the Philippines. Arthur MacArthur thought Funston's experience as a Cuban guerrilla would be a great help in the new phase of the war.

At that time, the war was called the Philippine Pacification. Today, it is often called the Philippine Insurrection. Neither term is accurate.

At one time, there was a Philippine insurrection, but it was an insurrection against Spain, not the United States. It began in 1896, a year after the Cuban revolt began, and it was highly organized. The Filipinos drew up a constitution modeled after that of the United States and elected a congress and a president. Aguinaldo, one of the original leaders, was elected president. There was a short lull in the fighting on December 27, 1897, and Aguinaldo went into exile in Hong Kong. When the Spanish-American War began on April 25, 1898, Commodore George Dewey sank the Spanish fleet in Manila Bay and returned Aguinaldo to the Philippines. Almost all of Spain's resources were tied up in Cuba, and the Filipinos under Aguinaldo almost drove the Spanish into the sea. When the war in Cuba ended, the Spanish were still holding out in Manila and a few other seaside cities on the main island, Luzon, but the Filipinos (known to the Spanish as *los insurrectos*) held the rest.

The United States ostensibly began the war simply to free the Cubans from Spanish domination. However, Mark Hanna, chairman of the Republican National Committee, wanted colonies, because in those days, colonies were believed to increase trade. Theodore Roosevelt, the powerful assistant secretary of the navy, wanted coaling stations for the fleet, and he wanted an American presence in the Far East. He also wanted a war. In an address at the Naval War College, Roosevelt said, "All the great masterful races have been fighting races. . . . No triumph of peace is quite so great as the supreme triumphs of war . . . the diplomat is the servant, not the master, of the soldier."[2] Roosevelt arranged to have Dewey, an ancient fire-breather, assigned to the China Squadron so that when war with Spain broke out, he could dash to the Philippines and seize Manila. President William McKinley, though, denied any territorial ambitions.

"We want no wars of conquest; we must avoid the temptation of territorial aggression," McKinley said in his inaugural address.[3] But McKinley was in the habit of writing memos to himself. In one, he scribbled, "While we are conducting war until its conclusion we must keep all we get; when the war is over, we must keep what we want."[4] A large portion of the American public, however, wanted no colonies.

Senator Henry M. Teller of Colorado slipped an amendment into the bill authorizing the United States to intervene in Cuba. It prohibited the United States from exercising "sovereignty, jurisdiction or control" in Cuba. That amendment pleased neither Hanna, Roosevelt, nor McKinley.

The amendment did not mention Puerto Rico, Guam, or the Philippines. The Puerto Ricans were happy with Spain, and to most Americans, the Pacific islands were just "South Sea Islands," inhabited by hula dancers and cannibals, and of no use to the United States American newspapers, like the anti-imperialist Chicago *Chronicle*, which ran cartoons showing Filipinos

Kansas Volunteers open fire on *insurrecto* positions during the Philippine War.
NATIONAL ARCHIVES

as grass-skirted savages, or like the imperialist Detroit *Journal,* which portrayed them as the caricature blacks of that era with enormous lips and pie-eyes.[5]

The Philippine insurrectos did not wear grass skirts. They wore military uniforms, had a command structure similar to that of the U.S. Army, and some of them had better rifles than the Americans.[6] Their supply of Model 1893 Spanish Mausers was limited, however, and most were armed with a variety of obsolete weapons. A few had only their work knives, called *bolos.*[7]

The war in Cuba was still going on when Funston's regiment was moved to the Philippines. McKinley called this force an "army of occupation," as if the insurrectos who held almost all of Luzon didn't exist and the only fighting that had taken place was the Battle of Manila Bay. Funston's disappointment was huge: he was sure his experience in Cuba would be helpful, and he wanted to fight.

He soon got his chance. McKinley arranged to buy the Philippine Islands, Puerto Rico, and Guam from Spain for $20 million. In announcing his decision to annex the Philippines, McKinley said:

> I walked the floor of the White House night after night after night until midnight; and I am not ashamed to tell you, gentlemen, that I went down on my knees and prayed to Almighty God for light and guidance more than one night.
>
> And one night it came to me this way—I don't know how it was but it came: (1) that we could not give them back to Spain—that would be cowardly and dishonorable; (2) that we could not turn them over to France or Germany—our commercial rivals in the Orient—that would be bad business and discreditable; (3) that we could not leave them to themselves—they were unfit for self-government—and they would soon have anarchy and misrule over there worse than Spain's was; and (4) there was nothing left for us to do but to take them all, and educate the Filipinos, and uplift and civilize and Christianize them.[8]

At the time, the Philippines were the only predominantly Christian country in the Far East, and they had been exposed to European civilization for three or four centuries. Manila had electric lights and electric streetcars, which most American cities did not.

Some of the Filipino leaders wanted to declare war on the United States when they heard about the agreement, but Aguinaldo told them not to be hasty. The U.S. Senate had not yet ratified the treaty with Spain. Tension between the "army of occupation" and its Filipino "allies" was increasing, however. The Americans called the Filipinos "niggers," searched their houses without warrants, set up checkpoints, and knocked down any Filipino who didn't show them respect but showed no respect for Filipina women when they searched them. Of the natives, one American soldier wrote home, "We have to kill one or two every night."[9]

On the night of February 4, 1899, thirty-six hours before the Senate was to vote on the treaty, a group of drunken Filipinos approached a U.S. Army checkpoint.

"Halt!" commanded Pvt. William Grayson.

"Halto!" one of the Filipinos called, mimicking Grayson.

"Well, I thought the best thing to do was shoot him," Grayson testified later. Grayson then shot another of the Filipinos, and a second sentry shot the third. Then Grayson ran back yelling, "Line up fellows; the niggers are in here all through these yards."[10]

Firing became general. The Filipinos could not match the machine guns and artillery of the American soldiers, plus the naval gunfire from the warships in the harbor. When the fighting ended, 3,000 Filipinos and 60 Americans were dead. The so-called Philippine Pacification was exactly the opposite. Except for the sieges of a few Spanish strongpoints, the islands were peaceful until the Americans arrived.

Aguinaldo proposed to Gen. Elwell Otis that they establish a neutral zone between the two armies.

Otis refused. "[The] fighting having [once] begun, must go on to the grim end," he said.[11] And so began—a day before the Senate ratified the treaty with Spain—what McKinley called the "benevolent assimilation" of the Philippines.

The United States shipped 100,000 more soldiers to the Philippines, and in the fighting that ensued, Funston won his Medal of Honor and his promotion. That fighting was essentially classical warfare. The Philippine Army was a bunch of guerrillas who tried to re-form as a regular force. The Filipinos did—in a way—what Mao Zedong is given credit for accomplishing many generations later. But it dawned on their leaders that they didn't have the equipment, organization, resources, or manpower to match the United States in regular warfare. While Funston was in the United States, they doffed their uniforms and went back to the guerrilla warfare they had practiced against the Spanish. Aguinaldo was hiding in parts unknown, but controlling his forces by sending orders by courier. And that's why MacArthur wanted Funston back in the Philippines.

Back in Luzon, Funston found himself in command of a military district in the center of the island. The district was a mess. It was staffed by elements of six regiments, all with headquarters somewhere else. The supply system was in disarray. The troops had been living on water buffalo meat and rice or on bacon and hardtack. They were exhausted and sick. Twelve percent of

Funston's command was in the hospital. The guerrillas were cutting tele-graph lines, ambushing small parties, and preparing for a major assault. Funston's first order of business was to consolidate his command, get supply and communications in order with aggressive patrolling, set up outposts, and patrol the areas between them intensively.

Unable to find the guerrillas, American troops had burned down whole villages in reprisal for attacks. They had been trying to gather intelligence by torturing villagers. The "water cure" was a favorite method. Water was poured into a victim's mouth until his body became distended. The inter-rogators forced the water out by kicking the victim. Then they filled him with water again. One report told of a priest who after the "treatment" had not given any information. "Give the nigger another dose," an officer ordered. But the interrogators couldn't. The victim was dead. Hanging a subject until he almost strangled to death, then stringing him up again was another favorite technique. Other unfortunates were dragged behind gal-loping horses. Some victims were tied to trees and then shot in the legs. After spending a day and a night tied to the tree, the subject was again ques-tioned. If he still gave no information, he was again shot.

Funston's methods were different. Historian Brian McAllister Linn writes: "Although a vocal advocate of repression, his actual conduct was characterized by lenient surrender terms, rewards for collaboration and per-sonal friendship."[12]

Funston was a vocal advocate of repression when talking to reporters. But he was also a vocal opponent of wholesale torture and group punish-ment when talking to superior officers—something that added to his unsa-vory reputation among the army brass: they said he was soft on the guerrillas. Funston also praised the courage of Filipino fighting men and criticized the brass for not enlisting more of them.

From his time in Cuba, Funston could speak fluent Spanish, the second language of most Filipinos, and he understood the Spanish colonial social structure. Society in the Philippines was similar to that of Cuba. People deferred to the *principales*—important people—in the towns as well as in the guerrilla organization. Funston courted the principales in his district. He befriended former guerrillas, and he used native troops extensively.

These practices paid off on February 4, 1901, when Funston got a mes-sage that some of his troops had captured a guerrilla courier with messages from Aguinaldo. Funston ordered that the man be sent to his headquarters with all his messages. Then he sent for Lazaro Sergovia. Lazaro Sergovia y Gutierrez was a brilliant Spaniard who had served in the Spanish Army in the Philippines. When the Spanish-American War ended, he found he could not take his Filipina wife back to Spain. So he joined Aguinaldo's army. He quickly saw how the war with the Americans was going, and he also heard about the maverick American officer who seemed, unlike most soldiers, to be a man with imagination. At the first chance he got, he surrendered to Funston personally. Sergovia had earned a bachelor's degree when he was only fifteen. Funston would not let brains like that go to waste. He made Sergovia a member of his personal staff—a strange and unauthorized collection of U.S. officers, native scouts, reformed bandits and former insurrectos. Among his other talents, Sergovia could read and speak Tagalog, the most common language in Luzon.

It turned out that the courier, Cecilio Segismundo, was traveling with a group that one of Funston's patrols had ambushed. Segismundo escaped and found a village where he hoped to find shelter. The mayor of the village was one of the principales Funston had won over. He convinced the courier to give himself up to the Americans.

All of the letters were in Tagalog, but some were also in cipher. These were usually signed "Pastor" or "Colon de Magdalo," two aliases Aguinaldo often used. Funston and Sergovia worked all night on the ciphered letters (Segismundo had no idea what they were about).

The decoders hit pay dirt in a letter from Aguinaldo to one of his cousins. *El presidente* asked his kinsman for reinforcements. "Send me about 400 men with a good commander; if you cannot send them all at once, send them in parties. The bearer can serve as a guide to them until their arrival here; he is a person to be trusted."[13]

Funston answered the letter. Earlier, he had raided the headquarters of Urbano Lacuna, the insurrecto chief in his district. Among other things, they captured Lacuna's stationery and documents he had signed. Sergovia wrote on Lacuna's stationery that, following the cousin's orders, he was sending some men and more would follow. Then he forged Lacuna's signature.

The men, though, would not be reinforcements. They would be U.S. Army Macabebe Scouts. The Macabebes were a minority group that had long been at odds with the majority Tagalogs. According to legend, they were descendants of Mexican Indians the Spanish had enlisted centuries before to help them in the Philippines. Even in modern times, the Filipino units in the Spanish Army were largely Macabebes. Funston planned to have the Macabebes pretend to be insurrectos. Segismundo, the former courier, would guide them to Aguinaldo's headquarters. Ostensibly leading them would be an insurrecto officer, Lt. Col. Hilario Placida, who had come over to Funston. Actually commanding them would be Sergovia. The Macabebes would say they were bringing five American prisoners to headquarters.

One of the prisoners would be Funston.

Funston had to get MacArthur's permission for his coup. MacArthur, now commander of all American troops in the Philippines, was most reluctant. But Funston's idea could end the Philippine War at a stroke, so he gave in.

"Funston, this is a desperate undertaking. I fear I shall never see you again," MacArthur said as Funston was preparing to leave.[14]

A navy gunboat dropped Funston's party off on the coast near the town of Casiguran. Then they marched to the mountain town of Palanan. The mountains were almost uninhabited. Nobody lived there but a few Negritos, an extremely primitive nation of hunters similar to the Australian Aborigines. The Negritos would warn Aguinaldo of any strangers, so Funston's people played their roles constantly. The Macabebes spoke only Tagalog, instead of their own language, and spoke as little as possible. Segovia did most of the talking. Only one white man in history, a Spanish priest, had ever made the journey from Casiguran to Palanan.

Aguinaldo sent messages to the false insurrectos by runner. His people and Sergovia kept up a lively correspondence as the "insurrectos" and their "prisoners" struggled through the jungle (although the insurrectos thought they were corresponding with Placida). When Funston's party ran out of food, they got insurrecto headquarters to send them some. Aguinaldo sent a column to collect the prisoners, but Funston managed to evade it. Finally, on March 23, 1901, the false insurrectos and their "captives" marched into Aguinaldo's headquarters.

The Philippine president had an honor guard drawn up to welcome them. The Macabebes opened fire on the honor guard. In his office, Aguinaldo heard the firing and thought the troops were celebrating. He ran to a window and yelled, "Stop that foolishness! Do not waste your ammunition!"[15]

At that moment, Sergovia burst into the office, revolver in hand, followed by Funston. Aguinaldo looked at Funston and asked him in Spanish, "Oh, tell me, is not this a joke?"[16] Funston and his people arrested Aguinaldo and his staff. The Macabebes killed or drove off all of the tiny garrison of the headquarters, and they took Aguinaldo and his staff back to Manila.

There was a chorus of screams from the United States to hang Aguinaldo, but MacArthur treated the ex-president as an honored guest. Aguinaldo decided that it was useless to go on fighting, so he ordered all units of the insurrecto army to surrender.

Most of them did, and the steam went out of the First Philippine War.

Funston had to go home for his health before all traces of guerrilla activity had been eliminated. That was most unfortunate, because the counterguerrilla campaign now was conducted by men with methods very different from Funston's. On the island of Samar on September 28, 1901, guerrillas, using bolo knives smuggled to them in coffins, chopped up a company of unarmed American soldiers eating breakfast.

On hearing of the incident, Brig. Gen. Jacob "Hell Roaring Jake" Smith said, "I want all persons killed who are capable of bearing arms in actual hostilities against the United States."

A subordinate asked, "I would like to know the limit of age to respect, sir."

"Ten years."

"Persons of ten years and older are those designated as being capable of bearing arms?"

"Yes."[17]

Smith's men didn't completely carry out his order. But they tried. One-third of the population of Samar—men, women, and children—was killed. Smith was eventually court-martialed. His sentence: early retirement with a brigadier general's pension.

There was no court-martial for Brig. Gen. J. Franklin Bell, who, like Kitchener in South Africa, adopted the idea of Spanish general Valeriano Weyler in Cuba and established concentration camps in the province of Batangas, where he was the commanding officer. He ordered all civilians to take themselves and "all their movable property," including food, to the camps. The inhabitants' original houses were burned, their livestock slaughtered, and their crops destroyed. As had happened in Cuba and South Africa, hundreds of civilians perished from starvation and disease. In an order to his subordinate commanders, Bell wrote:

> Natural and commendable sympathy for suffering and loss and with those for whom friendly relations may have been maintained should . . . [be relegated] to a place subordinate to the doing of whatever may be necessary to bring a people who have not as yet felt the distressing effect of war to a realizing sense of the advantages of peace.[18]

The War Department reported: "Within a comparatively few weeks after this policy was inaugurated [on December 25, 1901] . . . guerrilla warfare ended."[19]

It really didn't, but President Theodore Roosevelt, who took office after McKinley's assassination, wanted it to end, so the War Department said it did. On July 4, 1902, Roosevelt announced the end of the war. But the guerrilla war continued. Americans set up more concentration camps in the provinces of Albay in 1903 and Cavite and Batangas (again) in 1905.

In the northern islands, the guerrilla war gradually petered out. Macario Sakay, the last important guerrilla leader, surrendered in 1906. If the other American regional commanders had copied Funston's methods, the war might have ended sooner. But by the early years of the twentieth century, it had merged with a new war—this time against the Moros of the southern islands.

The Moros (Moors in Spanish) were Muslims who lived in the big southern island of Mindanao and in the Sulu Archipelago. Many Americans have the idea that all of the fighting in the Philippines was against the Moros. Many gun fanciers, for example, say that the .45-caliber pistol was adopted because the regulation .38 did not have enough "stopping power" to knock down "the fanatical Moros of the Philippines." Maybe that's because many people found it easier to attribute fanaticism to Muslims than to Christians. The hardest and bloodiest fighting in the Philippines, however, was between Christian Americans and Christian Filipinos. The inadequacy of the .38-caliber revolver was clearly demonstrated during that fighting. Maj. Gen. Julian Hatcher, who was the U.S. Army's leading small-arms expert, cites the case of Antonio Caspi, a Christian prisoner on the island of Samar who tried to escape on October 26, 1905. Caspi was shot four times in the chest with a .38-caliber revolver during a hand-to-hand struggle but, apparently uninjured, continued to fight until hit on the head with the butt of a carbine.[20]

The Moros had been waging a kind of low-level guerrilla war against the Spanish for more than three centuries. As happened in the northern islands, the Spanish-American War gave the Moros a chance to drive the Spanish away. When the Americans arrived in the southern islands, the Spanish were barely hanging on to a few seaside locations. There were two major Moro sultanates in 1899—Mindanao and Sulu. Sulu was a group of small islands ruled by a sultan on the island of Jolo. Under both sultans there was a collection of feudal chiefs called *datus*. Quite a few datus were little more than pirates or bandits.

The Americans reached an agreement with the Sultan of Sulu that involved monthly payments to the Sultan and nine subchiefs, American sovereignty over the islands, but a guarantee of freedom of religion and respect for the Sultan and his datus. It also suppressed piracy, allowed slaves to buy their freedom, and provided for local rule by the Sultan and his datus.

On Mindanao, the Moros were not so agreeable. Each datu had a fortress and the Americans had to take them one by one. Capt. John J. Pershing made a name for himself here by using a combination of diplomacy and force to bring datus into the fold. Pershing was so successful headquarters assigned more troops to his command until, although a mere captain, he was leading a small army. Eventually, he was promoted to brigadier general, although the fact that his wife was a senator's daughter didn't hurt, either. (See Chapter 3.) The Moros were hampered by the apparent inability of the datus to unite against the Americans. And although all Moro men considered themselves warriors, they lacked modern weapons. Every man carried a Moro kris, a sword that looked like a Malay kris (or *keris*) on steroids, in addition to a variety of other bladed weapons, but the only firearm many of them had was a "cigarette gun," a homemade muzzle loader fired by applying a cigarette to the touchhole. Some of the American troops in the Moro War must have thought they had been transported back in time to the sixteenth century. Many of the Moros wore armor—brass helmets copied from Spanish models and brass mail.[21]

One of the biggest problems the Americans had was that the Moro chiefs kept changing their minds. Another was that individual Moros would take an oath to kill Christians or die in the attempt. These *juramentados* (Spanish for someone who has taken an oath) were liable to go berserk at any time. And they really were hard to stop. American soldiers in Moroland went on guard duty three at a time. One had a .30 rifle; one had a 12-gauge shotgun, and one an old .45-70 Springfield. The old Springfield was slow and smoky, but its huge lead bullet had stopping power. In one case, a Moro managed to kill several people although he was hit thirty times by all three weapons.[22]

But, as in the north, in the conflicts between the Americans and the Moros, the Moros usually suffered disproportionate losses. One example is what is called the Moro Crater Massacre. This took place March 12, 1906, on the island of Jolo following a fight with troops of the Sultan of Sulu.[23] Some 600 Moros, men, women, and children, tried to find refuge in the crater of an extinct volcano. The Americans, commanded by Maj. Gen. Leonard Wood, climbed the mountain, dragging up artillery.[24] They lined the rim of the crater and fired into it. They killed all the Moros. There was no court-martial for Wood. He later became army chief of staff.

Raids, uprisings, and individual juramentado attacks continued for years. The Sultanate of Sulu, which made the first treaty with the Americans, was particularly troublesome. In 1913, Pershing, recently promoted to brigadier general, led an army against the Sultan's troops. He defeated them on Bagsak Mountain, an event that is usually considered the end of the Moro War. But intermittent guerrilla war went on and on. As a matter of fact, it's still going on against the independent Philippine government.

Fred Funston showed us how to end the war in 1901.

But we blew it.

CHAPTER 3

Unwelcome Liberators: Veracruz and the Villa Expedition, 1914–1916

For more than thirty years, Porfirio Díaz, who had been one of Benito Juarez's generals in the war against the French, ruled Mexico as if it were his personal property, a period Mexicans call the *Porfiriato.* Díaz took command of a primitive, agricultural nation and turned it into a modern state with a booming economy. Foreigners considered him a miracle worker. Leo Tolstoy called him "a prodigy of nature." Andrew Carnegie said he "should be held up for the hero worship of mankind." President Theodore Roosevelt described him as "the greatest statesman now living."

Roosevelt's successor, William Howard Taft, was somewhat less impressed. Taft, as governor general of the Philippines, had shown sympathy for ordinary Filipinos—farmworkers, fishermen, seamen, and the like—who always escaped the notice of fire-breathers like Roosevelt. Díaz never tried to help the ordinary people of his country. In fact, he took measures that made their lot considerably worse. Most Mexicans worked small farms that their ancestors had been working before Cortés arrived, but they had no deeds to that land. Villages had common land, plots called *ejidos,* also undocumented. Díaz had all of this "public" land surveyed. He gave some of it to the surveying companies and sold the rest, often to foreigners. Native millionaires also took advantage of Díaz's sales. The extended Terrazas-Creel family (descendants of an American citizen who moved to Mexico) owned almost the entire state of Chihuahua—not only land but mines, factories, granaries, railroads, telephone companies, meatpacking plants, and sugar mills. Don Luis Terrazas owned eight times as much land as the King Ranch at its peak. His son-in-law, Don Enrique Creel, after several terms as governor of Chihuahua, had served as Mexico's foreign minister.

Working for these millionaires were millions of *péons.* Péons were people who, to pay off debts, were required to work for free for the *patrón* who owned the land. They could work their own land only after the sun set. Under those conditions, they made so little that they were perpetually in debt to the hacienda store—and they were allowed to trade at no other store. The main difference between an agricultural péon and a medieval serf was that the serf had some rights. The péon had none.

Industrial workers and miners were not much better off. On June 1, 1906, 5,000 Mexican miners went on strike against the American-owned Cananea Consolidated Copper Company. They had been making $1.50 a day for an eleven-hour day. They asked the 2,000 American miners to join them. The Americans were making $3 a day for a shorter workday. There was no solidarity of labor in Mexico. The Americans not only refused to join their Mexican coworkers, they shot at them. The governor of Sonora sent troops and police to the mine. The troops killed twenty-three Mexican miners and wounded more than a score more. Díaz and his subordinates always favored foreigners, especially Americans. Díaz wanted foreign capital.

Anita Brenner, a daughter of Swiss immigrants, who later moved to the United States and became an American citizen, described life during the Porfiriato:

> Justice was carried out according to an unwritten, unbreakable law which required that a case be settled in rigid observance of who the attorney was, who the client. Cases involving a foreigner against a Mexican were decided according to the principle that the foreigner must be right, unless word came from Don Porfirio, exceptionally, to discover otherwise. In the remotest places judges understood the fine points of these usages, and could interpret skilfully the precept taught by the U.S. State Department that Americans were guests and must be spared the judicial annoyances unavoidable to Mexicans; that every American living and working in Mexico, from plant manager to gang foreman and oil driller, and every company that had American money in it—even if it were only one red cent, said the Embassy—had the right to this same kind of extraterritorial immunity.[1]

In the United States, President William Howard Taft felt as if he were trapped. He deplored Díaz's actions, but the U.S. ambassador, Henry Lane Wilson, a corporation lawyer, was a strong supporter of Díaz as were scores of American corporations doing business in Mexico. And the United States had received some concessions from Mexico that Taft wanted to keep. At the same time, he tried to keep Díaz at arm's length. In 1909, with the Mexican population growing restless, Díaz thought "full friendship and support" from the big republic to the north would be helpful. He asked to meet Taft at the border. The meeting turned out to be a true "Mexican standoff." Taft asked for a renewal of the leases for naval bases in Baja California. Díaz said that because of anti-American feeling in Mexico that would be impossible at the time. He asked for material aid. Taft gave him some flowery rhetoric but no definite promises.

In 1910, the Mexican people decided that they had had enough of the Porfiriato. Spontaneous riots broke out all over the country. In the state of Morelos, an agrarian reformer named Emiliano Zapata was already leading a revolt. Then an immensely wealthy landowner, Francisco Madero, raised an army and announced his intention to overthrow Don Porfirio. In the state of Chihuahua, a bandit leader called Francisco "Pancho" Villa called his old gang together and said he was joining Madero.

Pancho Villa became a major player in Madero's campaign. He was no ordinary bandit. Born Doroteo Arango to péon parents on a hacienda in the state of Durango, he had little love for *hacendados*. When he was sixteen, he killed the son of the hacendado after the crown prince raped his sister. He left the ranch, changed his name to Francisco Villa, and traveled north to Chihuahua, where he joined the bandit gang of Ignacio Parra. In Parra's forays Pancho (Frank) Villa was the first man into every dangerous situation. Among people who adore machismo, he was the most macho any of the gang had ever seen. When Parra was killed in a stagecoach robbery, the gang chose the young Villa to lead them.

Villa robbed banks and rustled cattle, especially the latter. He may have been the greatest cattle rustler in history. Certainly, he gave more free meat to the péons than any other person in history. He was celebrated as the

Pancho Villa (third from right) and some of his officers. NATIONAL ARCHIVES

Mexican Robin Hood, the subject of dozens of ballads. His one political idea at this time was the formation of national butcher shops that would sell meat to starving péons at nominal prices. He actually put this idea into practice. He became a butcher in Ciudad Chihuahua and sold meat at prices determined by the customers' ability to pay. Even when he gave food away, he didn't lose money. The meat came from cattle his gang had stolen. And the butcher shop gave Villa a respectable front. He became friendly with civic leaders and rich landowners. One of them, Abrahán González, told him about the Madero campaign. Villa joined the revolutionary army as a captain. Two years later, he was a colonel and played a key part in the decisive battle of Ciudad Juárez. Díaz took a ship for Europe, and Francisco León de la Barra became interim president. Then, in the first honest national election in more than three decades, Madero was elected president.

Madero has been praised as an idealist. He was, but he didn't really relate to the people, and he didn't have good sense. He ignored Zapata and the crying need for land reform. He slighted another revolutionary leader, Pascual Orozco. And he made Victoriano Huerta commander of the army. Huerta was a brilliant general: he defeated Orozco repeatedly when that former Madero partisan rebelled, and Pancho Villa, who hated him, had to concede that *"el borrachito"* (the little drunk) was a first-class military man.[2] But Huerta was an ardent admirer of the exiled Díaz, an utterly ruthless leader, and an inveterate plotter. Under Madero, Mexico became a mind-boggling mess of conspiracies, betrayals, and murders. At one point, Madero's brother, Gustavo, arrested Huerta for plotting with Díaz's nephew, Félix Díaz, to overthrow the president, but Francisco Madero ordered the general's release. Two days later, Huerta had Madero and his vice president, José Pino Suárez, arrested. National police then assassinated them, presumably on Huerta's orders.

Meanwhile, the United States had been involved in one of its more unusual elections. Taft was seeking another term, but his old ally, former President Theodore Roosevelt, dissatisfied with his successor's policy, was running against him on the "Bull Moose" ticket. The Democratic candidate was a New Jersey governor named Woodrow Wilson. What made this election unusual, aside from the fact that there were three candidates, each of whom had a good chance of winning, was that all three were considered liberals.

Roosevelt's candidacy so split the Republicans that Wilson became only the second Democrat elected since the Civil War.

Wilson, in spite of his liberal reputation, was perhaps the most racist president in American history. African Americans, he seemed to believe, were definitely inferior to whites and must be "kept in their place." Because of his liberal reputation, Wilson had won the majority of African Americans away from "the party of Lincoln." He then proceeded to bring Jim Crow to the city of Washington and spread segregation all through the federal government. This snobbery extended beyond race. Later, during the Versailles peace conference, he refused to see delegates from the newly proclaimed Republic of Ireland. Asked why, he said, "You have touched on the great metaphysical tragedy of today. When I gave utterance to those words [his call to free small nations] I said them without the knowledge that nationalities existed which are coming to us day after day."[3] An American president who had never heard of the Irish? As for Mexicans, he thought they were not quite civilized and needed guidance. And, it must be admitted, Huerta, who had imprisoned, assassinated, and executed scores of his political enemies, gave him reason to think that way.[4]

As far as Huerta was concerned, Wilson was all for regime change. Wilson demanded that Huerta, who had become president of Mexico legally, but through a most unethical manipulation of Mexican law, hold a new election in which he would not be a candidate.[5] He said, "We are seeking to counsel Mexico for her own good." Federico Gamboa, Mexico's foreign minister, called Wilson's note "humiliating and unusual."[6]

Wilson drafted a new note. This one attempted to bribe the Mexican government. If Huerta accepted Wilson's counsel, the U.S. government would use its influence with American bankers to give the Mexican government an immediate loan. Gamboa indignantly rejected the proposal, adding, "When the dignity of the nation is at stake, I believe that there are not loans enough to induce those charged by the law to maintain it to be lessened."[7]

Wilson refused to recognize Huerta's government. "Mexico has no government," he said.[8] Secretary of State William Jennings Bryan wrote to the chargé d'affaires in Mexico, Nelson O'Shaughnessy, "The present policy of the Government of the United States is to isolate General Huerta entirely; to cut him off from foreign sympathy and aid and from domestic credit, whether moral or material, and to force him out."[9]

To Wilson, Huerta was a bloody monster who was oppressing Mexicans. The U.S. president was resolved to use any means short of war to liberate the people of the republic south of the Rio Grande. Even means that were not far short of war.

During the Mexican Revolution, U.S. Navy ships routinely patrolled waters off the Mexican coast in case American citizens needed help. On April 10, 1914, eight sailors and the paymaster from the U.S.S. *Dolphin* took a whale boat to Tampico to pick up a supply of gasoline that had been previously ordered. When they landed, a Mexican Army captain and a squad of soldiers arrested them. The captain said they had entered a restricted military zone. As the captain was marching his prisoners up the street, another Mexican officer appeared, ordered him to release the sailors and apologized profusely to the Americans. That apology was followed by one from the commander of the Tampico garrison.

That apology was not enough for Henry T. Mayo, the admiral commanding the squadron off Tampico. Without consulting anyone in Washington, Mayo sent an ultimatum to Huerta himself, demanding that he "publicly hoist the American flag in a prominent place and salute it with twenty-one guns."[10]

When Wilson heard of the ultimatum, he backed up Mayo. Huerta, however, was not going to salute the flag of a government that refused to admit the existence of *his* government.

Meanwhile, the U.S. government learned that a German ship loaded with arms and ammunition for Huerta was en route to Veracruz, Mexico's largest Atlantic port. Germany was interested in keeping the Mexican Revolution going because it could distract the United States from Europe, where tensions were rising and a major war looked likely. Wilson decided that Huerta would not get those German guns. He ordered the U.S. Navy to occupy Veracruz. On April 21, U.S. sailors and marines streamed ashore at Veracruz. General Gustavo Maass, the garrison commander, handed out rifles to the crowds of civilians around the armory, released military prisoners and armed them, then took his 600 regulars out of the city.

The prison at Veracruz was filled with political prisoners as well as criminals. "We opened the jail and let them all out," said a sailor in the landing party. "Some were political prisoners; some were gangsters. We let them all out. They were delighted to see us."[11]

Not all residents of Veracruz were delighted to see the Americans. The civilian population opened fire on them with rifles and revolvers, government-issued and privately owned, from windows and rooftops. They built barricades on the streets. The teenaged cadets at the naval academy resisted furiously and heroically. But the machine guns of the landing party and the big naval guns of the warships ensured that the resistance would be brief and bloody.

When the German ship entered Veracruz harbor, its captain was informed that he could either give his armaments to the American forces or he could take them back to Germany. He did neither. He slipped out of Veracruz and landed his cargo farther down the coast, from where it was sent by train to Huerta.

Wilson decided that this landing would be no one-night stand. To maintain a long-term occupation, he sent army troops to Veracruz and appointed the army's most colorful and successful general, Brig. Gen. Frederick Funston, to command them.[12]

The occupation provided a setting for a future American hero to exercise a bit of derring-do. As relations between the United States and Mexico became more strained, war became a distinct possibility. Secretary of War Henry L. Stimson told Maj. Gen. Leonard Wood, the army chief of staff, that he might have to lead an expeditionary force into Mexico. Wood decided he needed more intelligence on conditions around Veracruz. He sent his aide, a captain named Douglas MacArthur, to the Mexican port on a secret mission. MacArthur was not to tell even Funston about it.

One problem was apparent to everyone: Veracruz was a rail center, and there were many cars on the tracks there, but no engines. The American forces definitely needed engines. MacArthur found a railroad engineer and two firemen and bribed them to show him where the engines were. He let them search him to prove he had no more money, so killing him would be profitless. He had no weapon but a small Remington derringer—a tiny, double-barreled pistol that was a favorite arm of gamblers in the Old West.

MacArthur and his Mexican confederates traveled by handcar thirty miles into Huerta-held territory with MacArthur wearing his uniform so he could not be accused of being a spy. They found five locomotives. During the return trip, they ran into hostile troops three times. One of the Mexicans with MacArthur was wounded. Several bullets put holes in the captain's clothes, and he reported that he had hit seven of Huerta's men with his little derringer.

Wilson was flabbergasted by the reaction to his liberation of Veracruz. All Mexico—in fact, all Latin America—was outraged. Even Mexicans who were actively engaged in fighting Huerta's army. Venustiano Carranza, the governor of Coahuila, who was leading the largest rebel army, sent a note to Wilson: "The invasion of our territory and the permanency of your forces in the Port of Veracruz are a violation of the rights that constitute our existence as a free and independent sovereignty and will drag us into an unequal war which until today we desired to avoid."[13]

That was definitely not the kind of reaction a "liberator" expected.

Actually, the Mexicans were well on the way to liberating themselves—at least, of liberating themselves from Huerta. Zapata, in Morelos, south of Mexico City, had never stopped fighting. Carranza was leading a large army south toward Mexico City from Coahuila, the state east of Chihuahua. Carranza was a politician, not a general, but he was closely allied with Álvaro Obregón, a farmer from Sonora, west of Chihuahua, who turned out to be a talented amateur general. Between these two leaders was Pancho Villa, a veteran of the original revolt against Díaz.

Villa had been a colonel in the army when Huerta, the commander-in-chief, ordered him to return a horse one of his men had stolen. Villa refused. Huerta had him arrested and sentenced to death. He was standing in front of an open grave and looking at a firing squad when Raúl Madero galloped up with a reprieve signed by his brother, the president. Villa was imprisoned, but a short time later he managed to stroll out of the jail wearing no disguise but a pair of sunglasses. He was hiding out in El Paso, Texas, when he heard of Madero's execution. He went berserk with rage, rounded up four companions and rode back into Chihuahua.

Robin Hood had returned!

Everywhere, péons picked up their rifles, revolvers, and machetes and joined his merry men. They rode north, south, east, and west through every town in Chihuahua, singing the sardonic *"La Cucuracha"* and the plaintive *"Adelita."* They also chanted a ditty translated as:

> Companeros of the plow,
> Starving, tired and dirty,
> There's but one road to follow now,
> So grab your thirty-thirty.[14]

In thirty days, Villa had 3,000 cavalrymen. Before long, Huerta's forces held only three towns in Chihuahua—Torreón, Ciudad Chihuahua, and Ciudad Juárez. On October 1, 1913, Villa's cavalry, known as *Los Dorados* (the Golden Ones) launched a wild charge on government troops and burst into Torreón. A month later, they appeared outside of Ciudad Chihuahua, 300 miles north. This time, the wild cavalry charge was met by massed rifle and machine-gun fire. Villa decided that charging machine guns might be macho, but it wasn't war. Instead of repeating his mistake, he captured a troop train en route to Chihuahua from Juárez. Forging the train commander's name, he telegraphed the train commander's superior in Juárez, saying his engine had broken down and he needed a new locomotive and five more boxcars. When the new engine and additional cars arrived, he sent another message to Juárez: "Large forces of rebels approaching from south. Wires cut between here and Chihuahua. What shall I do?"

"Return at once," was the reply.[15]

Villa loaded his troops onto the train and went back to Juárez. The Villistas arrived November 15 in the wee hours of the morning, jumped out, and took over the city while most of the garrison was asleep. A week later they bloodily repulsed a federal counterattack. On December 8, 1913, Ciudad Chihuahua surrendered, and Villa made himself governor of the state of Chihuahua. One of his first official acts was to give anyone who asked for it seventy-five acres, nontransferable for ten years. The land came, of course, from the big haciendas. Villa also started to establish a chain of public butcher shops.

Obregón joined Carranza, becoming, in effect, his chief of staff. Villa reported to Carranza only theoretically. To Villa, Carranza, a senator during the Porfiriato, was a typical arrogant hacendado. To Carranza, Villa was just a bandit. Villa's natural ally was Zapata, the Indian agrarian reformer.

In Washington, Wilson had placed an embargo on any munitions for Huerta's forces but put no restriction on weapons for the rebels. Villa purchased thousands of rifles in the United States, using money gained from the sale of stolen cattle and bank robberies. Villa was a hero to the American public. He had one brigade composed entirely of American volunteers, and newspapers were full of stories of Villa's courage, compassion for the poor, and sunny disposition. Carranza, though, was the only rebel leader who openly aspired to become president. Wilson sent the would-be president another message. He offered to help the Carrancistas by sending warships to blockade ports and prevent any supplies from reaching Huerta and by sending American troops to strategic locations in Mexico, ostensibly to protect American lives and property. This action, he said, would be kept unilateral by invoking the Monroe Doctrine.

Neither Carranza nor any other Mexican recognized the Monroe Doctrine as anything but an excuse the *Norteamericanos* used to dominate Latin America. He told Wilson's messenger that his "Constitutionalists" wanted guns, not guidance, and any American troops sent to Mexico would be met with bullets.

Although Carranza rejected him, Wilson felt that he could support no one else in Mexico. Villa was a bandit. Zapata was a radical, and his enemies said that he, too, was a bandit. Wilson shut off aid to anyone in Mexico except Carranza and his subordinate, Obregón.

Huerta fled to Spain.[16]

The rebels raced to be the first to enter Mexico City. Carranza and Obregón won the race, because Carranza had cut off Villa's supply of coal, so his 40,000 Dorado cavalry had to ride there on horseback instead of taking trains. Carranza sent Obregón to appease Villa. Villa welcomed Obregón with a firing squad, but the general from Sonora persuaded Don Pancho that executing him would dishonor the "Centaur of the North." Villa dismissed the firing squad and invited Obregón to dinner. He was later to bitterly regret his change of heart.

Villa, Zapata, Carranza, and Obregón met in Xochimilco, but fighting soon broke out among their followers. Carranza and Obregón moved to Veracruz, from which Wilson thoughtfully removed American forces. Villa and Zapata dawdled while Obregón, with the aid of German advisers, reorganized the Carrancista army.

Obregón drove Zapata's army back to Morelos and then fortified the town of Celaya with zigzag trenches, dugouts, and artfully sited machine guns and fieldpieces. He challenged Villa to do something about it. It was a challenge no macho man could resist. Villa sent wave after wave of Dorado cavalry charging Obregón's barbed wire while singing *"La Cucuracha."* The machine guns and artillery mowed them down. Finally, Obregón sent his carefully sheltered cavalry against the exhausted Villistas and drove them from the field. The Villa of 1913, creator of the Trojan iron horse, would have done something quite different. It would have been easy to surround Celaya and starve out its garrison, but the Villa of 1913 was dead, buried under tons of adoring newspaper stories and magazine articles. The Villa of 1915 believed his own press clippings.

Two months later, Villa attacked Obregón at León, sixty miles north of Celaya. It was a replay of Celaya, and the Dorados were almost annihilated. The Northwest was still mostly Villa country, but in October 1914, some fifteen hundred Carrancistas fortified the little town of Naco, Sonora. Naco, Sonora, is contiguous with Naco, Arizona. Gen. José Maytorena, a Villista and governor of Sonora, attacked the Carrancistas. Bullets were soon flying into the United States and hitting American citizens. Detachments of the 9th and 10th Cavalry Regiments, the famed African American "Buffalo Soldiers," were stationed in Naco, Arizona, but they had orders not to fire at the Mexicans, no matter what the provocation. They did not fire although a trooper in the 10th was killed and eighteen more wounded. Altogether fifty-four Americans were killed or wounded by stray bullets from Sonora. Brig. Gen. Hugh Scott, the army chief of staff, went to Naco to talk with the Mexican leaders. The Carrancistas agreed to stop, but they were already on their last legs. Maytorena refused to stop. Scott wired Villa requesting a meeting in Juárez. Eventually, Villa agreed with Scott's proposal: Both sides would leave Naco. The Villistas would have a port of entry to the United States at Nogales, and the Carrancistas at Agua Prieta, opposite Douglas, Arizona.[17]

Villa's next target was Agua Prieta. This time, he planned his campaign more carefully. He controlled all the lines of communication from Agua Prieta to Carrancista forces in the south. And there would be no more daylight charges. This would be a night attack. He considered everything. Except Woodrow Wilson.

The American president allowed Carranza to move troops across U.S. territory to Douglas, Arizona. They crossed the border to Agua Prieta, Sonora, and hooked powerful searchlights to electrical lines in Arizona. When Villa's men reached the Carrancista barbed wire, the searchlights suddenly illuminated them against the night sky. They were slaughtered.

On January 10, 1916, Villista colonel Pablo López stopped a train carrying American and Mexican mine engineers to an American-owned mine that had been closed. Obregón had convinced the mine owners to reopen it, promising government protection. Villa had ordered López to steal the mine's payroll.

López decided to do a bit more. He killed all the American citizens except one engineer who managed to escape. Villa probably did not order the murders, but he must have thought killing Americans was a good idea, because two months later, on March 9, he led what was left of his army across the border and attacked the sleeping town of Columbus, New Mexico, population 300.

The 500 Villistas, dismounted and with the vanguard silently leading their horses, split into two columns. One column crept into the town and the other moved into the adjacent cavalry base, Camp Furlong. The streets in both the town and the camp were dark. Columbus had no electricity. Kerosene lamps provided what light there was, and most of them had been blown out hours before. Pvt. Fred Griffin of K Troop, 13th Cavalry, heard a noise while standing guard. He whirled around and faced the noise.

"Halt! Who's there?" he challenged.

The answer was a rifle shot that hit him in the stomach. Griffin leveled his rifle and fired shot after shot into the darkness, working the bolt of his weapon with a speed born of long practice. Then he lost consciousness and died. The next morning, three dead Mexicans were found near his body.

Lt. John B. Lucas had just gone to bed after arriving from Fort Bliss, outside El Paso, where he had been playing polo with other cavalry officers. When he heard the shots, he grabbed his loaded .45 automatic and dashed barefoot to his company, Machine Gun Troop.

Lt. James P. Castleman, the officer of the day, was, of course, fully dressed and armed when he heard the shots. He dashed out of the guard shack with his .45 in his hand and right into a Mexican raider. Castleman shot the Mexican almost by reflex and met members of F Troop, half dressed but fully armed. He led them toward the center of town, thinking the raiders were attempting to rob the bank.

Lucas roused the members of Machine Gun Troop and got the machine guns out of the guard shack. The machine guns, known in the U.S. Army as the Benét-Mercié machine rifle, were a new weapon, invented by an American, Laurence V. Benét, and a Frenchman, Henri Mercié, at the French Hotchkiss factory, founded by another American, Benjamin Hotchkiss. The Ben-A, as the troops called it, was a popular weapon. In the British Army, it was called the Hotchkiss Light Machine Gun Mark I, and in the French Army, it was the Model 1908. Like many early machine guns, it could be tricky to handle, especially if it had to be loaded in the dark. Lucas and a gunner, Cpl. Michael Barmazel, grabbed one of the four machine guns and set it up. Lucas shoved a clip into the gun, and Barmazel fired. The gun jammed after a couple of rounds. The lieutenant and corporal ran back to the guard shack and got another gun. This one didn't jam. The rest of Machine Gun Troop set up the other two guns and cleared the jam on the first one.

Machine Gun Troop was an even newer organization than the gun they operated. Men were pulled from other companies and troops and designated Machine Gun Troop (or Company).[18] They were usually selected in the traditional army way. The "route-steps," nonconformists, and other odd-balls formed the new unit. In Columbus, New Mexico, on March 9, 1916, the oddballs performed magnificently. During the rest of the night, Lucas's men fired 20,000 rounds into the Mexicans with devastating effect.

Early reports about the fighting said that the machine guns had jammed and were useless. Julian S. Hatcher, an ordnance officer involved with training gunners and who later became a major general and field ordnance service chief, later wrote that the Ben-As were "a decisive factor in saving the town."[19]

Villa's men hid behind the thick-walled adobe cook shacks when the machine guns opened. Inside the shacks, the cooks and KPs had been up making breakfast before the raiders arrived. Each shack had a pump-action shotgun the cooks used to kill fresh game. They used these on the Mexicans. At one shack, the raiders broke down the door. The first cook threw a pot of boiling water in their faces while a KP used a wood-chopping hatchet on their skulls. The raiders were looking for horses at Camp Furlong. They found only grief.

In the town, they robbed and then killed a number of citizens in cold blood. When they entered the hotel, one tenant told them he'd give them all his money and threw bills and coins on the floor. While the Mexicans were picking up the money, he went into his room and down a fire escape.

The raiders burned the hotel and many other buildings. One of the men rescuing people from fires was a young customs agent named Jolly Garner, the younger brother of John Nance "Cactus Jack" Garner who later was vice president in Franklin D. Roosevelt's first two terms. A pair of cowboys, Buck Chadborn and Jack Taylor, living on a ranch outside town, heard the shooting and rode in to investigate. They found a friend of Chadborn's, Dick Rodriguez, and then all three started organizing citizens to fight back.

When the sun came up, the Mexicans saw all the bodies of their fellow raiders and started to leave the town. Maj. Frank Tomkins got permission from the fort commandant, Col. Herbert J. Slocum, to mount up Troop H and pursue the raiders. Tomkins and fifty-six troopers chased between 300 and 400 Villistas fifteen miles into Mexico, firing at them with Springfield rifles at long range and driving them from four defensive positions with mounted pistol charges. Finally, with ammunition and water running low, they returned to Columbus. On the way, they counted about a hundred Mexican bodies and captured two machine guns. When they got to Columbus, they saw that sixty-seven more Mexican bodies were being burned. American losses came to seventeen—nine civilians and eight soldiers.

Wilson ordered the army to send a task force into Mexico and bring back Villa dead or alive. To lead it, Gen. Hugh L. Scott, the chief of staff, picked Brig. Gen. John J. Pershing, a soldier who demonstrated a talent for diplomacy while campaigning against the Moro tribes in the Philippines. (That talent, though, would not be much in evidence during Pershing's time in Mexico.) Pershing had married the daughter of Senator Francis E. Warren (R, Wyoming) in 1905. Helen Frances Warren was twenty years his junior. In 1906 Pershing received a breath-taking promotion—from captain to brigadier general—over the heads of 862 superior officers. Some said it was the result of being a senator's son-in-law. But President Theodore Roosevelt, who had introduced Pershing to his wife and later promoted him, said it was because of his work in the Philippines.[20]

Pershing chose troops for the "punitive expedition" carefully. For cavalry, the essential arm, he picked the 7th, 10th, 11th, and 13th regiments. The 7th Cavalry was famed as George Armstrong Custer's old outfit. Pershing had strong ties with the 10th, the all-black (enlisted men) regiment that he had fought with in Cuba, where the African American troopers saved Roosevelt's Rough Riders at Guásimas and beat them to the top of Kettle Hill.[21] The infantry, from the 6th and 16th regiments, would be mainly used for manning outposts guarding the expedition's supply lines. Pershing also had two batteries of the 6th field artillery manning eight 75mm pack howitzers, which could be quickly disassembled and loaded on mules. For scouting, Pershing's column got something revolutionary for the U.S. Army—airplanes. Unfortunately, the planes were JN-2s, the "Jenny," an underpowered, unstable craft that couldn't climb over the mountains of Chihuahua.

The Americans marched deep into the heart of Chihuahua and split up to scour the countryside, but they never caught sight of Villa. They fought some skirmishes with Villistas. During one of these, Second Lieutenant George S. Patton Jr. led a foraging party against a ranch house where he believed Villistas were hiding. Three Villistas dashed out shooting, and Patton killed one with the Colt Single Action he carried instead of the regulation .45 automatic.[22] He shot the horse of another, then shot the unhorsed Villista, who continued firing in spite of a mortal wound. That determined antagonist turned out to be Gen. Julio Cárdenas, onetime commander of *Los Dorados*. He was finally silenced by the infantry in Patton's detachment, as was the third rider. Pershing was so pleased he promoted Patton to first lieutenant.

The main reason the Americans could not find Villa was the almost universal refusal of the villagers to give them any reliable information. That was not because they loved Villa. They hated the "invaders." Don Pancho's charisma had thoroughly disappeared by this time. He tried to replenish his army by drafting young men in the villages he passed through. That proved to be an almost fatal mistake.

Villa decided to attack a Carrancista stronghold in Guerrero. He passed out some antique rifles and a few rounds of ammunition to his draftees. The draftees saw a chance to return home. "It was our intent to kill him and go over to the Carrancistas," said Modesto Nevares, one of the draftees.[23] When Villa led a charge against the Carrancistas, one of Nevares's companions shot at him with an old 11mm Remington rolling block rifle. The big lead bullet struck Villa in the leg, inflicting a serious wound. Unfortunately for the draftees who had been planning to join the Carrancistas, the Carrancistas decided to flee about the same time Villa had been hit. Don Pancho was taken away in a wagon driven, ironically, by Nevares, who had been assigned to that detail. From then on, Villa's whereabouts were completely unknown to both Americans and Carrancistas.

A Carrancista officer called on Maj. Frank Tomkins, leading a squadron of the 13th Cavalry, and invited him and his troops to visit Parral, where they could be refreshed. That was unusual. The usual attitude of Carrancista troops was surly hostility. On one occasion, they shot at Pershing himself. Tomkins entered Parral, and the garrison commander offered him a camp site. It was really a site for an ambush. After a running fight, Tomkins and his men were surrounded. They were rescued by a squadron of the 10th Cavalry under Maj. Charles Young—one of only three African American officers in the U.S. Army.

Carranza had stopped all rail traffic to Pershing's troops. In Washington, Scott used unauthorized funds to buy a fleet of trucks to supply Pershing. Pershing proposed taking over the state of Chihuahua and its railroads, and Funston endorsed the idea. The idea got nowhere. Villa could be anywhere in Mexico, not just Chihuahua, and the Americans were greatly outnumbered by the Carrancista army. Wilson initiated a series of negotiations with Carranza, but they got nowhere. The Americans were looking for cooperation from Carranza while Carranza wanted nothing except an American exit. The Mexican president deployed his troops on all sides of the American forces. Gen. Jacinto B. Trevino sent a message to Pershing that he had orders "to prevent the American forces now in this state from moving south, east or west of the places they now occupy."[24]

Pershing ordered Capt. Charles Boyd of the 10th Cavalry to take a couple of troops and observe the movement of Carrancista forces to the east of them. He told Boyd to avoid battle if possible. Boyd sought battle instead. He charged a much more numerous force of entrenched Mexicans firing machine guns. Twelve Americans were killed, ten wounded, and twenty-four captured. It was the worst defeat suffered by the "punitive expedition." Another round of peace talks began, and the Mexicans returned the American prisoners.

While peace talks were in progress, Pancho Villa returned. He sent a message to General Trevino in Ciudad Chihuahua that he was coming to shake his hand. Trevino ignored the threat. Villa burst into Chihuahua September 16 at 2:30 A.M. Most of Trevino's soldiers deserted and went over to Villa. The Villistas looted the city, massacred Chinese residents, and left seven hours later. Villa returned to banditry while the "punitive expedition" bivouacked in central Chihuahua. Pershing wasn't able to move in any direction but north, and he wouldn't do that. The Americans wanted Carranza to guarantee the safety of the border—something he could not do—and, if possible, restore peace among the warring factions, which nobody could do. Carranza wanted only to see the last of Pershing and his men. By January 12, 1917, the United States was close to entering World War I. Wilson withdrew Pershing's expedition.

The Mexican Revolution continued. Life on the border continued to be perilous. South of Mexico City, a Carrancista officer, Col. Jesús Guajardo, sent a message to Zapata that he wanted to change sides. To prove his sincerity, he attacked another Carrancista unit, and then executed his prisoners. He invited Zapata to come to his camp and take over his army. When Zapata arrived, Guajardo's troops were drawn up on the parade ground, presenting arms while Guajardo stood with raised sword to salute the general from Morelos. Guajardo's sword flashed down; the troops leveled their rifles and fired. Zapata had often quoted José Martí, the Cuban patriot: "It is better to die on your feet that live on your knees." Zapata had lived on this feet, fighting tyranny, and that was how he died.

Carranza had no patent on treachery. His trusted general, Obregón, decided he wanted to be president. So he paid Carranza's bodyguards to dispose of the old man. He made himself president and bought off Pancho Villa with a huge hacienda.

But Villa was still dangerous. He had charisma, a quality the wily Obregón lacked. On July 19, 1923, Villa came to Parral to spend the night with one of his many mistresses. On the same day, a group of Mexican ranchers and cowboys tied up their horses at a Parral hotel and took an upstairs room. When Villa's car passed the hotel, they opened fire on it with Mondragón semiautomatic rifles. The Mondragón, an invention of Díaz's rapacious chief of ordnance, was the first semiautomatic ever used in war.[25] It was not widely owned by Mexican civilians. The organizer of the assassination said he had a dispute with Villa over money. It was a private quarrel, he said. He was sentenced to twenty years in prison. But Obregón saw to it that he was free in six months.

Three years later, while Obregón was chatting with friends in a restaurant, a young man walked up to him and put five bullets into his head. The youth belonged to the Cristeros, a Catholic faction in rebellion because of the government's persecution of their church.

With all the great revolutionaries dead, one of Obregón's hangers-on, Plutarco Elías Calles, took over Mexico. Calles, who richly deserved the nickname Mexicans had already given Huerta, *el Chacal* (the jackal), served one term as president and controlled the next three presidents from behind the scenes. He really founded the Party of Institutional Revolution, which ruled Mexico for seventy years. The fourth president, Lázaro Cárdenas del Rio, who took office in 1934, could not be controlled. He exiled Calles and put down the last armed uprising. At last, the Mexican Revolution was over.

Wilson wanted to develop real democracy in Mexico, and he wanted to bring peace to the country. He did neither.

The moral of the story is not that outside interference in the life of a country is doomed to fail. The interference of the French in the civil war now known as the American Revolution was anything but a failure.

Much depends on the attitude of the outsiders. The French did not try to shape the politics of the Americans. They did not try to instruct their allies. And when the British general O'Hara tried to give his sword to the French general, Rochambeau, at Yorktown, the Frenchman directed him to Washington, saying the French were not in command.[26]

PART II

World War I and Its Aftermath

CHAPTER 4

Most Irregular Regulars: von Lettow-Vorbeck in East Africa, 1914–1918

Early in 1914, a young German officer in German East Africa got tired of watching native *askaris* march on a dusty drill field. (The Arabic word for soldiers was universally applied to native troops, who in the German colonies were more formally called the *Schutztruppe*.) East Africa and all the other German African colonies were the back of beyond, the lieutenant believed. If war broke out—and it looked as if it might—matters would be decided in Europe, not Africa. And the colonial powers knew it. Not just Germany, but Britain, France, Belgium, and Portugal, all of them maintained colonial armies that had just enough firepower to maintain order in the native tribes. All of them were askari forces. And all the askaris were poorly armed and equipped. These black guys he was watching marched well, the officer thought, but their uniforms were patched, and they were shouldering the old Model 1871 Mauser, a single-shot rifle that used black powder cartridges. Every time the old coal burner fired, it belched out a cloud of white smoke, marking the firer's position for any enemy and making it impossible for the shooter to see the enemy. Any German officers in East Africa, in short, would be taking part in a useless sideshow.

The bored officer felt thirsty. He decided to go into town and get a beer. Walking along the dirt track, he met a middle-aged man chewing a piece of sugar cane. The young soldier complained of the boring routine and the waste of time here in this backwater of empire to the man he took to be a settler. He said he just had to take a break.

"I hope the new commander, von Lettow-Vorbeck, doesn't hear of it," the lieutenant said. "They say he's a real bastard."

Just then, the soldier and his companion turned a corner. Two other officers, both outranking the lieutenant, appeared. Before the young soldier could move, the two new officers snapped to attention and saluted the "settler." The lieutenant turned pale.

Paul von Lettow-Vorbeck turned to his young companion and said, "What you said was said to a comrade. No comrade would inform the commander, certainly."[1]

Lt. Col. Paul Emil von Lettow-Vorbeck could agree with almost everything the lieutenant said. Africa was certainly not going to be a decisive theater if war came. Lieutenant colonels do not command in decisive theaters. And his Schutztruppe certainly were neglected. New uniforms were coming, but no new rifles. The great general staff wanted all the modern rifles it could get in Europe. And the situation of the German colonies was perilous. The German High Seas Fleet was a mighty navy, but Britain's navy was larger and it seemed likely that the High Seas Fleet would never make it to the high seas. In that case, the British could drown all the German colonies with manpower from their empire, just as they had done to the Afrikaners a few years earlier.

Von Lettow-Vorbeck did not see duty in Africa as a waste of time, however. If war broke out, he would do his best to attract and hold as many British troops as he could, so they could not be used in the decisive theater.

The governor of German East Africa, Heinrich Schnee, did not agree with the new commander. He believed German East Africa could stay neu-

Paul Emil von Lettow-Vorbeck, a very Prussian regular who turned out to be a master of guerrilla warfare. He was the only German general who was still advancing when World War I ended. LIBRARY OF CONGRESS

tral. In 1885, all nations with African colonies met in Berlin and passed the General Act of Berlin, which declared that if war broke out in Europe, all European colonies in Africa would remain neutral, provided everyone agreed. The only European power that needed to agree was Britain, Schnee believed. The French colonies were too far away and neither the Belgians nor the Portuguese were likely to make trouble. Schnee talked with Norman King, the British consul in German East Africa. King said London would put nothing in writing, but it was inclined to honor German East African neutrality if the colony stayed strictly neutral.

Then the German cruiser *Königsberg* steamed into the port of Dar es Salaam. The *Königsberg* escaped from the Baltic just before war broke out and the British clamped a blockade on all routes from Germany to the Atlantic. The *Königsberg* was a commerce raider. On August 6, a week after the start of the war, the *Königsberg* captured the British ship *City of Winchester.* In British eyes, if a commerce raider was using Dar es Salaam as a base, the port was no longer an open city. Two British cruisers entered the harbor of Dar es Salaam and, not finding the *Königsberg,* shelled the radio tower. War had come to German East Africa.

Von Lettow-Vorbeck now took over. He had been preparing for this moment. He had recruited white settlers for an irregular force and sent askari officers and non-coms to native villages looking for Schutztruppe recruits. One of his notable recruits was Tom von Prinz, formerly Tom Prince, son of an English father and a German mother. When both parents died, he went, at age fifteen, to live with relatives in Germany. Unable to get a commission in the British Army, he went to the German military academy, where he met von Lettow-Vorbeck. With Lettow, he took part in Germany's colonial wars. The Africans called him Bwana Sakharani, something like Lord Berserker. The Germans gave him a "von," and he Germanized his name to Prinz. At this crisis, he raised an irregular force of both blacks and whites and offered it to von Lettow-Vorbeck. After the shelling of Dar es Salaam, von Lettow-Vorbeck sent Prinz and his men to the Kilimanjaro area and told them to raid British outposts, cut telegraph and telephone lines, and tear up and mine the Uganda Railway. That would cause the British to send troops to Africa—troops that would be more dangerous in Europe.

Another notable recruit was Kurt Wahle, a retired major general in the army of Saxony, who was visiting his son in Africa. He outranked Lettow, but he put himself at the lieutenant colonel's disposal. Von Lettow-Vorbeck put him in charge of transportation. Wahle greatly improved the colony's ramshackle supply system. Next, von Lettow-Vorbeck gave the general 600 men and had him attack Kisumu, a port city on Lake Victoria that was the terminus of the British Uganda Railway. British scouts learned of the move, and a British ship loaded with troops steamed up the lake to destroy the German expedition. But German scouts were also active. The German armed tug *Muanza* drove the British steamer away. Finally, the British South African Mounted Rifles rode up and attacked Wahle's men. The British had repeating rifles using smokeless powder. Wahle was driven off after losing a quarter of his officers. But von Lettow-Vorbeck had drawn more enemy troops away from Europe.

Meanwhile, Capt. Max Loof, the *Königsberg's* skipper, had been hiding his commerce raider in the labyrinthine creeks in the swampy delta of the Rufiji River. Von Lettow-Vorbeck thought that the *Königsberg* might be able to land some of his troops at Mombasa, the big port of British East Africa (now Kenya). When he asked Loof about that, he learned that recently the *Königsberg* had slipped out of the delta and had sunk a couple of British warships in Zanzibar harbor. The British now had a fleet outside the delta waiting for the German cruiser's next appearance.

The British, too, had thought about attacking from the sea. Their attack would not be a mere raid: it would be a conquest. Most of the other German African colonies had already been conquered. The ease of those campaigns led the British to underestimate the potential opposition in German East Africa. The British plan called for two columns, one to strike in the west at the Kilimanjaro area, the other to land at the port of Tanga. They would then converge on the Germans. To man these columns they sent a partially trained battalion of the North Lancashire Regiment and 10,000 third-rate troops from India.

"They constitute the worst in India," wrote Richard Meinertzhagen, the British intelligence officer for the expedition, "and I tremble to think of what may happen if we meet serious opposition."[2]

Von Lettow-Vorbeck knew most of the British plan. His African agents crossed the border between the German and British colonies regularly. No whites worried about what "simple niggers" might see—not even the articles about the coming invasion printed in all the British newspapers.

The commander of the King's African Rifles, an askari outfit, offered his men as prelanding scouts. Maj. Gen. Arthur Aiken said the KAR would be unnecessary. He planned to "thrash the Germans before Christmas."[3]

Capt. F. W. Caulfield, commanding the naval contingent of the landing force, seems to have heard of the talks between Norman King and Heinrich Schnee but not to have heard of the shelling of Dar es Salaam. He sent a ship with a white flag into the harbor to inform the Germans that the truce no longer applied. If von Lettow-Vorbeck didn't already know Tanga was a target that would have left no doubt. Then Caulfield sent minesweepers into the harbor to sweep nonexistent mines. Caulfield still thought there might be mines so, after all that, the British ships didn't enter the harbor. They landed the troops about a mile from town, behind a small headland.

At 9:30 P.M., November 2, 1914, two British companies landed in a swamp filled with crocodiles and poisonous snakes. The British continued landing all night. The landing resolved any doubts about whether the first strike would be at Tanga or Kilimanjaro. As the English and Indian troops were landing, Germans and German askaris were rolling down the rickety railroad from Kilimanjaro. But the two companies of Schutztruppe in Tanga were able to hold up the British force.

Outside town, the British attempted to outflank von Lettow-Vorbeck's men, but the brush was so thick they couldn't see anything. The German askaris didn't need to see anything. They just hosed down the brush with machine guns. Some British attempted to rush the machine guns. In 1914, soldiers hadn't learned that rushing machine guns is suicidal. The German askaris counterattacked. The German fire was so heavy, the British thought they were greatly outnumbered. British Brigadier Michael Tighe later reported that his 2,000 troops were opposed by "2,500 German rifles." Meinertzhagen said, "From what I saw, it was more like 250 with four machine guns."[4] He was right.

Von Lettow-Vorbeck got all his troops into Tanga by 3 A.M., November 4. He bicycled through the town, including parts supposedly held by the British. He had about 1,000 askaris and white settlers. The British had 8,000. At noon, the British attacked again. But by then, most of them had emptied their canteens. They advanced about 600 yards, but some of them were felled by heat exhaustion. One company of askaris had obtained modern Mauser Gewehr 98 rifles. They sniped at the Indians and English from the treetops. Other askaris set up their machine guns with interlocking fields of fire. During the house-to-house fighting, Meinertzhagen spotted a thin German officer who seemed to be in command. He fired at him and missed. The German fired back. He, too, missed.

"This was my first social contact with my friend Meinertzhagen," von Lettow-Vorbeck noted in his memoirs.[5] After the war, the two became fast friends.

The British force slowly fell back. During the retreat, the men of the Lancashire Battalion passed through a grove filled with wild honeybees. These "African killer bees" of later horror stories reacted to the disturbance by attacking the soldiers. The English believed that von Lettow-Vorbeck had wired the beehives. The attack was really the bees' idea, but it boosted the Prussian colonel's reputation as an evil genius.

By November 6, the British had evacuated. They lost 800 killed, 500 wounded, and hundreds missing. The biggest German loss was von Lettow-Vorbeck's old friend, Tom von Prinz. The berserker lord had fought his last battle in the streets of Tanga.

The Germans captured hundreds of rifles, 16 machine guns, and 6,000 rounds of ammunition.[6] The capture of arms and ammunition was extremely important in this campaign, because none could be sent from Germany. Lack of supplies from Germany was a serious handicap, but as the war continued, von Lettow-Vorbeck's troops became almost self-sufficient. They learned how to make fuel for motor vehicles from coconuts. They made tires from rope covered with raw latex from rubber trees. They built a gunpowder factory, a brewery, and a whiskey distillery. They distilled salt from wild plants. They ate wild plants, got food from the villages, and shot wild game. Women made homespun uniforms colored khaki with home-made dye. Farmers made soap and candles. Shoemakers made shoes from buffalo hide. The Amani Biological Institute, one of the world's leading research centers for tropical diseases (and Heinrich Schnee's pride and joy), made a quinine substitute.

But the attack on Tanga was only half of the British invasion plan. The second British attack took place after the landing in the Kilimanjaro area. A German force under a Major Kraut was still there, as von Lettow-Vorbeck's order to move to Tanga had not reached them. That was a stroke of luck. Kraut had 600 askaris and 86 settlers to hold off 1,500 Indians. The Indians charged the German machine guns bravely, if—as always—futilely. What decided the battle was a stampede of mules carrying water and other vital supplies for the British. That night, the Indians had to withdraw.

British warships again bombarded Dar es Salaam, and the Germans resumed raiding the Uganda Railway. Troops of the Indian Army took the German-held town of Jasin, and Lettow counterattacked. The Indians restored the honor of the Indian Army. Although he retook the town, von Lettow-Vorbeck's losses were heavy, including six regular officers who could not be replaced. Militarily, the town was worthless. The German commander realized that in the kind of war he was fighting, land was expendable; men were not.

He reorganized his army. The largest unit was now a platoon with thirty rifles and two machine guns. The reorganization showed that von Lettow-Vorbeck was well ahead of the German Army and all other armies in his grasp of machine gun tactics. In 1916, a year after Lettow's reorganization, each German division contained seventy-two machine guns.[7] That's about one gun for each 139 men. In the East African Schutztruppe, there was around one gun for each 18 or 20 men. Moreover, in Europe most machine guns were grouped together in companies or battalions, rather than split up among platoons.

The capture of British machine guns at Tanga helped von Lettow-Vorbeck develop this organization. The British Vickers and the German Maxim were both developments of the original Maxim and were only slightly different. A man trained on the Maxim had no trouble learning to use the Vickers. The askaris who manned the machine guns hired bearers to carry the guns. Neither type of gun was a lightweight. The Maxim weighed thirty-one pounds and was fired from an eighty-three-pound, four-legged mount, the legs of which could be raised to the horizontal like the handles of a stretcher. Two men could carry the gun, already mounted, easily. The Vickers gun, with a filled water jacket, weighed about forty-four pounds. It was fired from a tripod considerably lighter than the German mount, but gun and tripod were carried separately.[8] The askaris were expert at setting up fields of fire, and their bearers learned to prepare the guns for firing or for moving in a few seconds. The Maxim was especially well adapted for quick setting up and moving.

In the reorganized Schutztruppe, each platoon would support patrols of no more than three or four men. Soldiers would carry their own food and ammunition. Only on large-scale operations would civilian porters be used to carry supplies.

The British, too, turned to an irregular war of raids and ambushes. Meinertzhagen led British reconnaissance patrols. Once, he got inside a camp with 1,400 sleeping German troops. Challenged by a guard, he spoke in Swahili, pretending to be a German officer until he got close enough to bayonet the guard. He then swam a crocodile-infested river to reach safety. To discourage German patrols in one sector, he put a lot of dead birds and animals around a water hole and erected a sign saying the water was poisoned.

General Tighe, who now commanded the British forces, begged to be allowed to take the offensive. London ordered him to take Bukoba, a German port on Lake Victoria. He got reinforcements, the 2nd Rhodesian Regiment and the 25th Battalion of the Royal Fusiliers. Both regiments were mostly composed of British African settlers. One of them was Frederick Courteney Selous, a famous big game hunter and author who was also well over sixty at the time. The British, who outnumbered von Lettow-Vorbeck's askaris two to one, took Bukoba after a much harder fight than they expected. They celebrated the victory with a drunken orgy of pillage, rape, and murder. One soldier "liberated" a parrot who could only say—appropriately—*"Ach, du Schwein."*[9]

In July 1915, von Lettow-Vorbeck occupied two hills in the Kilimanjaro area. The British tried to retake them. In each case, the British charged against machine guns. And, as always, the machine guns won. After each victory, more volunteers joined von Lettow-Vorbeck. In irregular war, nothing succeeds like success.

Meanwhile, Max Loof on the *Königsberg* found a stream in the Rufiji Delta that the British were not watching. He radioed Berlin that if he had coal, he could steam out of his hiding place and get back into the war. Berlin sent a blockade runner loaded with coal. As an afterthought, they also loaded on weapons and supplies for von Lettow-Vorbeck. The blockade runner almost made it. The British spotted it and pursued. The German freighter, flying the Danish flag, ran aground near Tanga. British warships blasted it, and water poured into its hull. Lettow had men at the scene almost immediately. They unloaded 1,800 brand-new Mauser 98 rifles, 4.5 million rounds of ammunition, several dozen machine guns, artillery field-pieces, cannon shells, medicine, food, clothing, and tents. But the *Königsberg* crew was out of luck. The coal had been soaked with seawater and was now useless. The British made sure that the cruiser would never leave the Rufiji. Pieter J. Pretorius, an Afrikaner ivory poacher now a British major, who had hunted in the Rufiji Delta for years, found the camouflaged *Königsberg* and plotted a route for shallow-draft British monitors to approach the ship. The monitors destroyed the *Königsberg*. That was a loss for the German Navy, but not for von Lettow-Vorbeck. He got ten 105mm guns from the cruiser and mounted them on makeshift field carriages. He also got 320 more fighting men, hundreds of rifles, and more machine guns.

Because Loof, a navy captain, outranked von Lettow-Vorbeck, an army lieutenant colonel, Governor Schnee tried to get the sailor to take over the German military effort in East Africa. Loof was not that foolish. Von Lettow-Vorbeck had thousands of men who would march through hell for him, and if he didn't want to give up command, he wouldn't. Instead, Loof offered his services to Lettow, who gave him command of Dar es Salaam. By the summer of 1915, von Lettow-Vorbeck had 3,000 European and 11,000 African troops.

By the end of 1915, the British were ready to make an all-out effort to solve the East Africa problem. The Union of South Africa donated 20,000 troops to the effort. With them went Jan Christiaan Smuts, a guerrilla leader in the South African war and a successful politician. Before Smuts arrived, the English, Indian, and South African troops already in East Africa decided to take the hills von Lettow-Vorbeck was holding and give them to their new commander as a present. They concentrated on Mount Oldorobo, commanded by the reliable Major Kraut. The 6,000 English, Indians, Rhodesians, and South Africans outnumbered Kraut's troops five to one. The British opened with a terrific barrage on the German trenches and charged. They found that the trenches were empty. Then German machine guns hidden in the brush behind the trenches cut them down.

In spite of the British lack of success against Lettow, Smuts was not impressed with his foe. Most of the enemy troops were black. "Damned Kaffirs," he told Meinertzhagen, "I'll drive them with a whip." He didn't rate the Indians much more highly. They were only "coolies."[10]

The next time the British hit Mount Oldorobo, the Rhodesians, English, and Indians attacked from the front and the South Africans from the flank. German machine guns covered both sectors. After shooting up the South

African flankers, the German "kaffirs" charged them with bayonets. The South Africans were rescued by "coolies" from Baluchistan.

Smuts decided on wider flanking movements. The next time he attacked, he opened with a frontal assault meant only to hold the enemy in place. Brig. Jacobus van Deventer was to deliver a blow from the flank. But the new element was a wide sweep to the Germans' rear, delivered by Brig. James Stewart. Stewart's move was noted by von Lettow-Vorbeck's scouts. Askari snipers harried the British, destroyed bridges in front of them, and set up ambushes. Giraffes took care of the telephone lines the British laid behind them. These enormously powerful beasts, which can decapitate a lion with one kick, simply walked through the phone lines and broke them. By the time Stewart got to his blocking position—four days late—the Germans were gone.

Smuts sent bombing planes against the Germans. He expected to terrify the simple savages in the Schutztruppe. But the simple savages had shot down a plane before. They knew it wasn't a magic beast. It was a machine, and not, at this time, a particularly dangerous one.

The fighting began to fall into a pattern. The British would attack, struggling through thick thornbushes while rifle and machine-gun fire cut them down. The Germans would appear to counterattack. Then the firing would cease. When the British advanced again, they found the Germans were gone. The British gained land at the cost of many casualties. The Germans gave up land but suffered few casualties. Smuts outnumbered von Lettow-Vorbeck more than three to one, but he could see no end to the war. He raged at his subordinates. He was developing an obsession with von Lettow-Vorbeck.

When he reached the German northern railroad, he planned to push down it to Tanga. Lettow would undoubtedly oppose him with his main force. When he did, he could be encircled and destroyed. As Smuts struck east, the rainy season began. The rainy season in East Africa is like nothing in South Africa. When it begins, everything else stops.

Smuts's plan never varied: advance along the track and send out troops on wide sweeps to the rear. The trouble with wide sweeps in the rainy season is that much of the country is flooded. At one point, van Deventer, leading a sweep, became lost in a maze of unmapped bogs and lakes. Von Lettow-Vorbeck mounted one of the *Königsberg* guns on a railroad car and used it to blast the advancing British. The Germans ripped up the tracks behind them, heated the steel tracks over burning ties, and twisted them so they could not be used again. They destroyed all bridges. All this slowed Smuts's advance. When they reached a position that could not be easily flanked, von Lettow-Vorbeck's troops stopped long enough to inflict casualties on the British before moving on. Thanks to the rainy season, there were plenty of places that could not be flanked. In East Africa, flooded rivers meant that not only water, but crocodiles, hippos, and other interesting wildlife would be blocking your path.

Von Lettow-Vorbeck took his main body off the railroad and marched south, leaving Kraut to defend the rails. Smuts apparently still thought the main German army was on the railroad. He stayed on it and sent van Deventer after Lettow. Fighting south of the railroad also fit a pattern. The Germans would pick a position, set up their machine guns, camouflage themselves, and wait. The British would appear, and the Germans would greet them with a hail of fire, then leave on preselected hidden paths. Land mines made from the explosives in the *Königsberg's* shells slowed down pursuit.

All through this thornbush country there were wild animals—lions, leopards, crocodiles, rhinos, hippos, hyenas, and buffalo. Much worse, there were leeches, chiggers, mosquitoes, and tsetse flies. Tsetse flies carried *nagana,* an African disease that killed horses and mules by the thousands. They also carried sleeping sickness, which killed men. The mosquitoes carried malaria.

In British newspapers, with the Germans being pushed back continually, van Deventer's campaign looked like a triumphal march. If so, it was the most grisly triumphal march in history. At the end of the rainy season, only 1,500 of van Deventer's 10,000 men were able to walk. The North Lancashire Battalion came to Africa with 900 men. Now it had 345, and that included replacements. The 25th Fusiliers started with 1,200 men. Now it had 200. The 9th South African Infantry had dropped from 1,135 to 120 men. All van Deventer's animals were dead. All his motor vehicles were kaput. In the north, Kraut had evaded all encirclements and was joining von Lettow-Vorbeck.

Smuts was still dangerous, though. He now had 80,000 men because the British, as von Lettow-Vorbeck hoped, had sent him more men. Another British column was approaching from Nyasaland. The Belgians were sending a column from the Congo. Even the Portuguese were joining the war. The African campaign was not a sideshow. It was drawing in men who could have been fighting in Europe. Von Lettow-Vorbeck moved his headquarters back to the Rufiji Delta and struck at one column, then another, keeping his numerically superior enemies confused.

The Nyasaland column was weak—not a major problem. The Belgian Army could have been a problem, but the British did not encourage it to penetrate deeply into German East Africa. Britannia did not want to share the colony with allies. The askaris in the Portuguese column were all looking for a chance to desert. They were no problem. The main enemy was Smuts.

Von Lettow-Vorbeck was doing some personal reconnaissance when he saw a small man with a neat red goatee in front of the British lines. Jan Christiaan Smuts was in easy rifle range. Lettow didn't fire, because, he said later, it didn't seem sporting. War was different in Africa in those days. When Smuts learned that von Lettow-Vorbeck had been awarded the *Pour le Merite,* Germany's highest honor, he sent a messenger to his opponent under a flag of truce. And when von Lettow-Vorbeck was promoted to major general, making him the highest-ranking German in Africa, Smuts again sent him word. When Smuts was transferred to England, von Lettow-Vorbeck sent him his congratulations on the way he had conducted the war.

In London, Smuts said the war in Africa was all but over. But in Africa, the English general who replaced Smuts despaired over the wreckage of the army the Afrikaner general once commanded. He returned to England and van Deventer took command of the British forces.

Von Lettow-Vorbeck had one notion of what was "sporting." Frederick Courteney Selous had another. On January 4, 1917, the sixty-six-year-old hunter was in the Rufiji Delta. Selous was after the most dangerous game in Africa—the Prussian guerrilla leader who had been making fools of the Allies in Africa. Captain Selous (only two years before he'd been demoted from lance corporal to private in the Royal Fusiliers) was camouflaged in a tree with his faithful old gun bearer hidden in another. He knew that sooner or later, he'd see the now-legendary von Lettow-Vorbeck. But a German sniper saw Selous first.

While in the Rufiji Delta, von Lettow-Vorbeck noticed that army ants were on the march. They were leaving their nests in the swamp and moving to higher ground. That meant the rainy season was approaching and most of the delta would soon be submerged. Von Lettow-Vorbeck and his men followed the ants. When the rains came, they separated the Germans from their enemies with a seasonal lake ninety miles wide. When the rains ended, Lettow again reorganized the army. Because the British had been raiding the villages that supplied the Schutztruppe, he reduced the army to 1,900 fighters—200 German and 1,700 African—and sent the rest home.

For three years, von Lettow-Vorbeck had been holding out in Africa although cut off from all contact with Europe. With no more than 14,000 troops he had been keeping 150,000 Allied soldiers from the Western Front in France. He was one of Germany's heroes, but Germany had been unable to help him. Britain ruled the sea.

But how about the air?

Remember, this was 1917. In 1919, three American flying boats tried to cross the Atlantic. Only one of them made it—the first transatlantic flight. The NC 4, piloted by Lt. Commander Albert C. Read, completed the 1,300 mile trip to the Azores, refueled, and continued on to Portugal. The other two planes, all especially equipped for long-distance flight, had to land in the ocean where they were picked up by ships.[11] The distance from Europe to German East Africa is a lot greater than the distance from the United States to the Azores.

Someone in Germany thought he had the answer, though. The Germans built the world's largest dirigible, the L-59. It was 750 feet long and carried 50 tons of supplies. In its cargo were 30 machine guns, 311,900 boxes of ammunition, 61 bags of medical supplies, 2 sewing machines, and a case of cognac. It was to land at von Lettow-Vorbeck's headquarters, unload its cargo, and be cannibalized. Any extra fuel could power German vehicles or generators; the airship's engines could also power new generators; the fabric envelope could be turned into tents and uniforms, the leather catwalk into shoes, and the gas cell containers into sleeping bags. The troops could even use the girders for buildings.

The zeppelin, under Lt. Commander Ludwig Bockholt, took off from Bulgaria and headed south. It crossed the Mediterranean, flew over British-held Egypt and the Sudan and got within sight of Mount Kilimanjaro. Nothing could stop it. Then it got a message in the German naval code:

ABANDON UNDERTAKING AND RETURN STOP ENEMY HAS OCCUPIED GREAT PART OF MAKONDE HIGHLANDS AND IS ALREADY AT KITAUGARI STOP[12]

Bockholt turned the ship around and flew back to Bulgaria. He had flown 4,225 miles nonstop. But it was all in vain. The message was a fake. The British had learned the German naval code and used it to defeat an enterprise they couldn't physically touch. Von Lettow-Vorbeck was not in trouble.

The day the zeppelin turned back, the German army was invading enemy territory.

Von Lettow-Vorbeck had invaded Portuguese Mozambique. He quickly captured a fort and resupplied his troops. He then divided the force into three columns, all moving in different directions, to confuse the British and Portuguese. The Germans struck here and there in Mozambique. Von Lettow-Vorbeck resupplied the Schutztruppe from Portuguese and British supply centers and forts. He captured a river steamer, two fieldpieces, a load of medicine, ten machine guns, 350 rifles, and more ammunition than his troops could carry. At one supply dump, he killed 209 defenders and captured 540. In another battle, a British column surrounded Lettow's troops, but the Prussian fox turned the tables on them and captured most of the British unit, including its commander. On September 28, 1918, he recrossed the border into German East Africa. Then he invaded Northern Rhodesia.

On November 11, 1918, while the armistice was being signed in Europe, von Lettow-Vorbeck was taking over the Rhodesian town of Kasama and the supplies stored there.

Two days later, his men captured a British courier. The courier carried a message:

> Send the following to General von Lettow-Vorbeck under white flag. The prime minister of England has announced that an armistice was signed at 5 hours on November 11th. I am ordering my troops to cease hostilities forthwith unless attacked and of course conclude that you will do the same. Conditions of armistice will be forwarded to you immediately [after] I receive them. Meanwhile, I suggest that you remain in your present vicinity in order to facilitate communications. General van Deventer.

The war was over. Von Lettow-Vorbeck had not only never surrendered, he was on the offensive.

Van Lettow-Vorbeck did more than masterfully demonstrate proper use of terrain in an irregular war while pioneering machine-gun tactics. He planted, inadvertently, probably, the seeds to an idea that would bear fruit a generation or two later. He showed that black African troops, properly equipped, trained, and led, are as good as any in the world.

CHAPTER 5

The Triumph of the Outside Agitator: Lawrence in Arabia, 1916–1918

The young British officer was sick in body and soul. He had a fever, was exhausted, and had just had to preside over a court-martial for one of his followers who murdered another follower. Even worse, the Arab revolt seemed to be getting nowhere.

Captain T. E. Lawrence had been sent in 1916 from Cairo to Arabia to observe the revolt against the Turks and report on what aid the British could give the troops of the Sherif of Mecca. Any descendant of the prophet Muhammad was called a sherif, but the Sherif of Mecca was also King of the Hejaz, the strip of western Arabia that contains the holy cities of Mecca and Medina. Sherif Hussein's prestige as Guardian of the Holy Places far outweighed his military strength. To call the Sherif's men an army would be a gross exaggeration, Lawrence thought. They were a ragtag collection of Bedouin from many tribes.

Arabia had been part of the Ottoman Empire for centuries, but Hussein longed to get rid of the Turkish yoke. When Turkey entered World War I, Hussein looked for an opportunity to break loose. His sons, Abdullah, Feisal, Zeid, and Ali, were educated in Constantinople. Feisal had served in the Turkish Army and was a member of the Turkish Parliament. After the Allied attack on Gallipoli, Feisal had told his father that although the attack was a disaster for the British, it had left the Turkish Army seriously weakened. Hussein, who had been secretly gathering adherents from the mutually suspicious tribes around Mecca and Medina, declared his independence. The Turks sent a force, commanded by Hamid Fakhri Pasha, known as the Butcher of Armenia, down the Hejaz Railway. Fakhri drove Hussein's men out of Medina. He then showed that he could butcher Arabs as well as Armenians. That was not a brilliant move on Fakhri's part. To the Arabs of that time and place, killing women and children was an abomination, and revenge for injuries was almost a religious duty. The old Turk was practically guaranteeing that the revolt would grow.

Fakhri had no concerns about "winning hearts and minds," though. He intended to win a war by capturing the enemy's capital. He would take Mecca as he had taken Medina, the other holy city. First, though, he planned to capture Yenbo, a port where the Sherifian forces were receiving supplies from Britain.

The attack on Yenbo was foiled by the guns of the British navy, and Feisal, who was the Arab commander at Yenbo, consulted with Lawrence on how to capitalize on the Turkish defeat. Feisal, incidentally, was Lawrence's choice for a leader of the revolt—a choice he had no authority to make. His reasoning was more romantic than scientific. He saw the Bedouin as "incarnate Semites," and recalled that three of the world's great religions—Judaism, Christianity, and Islam—were founded by Semites living in the deserts of western Asia. Semitic prophets had gone into the desert, found God, and returned to gather crowds of Semitic followers. Lawrence decided that the best leader of this Semitic revolt would be a secular prophet. After meeting Hussein and his sons, Lawrence decided that Feisal made the best prophet material.

Feisal resolved to move the army to Wadi Ais, a valley with many springs that would let the Arabs threaten the Hejaz Railway, the only supply route for the Turks in Medina. To facilitate their own supply, the Arabs moved their base to Wejh, farther north on the coast of Hejaz and closer to the British base in Egypt.

The Turks suddenly switched to the defensive. They established a circle of trenches and strongpoints around Medina, a circle wide enough to make it impossible for the Arabs' light and obsolescent artillery to shell the city. Fakhri also set up outposts along the railroad and had patrols travel between them along the line. The Turkish army was still the same army that had driven the Arabs out of Medina, so the reason for this sudden switch to the defensive was not clear. Lawrence thought about that as he was riding up to Feisal's brother, Abdullah, to get him to coordinate his movements with those of Feisal. On the way, he was stricken with fever, boils, dysentery, and profound weakness. For ten days he lay in a tent at Abdullah's camp unable to do anything but think.

His thoughts at first were not happy. At Medina, the Bedouin had proved they could not hold a position against a regular army. Further, they had also demonstrated that they could not attack and hold a major enemy position. The Arab leaders and their British allies were all for them taking Medina, but Lawrence knew the Bedouin could not capture a fortified city. That, he thought, made them incapable of forcing a decision. Lawrence had studied all the classic European military writers, such men as Napoléon, Clausewitz, Jomini, and Moltke, and he could see no way the Arabs could win the war by following their principles. What strengths did the Arabs have?

Why would their position threatening the railroad make an old soldier like Fakhri Pasha go on the defensive?

One thing was sheer space. "I began to calculate how many thousand square miles . . . perhaps one hundred and forty thousand square miles. And how would the Turks defend all that?"[1] The Turks had planes, artillery, and armored trains, but even so, Lawrence calculated that they would need a fortified post every four square miles and each post would need a minimum of twenty men. That would take far more men than Fakhri Pasha had. And any one of those tiny posts could easily be overwhelmed by a fraction of the 50,000 men who followed the sherifs.

Lawrence compared regular armies to plants, fixed to their supply routes the way flowers were fixed to their stems. Consequently, they were immobile. The camel-mounted Bedouin, on the other hand, were relatively weak, but self-sufficient. The Arabs, Lawrence thought, were not plants but vapor, "blowing where we listed."[2]

The Turks and their German allies "would believe that rebellion was absolute like war, and deal with it on the analogy of war. Analogy in human things was fudge, anyhow."[3]

Lawrence believed the Turks were stupid. It seems, though, that Fakhri Pasha was not as stupid as the Englishman thought. The old Turkish general knew that his armored trains could not leave their tracks. The soft sand and waterless expanse of the desert made his horse-drawn artillery almost as immobile. Military airplanes in 1917 were slow, short-ranged, delicate, and had little firepower. Even if they spotted the Arabs in the desert, the Turkish ground forces could never catch up with the camel-riding Bedouin. Fakhri did about the only thing he could—fortify Medina and wait for the Arabs to come to him.

Lawrence thought the Arabs should take advantage of their mobility by raiding along the railroad at points as widespread as possible. That would force the Turks to extend their outposts and patrols along the full length of the railroad. The Arabs would not permanently cut the Turks' umbilical cord. They would allow some supplies to reach Medina, but not enough. Fakhri's men would have to eat their horses and mules, further reducing their mobility, and they would be too busy vainly trying to guard the railroad to take the offensive. Meanwhile the sherifs would be able to range far and wide, proselytizing the Arab tribes. (At this stage, the Arab Revolt was far from including all Arabs. Many tribes were pro-Turk; many more were neutral.) The Turks in Medina, Lawrence thought, were as good as in prison— better, in fact, because in prison they would require the Allies to provide guards, food, and medical care.

When he recovered, Lawrence tried to convince the Arab leaders and his own British superiors of his ideas. They still wanted to attack Medina.

Then the Arabs got a message from Cairo. The British had learned that Fakhri Pasha had been ordered to withdraw from Mecca. At this time, the British were preparing to invade Palestine, and they didn't want Fakhri's army to suddenly appear on their right flank. They desperately appealed to the Arabs to attack Medina. The Arabs had been getting more artillery and machine guns from the British, but Lawrence still didn't think they could take Medina. The more sophisticated weapons the British sent were mostly handled by Egyptian regulars. Lawrence thought this was not at all helpful.

"If there were professional soldiers present," he wrote, "the Bedouin would stand aside and let them work, glad to be excused from the leading part."[4]

At this point, a Bedouin leader appeared and joined the revolt. His name was Auda abu Tayi, and he had the reputation of being the greatest fighting man in northern Arabia. Lawrence persuaded Auda and 500 of his men to accompany him on an expedition against Aqaba, a port at the extreme northern end of the Red Sea. Aqaba's harbor was strongly defended, and the city was also heavily fortified on the west, the side facing the British in Egypt. Lawrence's plan was to make a 600-mile march through mountains and deserts and take Aqaba from the rear, striking out of the northeastern desert. The march would be difficult, and the Arabs could not take artillery or machine guns. Nor could they take the less mobile regular troops who manned them.

The expedition was a complete success. The Turks had never expected an attack from inland. Lawrence sent a message demanding their surrender and pointing out that the wild barbarians in his army were growing impatient. The Turks surrendered the next morning. The "wild barbarians" threat was typical of Lawrence. His campaign relied on propaganda as much as bullets, and it was directed against the mind of the enemy.

After Aqaba, Lawrence returned to Egypt and got the backing of his British superiors to be in fact, if not in name, the commander of the British effort in Arabia. He learned that the British under Sir Edmund Allenby were about to invade Palestine. Returning to Arabia, he persuaded Feisal to become commander of an Arab section of the British invasion army and to take orders from Allenby. Among the benefits to the Arabs were a couple of armored cars and some weapons especially useful in irregular warfare— Lewis guns, light machine guns that could be easily handled by one man, and Stokes mortars, light trench mortars that fired a shell as powerful as one from a full-size fieldpiece.

Fakhri Pasha gave up the idea of retreating into Palestine. With the sherifian forces in Aqaba, the Turkish general seemed to think that all the tribes along those hundreds of miles to the tip of the Red Sea must have joined the Arab revolt. And with the British and Arabs controlling the heavily fortified strongpoint of Aqaba, retreat would be suicide. All he could do now was sit tight in Medina and hope for the best.

Lawrence, Auda, and their men were not sitting at all. They were cutting the Turkish railroad in as many places as they could and blowing up trains. The activity involved a lot of traveling, but very little fighting. There was more fighting when they ambushed trains using electrically detonated mines and followed up with machine guns and mortars, but the duration of the fighting was short, the Arabs suffered few casualties, and the looting was wonderful. (Loot was important to the Bedouin, most of whom were accustomed to raiding other tribes for plunder. Lawrence's ally, Auda Abu Tayi, was a notorious robber and even engaged in dickering with the Turks to see if they could provide him more than the British.) These actions showed the local Arabs that the Hejaz army was operating successfully. In guerrilla war, Lawrence learned, success is the best recruiting tool. When Lawrence's expedition appeared before Aqaba, hordes of local hill tribesmen joined them in the assault on the Turkish port.

This guerrilla campaign was a kind of massive propaganda operation. Feisal, the "prophet" of independence, the capture of Aqaba, and the raids on the railroad were all calculated to convince the uncommitted tribesmen that Arab independence was the wave of the future.

Allenby was concerned about the Turkish garrison at Maan, the headquarters of the Turkish forces in southern Palestine. He wanted the Arabs to take care of it. Lawrence knew his troops were still not capable of assaulting a major fort, and they were equally useless for staging a formal siege. But they managed to immobilize the Turks in Maan the same way they had at Medina—by raiding their supply lines and their outposts. On a few occasions they also got British planes to bomb Maan and its satellite outposts.

The Turks facing the British were holding a line running from Gaza to Beersheba in southern Palestine. Allenby used a variety of tricks to make them think he was going to attack at Gaza, on the seacoast, and then he flanked the line at its eastern end, Beersheba. Lawrence tried to support the effort by destroying a railroad bridge at Deraa, far to the north in Syria. The raid failed because the Arabs carrying the dynamite dropped it in the river when the Turks opened fire. But in spite of that, Allenby captured Jerusalem. As the Arabs no longer had to depend on seaborne supplies, Lawrence moved his headquarters to the north end of the Dead Sea, a better base for striking deep into Syria.

As a civilian archaeologist, Lawrence had spent a good deal of time in Syria, spoke several Syrian dialects of Arabic, and thought Damascus was the natural site for the capital of all Southwest Asian Arabs. His interest fortunately coincided with the situation: Syria was the link between the Arab lands and Turkey. By raiding far and wide in Syria and enlisting Arab tribes

T. E. Lawrence, known as Lawrence of Arabia. He was an amateur archaeologist turned staff officer who showed that his real genius was in organizing a revolution. LIBRARY OF CONGRESS

in the area, he kept the Turks immobilized. A tactic he used frequently was to induce the Turks to attack when the Arabs were in a strong defensive position and could count on support from the local tribes.

By the end of 1917, the British were occupying Palestine and about to move deeper into Syria. Fakhri Pasha knew he had to retreat, regardless of the cost. The cost was heavy. As he moved his army along the rail line, the Arab army got behind him. He turned and attacked them from the north. The more or less regular segment of Lawrence's troops blocked the Turkish advance, while Arabs from the sherifian army and local tribesmen attacked from both flanks.

"Old General Hamid Fakhri collected his Staff and Headquarters, and told each man to take a rifle. 'I have been forty years a soldier, but I never saw rebels fight like these. Enter the ranks.' . . . But he was too late," Lawrence wrote later. "Rasim pushed forward an attack with his five automatic guns, each with its two-man crew. They went in rapidly, unseen until they were in position, and crumpled the Turkish left.

"The Aima men, who knew every blade of grass on these, their village pastures, crept, unharmed, within 300 yards of the Turkish machine guns. The enemy, held by our frontal threat, first knew of the Aima men when they, by a sudden burst of fire, wiped out the gun teams and flung the right wing into disorder. We saw it and cried advance to the camel men and levies about us."[5]

The Arabs charged from three sides and the Turkish force was routed and virtually annihilated.

Winter—freezing cold and snowy in Palestine and Syria—shut down Arab operations until spring. When warmer weather came, the British sent the Arabs more camels, weapons, and some Egyptian and Indian regular troops. But the Turks had been reinforced, too, and Ludendorff's offensive on the Western Front had drawn off men from Allenby's army. The Turks counterattacked and pushed the British back down the Jordan Valley. The Arabs stepped up their railroad and outpost attacks, which helped keep the Turks from renewing their offensive.

The Ludendorff offensive ran out of steam, and Allenby received more troops. Again, he arranged a huge deception, using empty tents, dummy horses, and dummy vehicles to convince Turkish aerial reconnaissance that the British were massing at the wrong point on the line. The Arabs helped by appearing at the phony breakthrough point and purchasing supplies and spreading rumors.

Allenby created a second tactical masterpiece, and swarms of Turks, along with German and Austrian troops, fled north. Lawrence's Arabs chopped them up. World War I was ending. The Central Powers, Austria, Bulgaria, Germany, and Turkey, collapsed almost simultaneously. Lawrence led his Arabs into Damascus, which he hoped would become the capital of vast new Arab state.

Britain and France had other ideas, though. They drew lines on a map that became the borders of Syria, Lebanon, Palestine, Jordan (Transjordan at that time), and Iraq—all of them under the domination of Britain or France.

Hussein was recognized as King of the Hejaz, but Abdul Aziz Ibn Sa'ud, the Wahhabi emir of central Arabia, conquered the Hejaz and its holy cities. The British put the refugee king on the throne of Transjordan. The French decided that Feisal, who had been installed as the King of Syria, was too independent, so they deposed him. The British then gave him a throne in Iraq. Lawrence, now a colonel, and Feisal went to the League of Nations to plead the cause of Arab independence but accomplished nothing. Lawrence did some writing and tried to disappear into the British military as an enlisted man. Shortly after he returned to civilian life, he was killed in a motorcycle accident still considered highly suspicious.

Lawrence's operations received a great deal of publicity, and some critics have contended that they accomplished nothing. The critics point out that Lawrence's Arabs never captured a major city, won few big battles, and never controlled territory. But they are making the same mistake Lawrence said the Turks and Germans made. They are equating war with rebellion.

Lawrence contended that they are not the same, and "war upon rebellion was messy and slow, like eating soup with a knife."[6]

Lawrence accomplished two things: (1) he immobilized a large number of Turkish troops who could have made British operations in the Near East far more difficult, and (2) he spread the idea of nationalism through all Arab lands. The second accomplishment is the more important. It has been shaking the world with increasing intensity since the end of World War I.

CHAPTER 6

The Russian Revolution and the Army without a Country, 1917–1918

"**A**nything is preferable to the state of anarchy that characterizes the present situation," Maurice Paleologue, the French ambassador to Moscow wrote early in 1917. "I am obliged to report that at the present moment, the Russian Empire is run by lunatics."[1] Actually, it had been run by lunatics or equally strange people for some time.

Tsar Nicholas II seemed unable to say "No" to his tsarina, Alexandra. And Alexandra hung on the words of Grigorii Yefimovich Rasputin, a monk and a self-appointed holy man. Somehow, Rasputin seemed able to stop the bleeding of the hemophiliac tsarevitch Alexis. Rasputin was a very strange holy man. He was usually drunk, never bathed, ate with his fingers, and stank. Nevertheless, he was able to seduce women wholesale. He seems to have been a master hypnotist, and he did do for the tsarevich what no doctor could. Alexandra thought Rasputin had a direct line to God. She relied on his advice on whom to appoint to high position in the government, and Nicholas meekly agreed with his wife's requests.

After a long line of thieves and incompetents had been appointed, some Russian nobles decided that Rasputin had to go. Prince Feliks Yusupov invited him to his palace for a late night meeting with him and his beautiful wife, Irina. Rasputin never rejected an invitation to meet a pretty woman. The prince and princess offered Rasputin some cakes that had been baked with potassium cyanide—enough cyanide, according to the doctor who baked them, to kill ten men. Rasputin didn't die. He didn't even get a stomachache. Yusupov asked Rasputin to look at a crucifix hanging on the wall behind him (apparently believing it would have the same effect on the monk as it reputedly had on vampires). When Rasputin turned to look, Yusupov shot him in the back. Rasputin fell to the floor. The other conspirators, hiding in the palace, heard the shot and ran to the scene. The doctor who prepared the cakes announced that Rasputin was dead. As the conspirators left the room, Yusupov's years of frustration exploded. He kicked the body of the monk.

Rasputin kicked him back.

Screaming in terror, the prince dashed out of the room. Rasputin followed him out of the palace and into the courtyard. Another conspirator, Vladamir Purishkevich, hearing Yusupov's screams, followed them into the courtyard. He shot Rasputin twice, once in the back and once in the head. Rasputin fell down again. Two soldiers carried the body back into the palace. Purishkevich, to make sure the man was dead, pounded him on the head with a blunt instrument—a steel pipe, a blackjack, or a set of brass knuckles—until he was totally disfigured. The conspirators then wrapped the monk's body in a curtain, tied it securely and drove it to the shore of the Neva River. They pushed it through a hole that had been previously cut in the ice and lodged it under the frozen surface.

The body was discovered hours later. There was water in the lungs, indicating Rasputin was alive when he went through the hole. And one of his arms was loose, showing that he almost got free of the cloth and rope binding.

Rasputin was buried December 22, 1916, but, according to the French ambassador, the country was still being "run by lunatics." And that was hardly Russia's only trouble.

Russia was the last major power to have an absolute monarchy. That began to change at the beginning of the twentieth century. In 1903, the tsar's government attempted to cope with widespread unrest in the traditional way—by inciting a pogrom to distract the population. An estimated 50,000 Russian Jews were murdered, but the unrest continued. The only noticeable effect of the pogrom was to accelerate the emigration of Russian Jews to America and to increase the interest in Zionism.

Russia's losses in the Russo-Japanese war seemed to make the discontented citizens think the government had become weak. On January 9, 1905, just a week after the Russians surrendered Port Arthur, mobs demonstrated outside the Winter Palace. Russian troops fired on them and charged them with cavalry. Thousands of people were killed and wounded on "Bloody Sunday." That touched off a series of mutinies in the armed forces that turned into a general revolt. Nicholas II issued his October Manifesto, promising a constitutional monarchy. That satisfied most of the rebels. The next year, though, the new prime minister, Pyotr Stolypin, instituted a reign of terror against suspected subversives.

Russian peasants, who formed the bulk of the population, had always been poor. Until 1861, they were actually serfs. The approach of World War I brought a tremendous change in the Russian economy. Railroads, oil fields, mines, and factories expanded enormously. Thousands of opportunities opened for people who for centuries had no alternative employment but working the land. But instead of improving the lot of the average person, the economic boom made things worse. So many peasants were absorbed by Russia's new industrial base that there weren't enough farmers. The railroad system, although greatly expanded, moved food and other goods less efficiently. The manpower to operate the trains came from barely trained peasants. Food became scarce. Expensive, too—the boom was financed by paper money. Inflation, combined with scarcity, raised prices for everything tremendously, especially bread, that staple of the Russian diet.

And then, there was the war. In all the belligerent countries, young men, filled with patriotic fervor and the desire to perform heroic deeds, joined their countries' armies. But heroic deeds were passé. Instead of great swords like Excalibur and Durenal, there was poison gas. Machine guns and barbed wire had eliminated any chance for heroic cavalry charges. Heroic warriors no longer exchanged challenges before meeting in lethal combat. Now the soldier seldom saw an individual opponent. Millions were killed by artillery completely out of sight.

By 1917, the war had entered the stage historian John Keegan calls "the breaking of armies."[2] The French Army experienced massive mutinies; the British Army, a number of smaller ones. The German army was about to break when the Russian broke first.

War was hell everywhere, but it was more hellish in Russia than anywhere else. In spite of Russia's industrial expansion, many soldiers were unarmed. They were told to pick up the rifles of fallen comrades. They were short of everything—weapons, ammunition, medical supplies, and even food. Even worse, letters from home told the soldiers that their families were starving. Desertion was becoming epidemic.

On February 23, 1917, 7,000 women walked out of a textile mill in Petrograd and marched down the street chanting "We want bread!" By evening, there were 70,000 demonstrators. The next day, there were 150,000. The third day a quarter of a million people were clamoring for bread, while the police struggled to keep them in check. The fourth day, the mob was even bigger, and troops got into the action.

Fedor Linde, a sergeant in the elite Finland Guards, later described what he saw:

> I saw a young girl trying to evade the galloping horse of a Cossack officer. She was too slow. A severe blow on the head brought her down under the horse's feet. She screamed. It was her inhuman, penetrating scream that caused something in me to snap. [I] cried out wildly: "Fiends! Fiends! Long live the revolution. To arms! To arms! They are killing innocent people, our brothers and sisters!"[3]

The vast majority of the 180,000 soldiers in the capital and the 150,000 stationed just outside joined the revolution. They had armored cars, machine guns, and artillery. They opened the prisons. Socialist politicians began organizing them. The mob elected the first Soviet (council) of Workers and Soldiers Deputies. Other soviets sprang up all over the country. On March 2, the tsar abdicated. The politicians in the Duma, which had hardly begun to function as a true parliament, tried to work with the many soviets to form a provisional government. Things were pretty chaotic until a provincial lawyer, Aleksandr Kerenskii, appeared.

Kerenskii, a spell binding orator, was a socialist, but unlike many other socialists, he believed the Russian people should unite to drive out the invaders. He became Minister of War and Marine. Kerenskii's position was that Russia must fight on, not for the land and indemnities that the British and French had promised, but to protect the revolution.

"For the sake of the nation's life," he said, "it was necessary to restore the army's will to die."[4]

The soldiers at the front had elected soviets, which interacted with their commanding officers as if they were labor unions. There was a great lack of warlike activity. The Germans had penetrated deeply into Russia; they occupied the best farmland and the most industrialized cities. They were commanded by the brilliant Maj. Gen. Max Hoffman, the brains behind the German tactical masterpiece, the battle of Tannenberg, which made Hindenburg a hero. The Germans were waiting for the Russian Army to collapse. To speed the process along, Gen. Erich Ludendorff, Germany's military dictator, in fact if not in name, smuggled into Russia a radical socialist who went by the name Nikolai Lenin. (His actual name was Vladimir Ilich Ulyanov. After he came into power he combined his real and assumed names and became V. I. Lenin.)

Meanwhile, Kerenskii was touring the front, talking to the soldiers. "Let the freest army in the world . . . prove that there is strength, not weakness in liberty. Let them forge a new iron discipline of duty."[5]

The inspired soldiers went on the offensive. But new spirit was little help when there were no new rifles. The Russian supply system was even worse than it was before the tsar was deposed. The "Kerenskii Offensive" was a disaster. Desertions became massive. Kerenskii appointed a new commander, Gen. Lavr Kornilov, who began hanging deserters at every crossroad. But a short time later, Kornilov attempted a coup d'état and was arrested. Kornilov's fall ended all discipline in the Russian Army. The troops deserted in masses, looting towns as they moved back to their homes.

Lenin saw his opportunity as Russia again began falling into anarchy. He invited another exiled socialist, Lev Davidovich Trotskii, then living in the United States, to join him. They began talking to soviets all over the country.

The Lenin-Trotskii wing of the socialists won majorities in the soviets of Petrograd, Moscow, and Kiev. Thereafter, they called themselves the Bolshevik (Majority) Party. On October 24, they rose and overthrew the Kerenskii government.

The Bolsheviks, knowing that it was impossible to continue the war, made peace with Germany—a peace that gave away a huge portion of their homeland: 34 percent of the population, 32 percent of the farmland, 50 percent of the industry, and 90 percent of the coal mines. They then prepared for a new war, one against Russian "counterrevolutionaries." Several generals, including Kornilov, had escaped to the lands of the Cossacks and prepared for civil war.

Meanwhile, the revolution had a serious effect on some Slavic prisoners of war. The strange multinational hodgepodge called the Empire of Austria-Hungary contained soldiers of many ethnic backgrounds. Two groups, the Germans and the Hungarians, provided the officers. The others, mostly Slavs speaking many Slavic languages, seldom got into the officer corps. Communications between different ethnic groups in the army were conducted in "Army Slavic," a lingua franca of seventy or eighty words taken from Slavic languages. Many of these Slavic nations resented the domination of the Germans and Hungarians.

Back in 1914, the Russians, inspired by the philosophy of Pan-Slavism as well as by the knowledge that Czechs and Slovaks hated the Hungarians and Germans, recruited Czech and Slovaks living in Russia for a Czechoslovakian army company. It was to be used for covert actions—what today we call "special ops." When war broke out, the Russians captured many Czech and Slovak prisoners of war. Capture was often not at all difficult. In some cases, the Slavs shot their Austrian and Hungarian officers and deserted en masse. The Russians also had many Polish prisoners. They came from both the armies of Austria-Hungary and the German Empire.

As Russia contained many different nationalities, the tsar's government did not want to encourage nationalism. Recruiting POWs to fight against their imperial masters would send the wrong message to Russia's own subject nations. But the early revolution's promise of freedom for all caused a change in policy. Russian authorities decided to use these Slavic POWs. They allowed the Czechs and Slovaks to join the established Czechoslovakian company, which rapidly grew into a brigade and finally achieved the size of an army corps. And they allowed the Poles to form another unit. In the chaos of the revolution, these ex-POWs had to decide which faction—if any—to join. The one thing they did not want was to be returned to Austria-Hungary or Germany, as the Central Powers demanded in the Treaty of Brest-Litovsk.

The Russian Empire was at least as diverse as the Austro-Hungarian Empire. With the Revolution, it began to break up. Finns, Lithuanians, Poles,

Ukrainians, and other nationalities saw a chance to regain their independence. Cossacks, those traditional defenders of the autocracy, had become virulently anti-Bolshevik. Both former imperial officers and dissident socialists were trying to set up independent states in Siberia. The Bolsheviks had established Red Guard units all over the country. The Red Guards, sometimes called the armed proletariat, took orders from the local soviets, which often disregarded orders from Trotskii, the People's Commissar of War. Red Guards, separatists, and Whites used weapons the deserters had taken home with them and weapons their agents were buying in other countries, notably Japan. The Red Guards also got rifles and machine guns from government arsenals. So did the Czechoslovaks and Poles. The Czechoslovaks preferred captured Austrian weapons, because they were familiar with them. The Russians had captured thousands of these along with millions of cartridges, so there was no logistics problem at first. Russian rifles and machine guns were a bit more plentiful than they had been during the war, more because of the massive desertions than the continued production of weapons. Later, the Czechs were to capture more Russian rifles in Siberia and receive Allied weapons that had been sent to support them in Siberia. The Japanese were particularly generous with rifles. They thought they could use the Czechs to obtain power in Siberia. The Czech and Polish "Legions" had far more cohesion than either the Red Guards or the scratch armies that counterrevolutionaries, known as Whites, were putting together in the south and in Siberia. They would be a formidable addition to any faction.

The Poles joined the Ukrainian separatists, who had ignored the Treaty of Brest-Litovsk that Lenin had signed. That was a mistake. The Rada, the

Bolshevik soldiers take over the streets of Moscow. The Russian Revolution turned Russia upside down and initiated chaos in Central Europe. LIBRARY OF CONGRESS

Ukrainian nationalist committee, made its own peace with the Germans and that ended the "Polish Legion."

The "Czech Legion" was adopted by a Czech government in exile in France headed by Tomas Masaryk. The exiled Czechs wanted the Czech Legion to fight on the Western Front, but the whole German and Austro-Hungarian armies lay between that war zone and the Czechs. Masaryk met with Lenin and negotiated a safe conduct for the legion to leave Russia at Vladivostok. That did not please the French, who wanted the Czechs and Slovaks to follow the example of the Poles and stay in the Ukraine to fight the Germans. It didn't please the British, either. They were hoping the Czech Legion would go north and help them defend the port of Murmansk, terminus for the supplies they were sending to their Russian allies.

And so the Czech Legion, officially the Czechoslovak Corps in Russia and numbering more than 60,000 men, began the longest fighting march of any army since the days of Genghis Khan. To reach Russia's Pacific Coast, more than 4,000 miles away, they used the Trans-Siberian Railway. Travel was slow, because most of the railroad is a single track, and the Russians were returning to Germany and Austria-Hungary the prisoners they had been holding in Siberia. And that caused other problems.

On May 14, 1918, at Cheliabinsk in western Siberia, a Hungarian ex-POW moving east threw a rock at the Czech ex-POWs. A fight broke out and the Czechs killed a Hungarian. The local Red Guards arrested the killer. Then the killer's comrades stormed the railroad station, freed him, killed the Red Guards, and took over the town. Trotskii ordered the Red Guards along the length of the Trans-Siberian Railway to disarm the Czech Legion. In fact, he said any legionnaire with a weapon was to be shot on sight. Disarming the legion seemed much easier in Moscow than in Siberia.

Because of the scarcity of trains and the difficulty of moving east on a one-track railroad while other trains were trying to move west, the Czech Legion was strung out over a long extent of track. They took over all the towns they were near and routed the local Red Guards. In the process, they captured eight carloads of gold bullion being moved from the imperial reserve in Kazan. They gave the Bolsheviks seven carloads in exchange for a new promise of safe conduct and kept the eighth to pay for ships to take them to the United States and thence to Europe. The Bolsheviks didn't keep their promise, but the Czechs also captured munitions of all kinds, including an armored train that contained cannons and machine guns in rotating turrets. That land battleship accomplished far more than the gold. Trotskii's hostility had changed the Czechs and Slovaks from neutrals to anti-Bolsheviks. They began moving east. "By midsummer 1918, both Siberia and the Urals had been lost to the Bolseviks."[6]

By late summer of 1918, the exploits of the Czech Legion were known all over the world. The Allies were determined to help them leave Vladivostok. Helping the Czechs also provided cover for another mission. Japan sent 40,000 troops into eastern Siberia, ostensibly to help the Czechs but also to expand westward from their base in Manchuria. The United States sent two regiments, the 31st and the 27th, to Vladivostok to smooth the way for the Czechoslovaks but also to keep an eye on Japan. When they finally returned to the States, the 31st became known as the Polar Bears and the 27th as the Wolfhounds. Little by little, the Allies had turned against the Bolsheviks. The British landed troops in northern Russia and the French in southern Russia, and both countries were actively supporting the White forces.

Meanwhile, the Czech Legion had allied itself with a group of dissident socialists who proclaimed an Autonomous Republic of Siberia. And farther west, Trotskii was busy turning the Red Guards into what became the Red Army. By October, the legion was the only competent military force in Autonomous Siberia. The Russian leadership in Siberia was divided by mortal hatreds: murders of political rivals became common. The leaders of the government were socialists, the Revolutionary Socialist Party, but the refugee imperial officers were the rankest reactionaries. The Czechs sided with the socialists.

"Within two days we can clear Omsk (the capital of Autonomous Siberia) of all these reactionary scoundrels," a Czech officer told leaders of the Siberian government.[7]

"The Directorate," one of those leaders replied, "does not shoot people and does not put them in prison."[8] The Czechs decided that they were tired of fighting for Russia.

On October 28, in Prague, Masaryk announced the birth of an independent Czechoslovakia. The army without a country that had conquered Siberia now had a country of its own. Most of the legion decided to go home. As the legionnaires were preparing to cross the Pacific, Admiral Aleksandr Vasilevich Kolchak seized the government and made himself dictator of Siberia. Some members of the Czechoslovak Legion stayed to help him, but they soon became disgusted by his high-handedness, his brutality, and the corruption of his subordinates. They returned to their newborn country after accomplishing one of the most unusual feats in modern military history.

CHAPTER 7

Chaos on the Continent, 1917–1921

In the spring of 1917, the Russian Empire began to disintegrate. In the fall of 1918, the other three European empires—the German, the Austro-Hungarian, and the Ottoman—followed suit. The map of Europe and the Near East changed completely and much of Europe plunged into chaos. What emerged from the chaos was a Europe radically different from anything seen before.

There was civil war and war between a host of new or reborn states. As in Russia, most of the fighting was guerrilla warfare conducted by irregular armies. Europe was filled with trained, battle-hardened soldiers, but most of them fought in units that never existed in the Great War, using the most motley collections of weapons. Four years of regular warfare had ground down the nations of Europe. Several years of guerrilla fighting transformed them.

Austria-Hungary was the first to crack. Early in October, after the failure of an Austrian offensive in Italy, the new emperor, Karl I, sent a message to U.S. president Woodrow Wilson proposing an armistice to discuss a peace based on Wilson's "Fourteen Points." Two weeks later, on October 16, he changed the empire into a federation of autonomous states. But his subjects were ahead of him. On October 6, the Serbs, Croats, and Slovenes created a new Kingdom of the South Slavs, which later became Yugoslavia. On October 28, Tomas Masaryk and Eduard Benes, the Czech leaders in exile, now in Prague, proclaimed the independence of Czechoslovakia. Two days later, Karl's German-speaking subjects announced the formation of a new all-German Austria. And two days after that, the Hungarians declared their independence. The other subject nationalities of Austria-Hungary began declaring their independence. And in many cases, soldiers of those ethnic groups then went home.

There was still an Austro-Hungarian army in Italy while Austria-Hungary itself was becoming extinct. That situation changed in November. The Italians had launched an offensive October 24 and drove their ancient enemies back over the mountains. With an Italian army on Austrian soil, the army of the empire sued for peace November 1 and declared a cease-fire

November 3. The Italians recognized the cease-fire on November 4, after they had taken 300,000 prisoners.

The Turkish Empire, except for an Arab revolt that spread from the Hejaz to Syria, had more or less held together, but it stopped fighting before Austria-Hungary. The Turks sued for peace on October 30. The British had flanked their line in Palestine in 1917, and the next year flanked it again in Syria. There was nothing to keep them from the Turkish homeland.

On the Western Front, Ludendorff's offensive had petered out. It had been planned to use the "storm trooper" tactics worked out on the Eastern Front. Army units were to bypass centers of resistance, push through weak spots in the enemy line, and disrupt enemy communications and command centers in the rear. But instead of bypassing strong areas, Ludendorff continued attacking them while the Allies merely rushed up reinforcements. These attacks cut down the Germans' original numerical superiority while new troops from the United States were pouring in to reinforce the Allies. Ludendorff began losing heart in August. On September 28, after a massive Allied attack, he told Hindenburg that Germany had to ask for an armistice. The stolid-looking Ludendorff actually had a mercurial temperament. He regained his belligerence in October, and he issued a proclamation to the troops defying the new chancellor, Prince Max of Baden, who was seeking peace. A staff officer, knowing what the reaction to the proclamation in Berlin would be, tried to suppress it, but word of it leaked out. The proclamation was as blatant a defiance of civilian authority as Douglas MacArthur's famous proclamation during the Korean War. But while MacArthur gloried in his defiance, Ludendorff tried to deny his. Nobody believed him. On October 26, the kaiser fired Ludendorff.

The wave of mutinies that had plagued France, Britain, and Russia in 1917 got to Germany in 1918. On October 30, the High Command ordered the German High Seas Fleet to go into the North Sea and fight one last battle for the honor of Germany. The German sailors were probably patriotic, but they weren't suicidal. Waiting for them on the blockade line were the combined British and American navies—the two largest navies in the world. The sailors refused to get up steam. When their officers tried to discipline them, they broke into the ships' arms lockers and into armories on shore. They took over the naval base and city of Kiel and called for a national revolution. Prince Henry of Prussia, the admiral commanding the port and the kaiser's brother, fled the city in disguise on November 3.

Bolshevik bands, mostly deserters from the army, roamed the streets of Berlin. The kaiser had left Berlin and gone to army headquarters. He believed he could lead the army back to Berlin and quash the rebellion. Soldiers and civilian officials, including members of the German royalty, tried to convince him that the only way to prevent civil war was for him to abdicate. On November 10, the kaiser abdicated and took a train for Holland, where he would live the rest of his life.

Prince Max resigned as chancellor and gave the office to Fritz Ebert, a Socialist but not a Bolshevik. Germany became a republic. It was a troubled republic, though. The Bolshevik leaders, Karl Liebknecht and Rosa Luxemburg, proclaimed it a "free socialist republic," by which they meant something like Russia. The Bolsheviks in Russia were actively working to promote a Communist revolution in Germany. Lenin had announced his aim "[t]o unite the proletariat of industrial Germany, Austria and Czechoslovakia with the proletariat of Russia and thereby create a mighty agrarian and industrial combination from Vladivostok to the Rhine, from the Finnish Gulf to the blue waters of the Danube."[1]

The German Army no longer existed, but not all the ex-soldiers had laid down their weapons and thrown away their uniforms. Bands of armed men, often wearing army uniforms, were everywhere. Most of these veterans knew no trade but soldiering, and many of them could not find civilian work anyway. Some were Bolsheviks, some were members of right-wing militias—the so-called *Freikorps*. These bands fought each other and, on Germany's eastern border, fought militias in newly independent Poland.

Liebknecht and Luxemburg organized the Spartacist League, named after Spartacus, the ancient Roman who led a slave revolt. The Spartacists attempted to overthrow the government in January 1919 but were crushed by Freikorps militia who captured and killed the two Bolshevik leaders. Other Communists proclaimed the Bavarian Communist Republic in April 1919, but it, too, was wiped out by the Freikorps.

Some of the Freikorps units went abroad to fight. The future general Heinz Guderian went to the Baltic with one Freikorps outfit to help the newly independent Baltic republics organize armies. Finland, Estonia, Latvia, and Lithuania had all declared their independence of Russia. In Finland, there was also a civil war between the Red Guards and the White Guards, which began before the Great War ended. Germany had units helping the White Guards. Russia sent the fledgling Red Army to Finland and the Baltic States. These northern wars were somewhat confusing affairs involving German regulars until after the Treaty of Versailles as well as German Freikorps and Russians, and native militia. The war in Lithuania also involved Poland, which claimed the city of Vilna. Finland and the Baltic states gained their independence in 1920.

More serious than these clashes was Russia's war with Poland. The Baltics and Finland were backwaters. Poland was Central Europe and the pathway to Germany. The Central Powers had arranged for the independence of Poland and set up a regency council to govern the country while the First World War was in progress. After Germany signed the armistice, the regency council appointed Joseph Pilsudski commander of the armed forces. Pilsudski then appointed himself head of the nation. Pilsudski aimed to restore Poland's borders of 1792. That led him to invade Lithuania and Ukraine. The Poles eventually withdrew from Vilna and made peace with Ukraine. Pilsudski then supported Ukraine against Russia.

Russia responded by sending in Mikhail Tukhachevskii, who had just defeated Admiral Kochak in the Russian Civil War. Tukhachevskii was a strange man who worshiped the ancient Slavic god of war, Pierounn.

"I have accepted Pierounn," he told a French POW when both were interned in a German POW camp, "because once Marxism is thrust upon Russia, the most devastating wars will be let loose. . . . We shall enter chaos and not leave it until civilization is reduced to total ruin."[2]

Tukhachevskii may have been crazy, but he was the most talented Russian general to appear in the Russian Civil War. He pushed Pilsudski's army back to the gates of Warsaw. There, in the most decisive battle of this postwar period, Pilsudski led his ragtag Poles and Ukrainians through the weak center of the Russian line and attacked the troops before Warsaw from the rear. The outnumbered Poles drove the Russians out of Poland.

Also in 1920, the Freikorps unit led by Wolfgang Kapp seized control of the German government in what was called Kapp's Putsch, but it was

Recruiting poster for a Freikorps, one of the freelance military groups that fought Communists in Germany and in the Baltic states. Soldier in nineteenth-century uniform offers swords. Poster asks who will protect the Fatherland and urges men proficient with weapons to join Freikorps Lutzow. LIBRARY OF CONGRESS defeated by the new German Army (mostly composed of former Freikorps members).

The Communists had a brief success in Hungary, where Bela Kun led a revolt in 1919. Kun attempted to annex parts of Czechoslovakia with heavily Hungarian populations, but the Romanian Army invaded Hungary in support of Czechoslovakia. Kun fled, and the country was taken over by Adm. Miklos Horthy. Horthy, an admiral in a country without a navy, became regent for a king he would not allow to enter Hungary.

Each of the new European states aimed to restore its "historic" boundaries, which usually meant the state's boundaries when they reached their greatest extent. As a result, western Czechoslovakia contained large numbers of Germans; eastern Poland held many Ukrainians and Russians; and western Poland, many Germans. Southeastern Finland included a substantial population of Russians. One of the most blatant cases of "historic boundary" grabbing involved Greece. Greece proposed to annex all the lands inhabited by Greeks at the time of the Peloponnesian War, at least all those lands occupied by what Greek leaders considered the worn-out nation of Turkey. Turkey surprised the Greeks. Reorganized under Mustafa Kemal, later Kemal Atatürk ("father of the Turks"), the Turks drove the Greeks out of their country. As a result, today one of the Greeks' greatest holidays commemorates the day they won their independence from Turkey, and one of the Turks' greatest holidays commemorates their defeat of the Greeks in 1922.

Turkey once had a vast empire in Arab lands, but western European powers had been whittling it away for a century. France had taken over all of North Africa from Tunisia to Morocco. Italy had conquered Libya, and Britain supplanted Turkey in Egypt. After the war, France took Syria and Lebanon; Britain took Palestine and Iraq. And an Arab conqueror appeared. Abdul Aziz ibn Sa'ud, a Wahhabi chieftain in Central Arabia, made himself supreme in most of the Arabian Peninsula and ousted Lawrence's ally, King Abdullah, from the Hejaz. Because they believed a king must have a kingdom, the British carved out a piece of desert on the east bank of the Jordan, named it Transjordan and gave it to Abdullah. The British pressured the French to make Lawrence's friend, Feisal, king of their protectorate, Syria. But in a short time, the French decided Feisal was too uncooperative. So the British gave him another throne in Iraq. So much for the Arab independence Lawrence and Feisal had fought for.

The Central Powers suffered heavy losses as a result of their defeat. Of the victors, the British and French made substantial gains to their empires. Italy was one of the victors, but its gains were modest. The war cost it 600,000 dead soldiers, but it gained only the city of Trieste, the South Tyrol, and the Dodecanese islands. The war effort had left Italy in an economic crisis. The crisis provided an opportunity for a socialist editor, Benito Mussolini.

Mussolini founded the Fascist Party, which included a militia called the Black Shirts. He became prime minister and, in effect, dictator of Italy. Mussolini and his methods were widely imitated by leaders in countries disrupted by the Great War and its aftermath. The most notable was a German painter who joined the German Workers' Party in 1920 and became its head in 1921. Under Adolf Hitler, the German Workers' Party became the National Socialist German Workers' Party and helped its führer foment an even larger and bloodier war than the last one.

CHAPTER 8

Black and Tans, Republicans and Staters: Two Irish Wars, 1918–1922

April 24, 1916, was a day Ireland never forgot. On that day, some 700 men (and a few women, like the extraordinary Countess Constance Markievicz) tried to drive the British Empire out of Ireland. Poorly armed, and trained in little but close-order drill, they seized a few buildings in Dublin and held out for five days against 5,000 British regulars (many of them as Irish as the rebels) who were armed with repeating rifles, machine guns, hand grenades, and artillery.

The "Rising," as it is known in Ireland, was a failure. It was organized by a clique in a secret society, the Irish Republican Brotherhood, which, unknown to most Irish people, recognized the president of that lodge as the true president of Ireland.[1] The rebellion followed a plan drawn up by an aristocratic young poet, Joseph Plunkett, who had no military experience, and it was led by another poet, the idealistic, charismatic, and completely impractical Padraic Pearse. Because of Pearse's bungling, what was supposed to be a nationwide uprising by thousands of men using modern rifles became a demonstration by a few hundred armed with old rifles and shotguns, some of them muzzle-loading flintlocks.

When the Rising was over five days later, the center of Dublin had been blasted and burned out. Scores of people were now homeless; hundreds were jobless. More than 3,000 persons had been killed or wounded. As the surrendered rebels were marched down the street, the crowds on the sidewalk threw stones and garbage at them. To the average Dubliner, the Rising was a supremely foolish act. There was no chance that it could have set Ireland free. The only possible result was that the people of Dublin, one of the poorest cities in Europe, would become poorer still.

Then the British proceeded to turn the rebels from villains into heroes.

First, there were the executions. The British commander, Sir John Maxwell, decided to execute all the officers of the rebels, who called themselves the Irish Republican Army (IRA). They were tried in secret before military kangaroo courts and shot by firing squads immediately. The executions dragged out over nine days. Everything was secret until the military released the names of the prisoners who had been killed. They shot Joseph Plunkett, who was dying of tuberculosis, ten minutes after they allowed him to marry his fiancée. They shot James Connolly, dying of the wounds he had received and so weak he could not sit up and had to be tied to a chair in front of the firing squad. The rank and file were all sentenced to life imprisonment.

Somewhat earlier, another armed militia group, the Ulster Volunteer Force, had threatened to fight if the government dared to give Ireland its own parliament. They were not shot or imprisoned. They were rewarded with the indefinite postponement of Home Rule, a law that the British Parliament had already passed, and they eventually got their own corner of Ireland—four counties where Protestants had a majority plus two more. The treatment of the two groups of rebels was so different that even the leader of the Ulster Protestants, Sir Edward Carson, pleaded for clemency for the IRA members.

Then there were the atrocities the army tried to hide. Dozens of civilians were shot, usually waving white flags, as they tried to leave the combat zones. At least fifteen men who had nothing to do with the rebellion were dragged from their homes, bound and shot or bayoneted, and then buried secretly. The authorities said reports of this atrocity were fabricated—until the bodies were dug up. The most notorious of the atrocities were committed by Capt. J. C. Bowen-Colthurst, scion of the family that owned Blarney Castle. Bowen-Colthurst had wandered the streets of Dublin with an escort of soldiers killing innocent people at random. A British army officer, Maj. Sir Francis Vane, who tried to get Bowen-Colthurst confined to his barracks was dismissed from the service.[2]

Then the British began enforcing the Defense of the Realm Act (known as "Dora") with a previously unknown fanaticism. Anyone criticizing the government could be shipped off to an English jail. In some cases, even speaking Irish instead of English was considered criticism of the government. More than three thousand, including many loyalists, were picked up and jailed.[3]

As a result of all this, people began to view the Rising in a new light. In elections, they turned away from John Redmond's Irish Parliamentary Party and voted for candidates of the nationalist Sinn Fein Party. Before the Rising, Sinn Fein had been considered an extreme, lunatic-fringe group. In the 1918 elections, Sinn Fein won 73 of the 105 seats in Parliament; the Irish Parliamentary Party won only six. When he saw Sinn Fein gaining power, British Prime Minister David Lloyd George offered John Redmond, still an active Irish politician, immediate Home Rule—with one catch. Six counties in Ulster would be exempted for an indefinite time. Four of the counties had Protestant majorities and the other two, Fermanagh and Tyrone, had

Catholic majorities, but without enough Catholics to give Catholics a majority in all six counties. Lloyd George told Redmond that the separation would be temporary, but the old Irish MP (member of Parliament) knew that he had also promised the Ulster Protestants that it would be permanent. Redmond rejected the offer.

Many of the voters knew very little about Sinn Fein except that it was nationalist. The British government (except for Lloyd George) knew almost nothing. It continually referred to the participants in the Rising as "Sinn Feiners." Actually, except for nationalism, Sinn Fein was opposed to everything the Rising stood for.

Sinn Fein was the brainchild of a journalist named Arthur Griffith. Although Griffith was a prominent nationalist, he was not a republican. He was a monarchist. His party, Sinn Fein (Irish for "Ourselves") took as its model the nonviolent Hungarian revolution that resulted in the Dual Monarchy, Austria-Hungary. Sinn Fein parliamentarians would not go to London. They would establish a separate parliament in Dublin. They would establish separate courts and separate banks and parallel every agency of the British government with Irish ones. The result, Griffith hoped, would be an Ireland that recognized the King of England as the King of Ireland, but would otherwise be entirely separate.

A few months after the Rising, the British released the IRA people who had taken part in it. The authorities concluded that there was no danger of another rising, and they were feeling pressure from the British public and from other countries, especially the United States, to let bygones be bygones. The Rising veterans received a tumultuous welcome in Dublin. The highest-ranking of them, Commandant Eamon de Valera, was elected president of the Sinn Fein Party. (De Valera's death sentence had been commuted because he had been born in the United States to an Irish mother and a Spanish father, and the place of his birth made him an American citizen.) De Valera's election marked a change in Sinn Fein. It was no longer pacifist and, in spite of Arthur Griffith, it was republican. It had not, however, forgotten Griffith's idea of a parallel government.

British prime minister David Lloyd George, known as the Welsh Wizard, understood Griffith's idea quite well, and he knew that Sinn Fein would certainly launch a shadow government. He saw a new challenge. This was not like the 1916 Rising. It could not be solved by sending a few soldiers to Dublin. Neither could it be handled the way Britain had handled the Boers at the beginning of the century. Britain could not flood Ireland with soldiers and imprison all the civilians in concentration camps. There were too many civilians, for one thing. For another, the army had been demobilized, and the public would not stand for conscripting the veterans of the Great War for a little war in Ireland. More important, Ireland was not some unknown land at the southern tip of Africa—literally the other end of the world. It was "John Bull's other island," part of the United Kingdom, and the Irish were fellow citizens. Further, the Irish economy was a vital part of the UK's. Lloyd George could not shut down the country, as Britain had shut down the South African Republic and the Orange Free State.

Lloyd George denounced Sinn Fein as a criminal conspiracy. A criminal conspiracy was a matter for the police. It was not a war. Soldiers could help the police, but they would not be fighting a war, and there would be no huge reinforcement of the troops already in Ireland. There were two kinds of police in Ireland—the local police in cities like Dublin and Cork, and the Royal Irish Constabulary. The RIC was a national police force, organized on military lines and often armed with carbines as well as revolvers. The prime minister's plan was for his police to arrest the Sinn Fein leaders and quash the independence movement at once. The police arrested a number of prominent Sinn Fein members, including de Valera. But they missed a highly talented, charismatic, but unknown leader named Michael Collins, another veteran of the Rising. Collins was eight years younger than de Valera (at this time, he was twenty-eight), boisterous while de Valera was reserved, but like "Dev," he was a natural politician and a born leader. He

Michael Collins, leader of the Free State forces in the Irish Civil War. Previously, in the Irish War of Independence (the "Black and Tan War") he had been in charge of the vital IRA intelligence operation.
LIBRARY OF CONGRESS

demonstrated his talents in 1919 when he organized an operation that broke de Valera out of prison.

As Lloyd George expected, after Sinn Fein swept the 1918 parliamentary elections, the new MPs set up the *Dail Eireann,* an Irish parliament, in Dublin. The Dail elected de Valera president and *Priomh Aire* ("First Minister" in English). De Valera appointed a cabinet. Countess Markievicz became head of the Labour Department, the first woman cabinet minister in either England or Ireland. De Valera appointed Michael Collins minister of finance, and empowered him to float a national loan. The Dail established its own courts and county councils. The Irish Volunteers became, like the soldiers of the Rising, the Irish Republican Army. De Valera himself, a wanted fugitive, went to America to raise money from Irish Americans.

The same day the Dail proclaimed Ireland an independent republic, the first shots of the Irish Revolution were fired near the town of Soloheadbeg. Eight Volunteers, or IRA soldiers, as they now were called, held up a cart that was carrying "gelignite," the British and Irish term for gelatin dynamite. Two RIC constables were killed. The IRA wanted the dynamite to make hand grenades. Using this powerful, but sensitive, explosive for hand grenades was a dangerous practice, but the Irish army, throughout its revolutionary war, was plagued by a shortage of weapons.

The war that followed the incident at Soloheadbeg was totally unlike the fighting at the Rising. The British population outnumbered the Irish about fifteen to one. Britain emerged victorious from the First World War with one of the world's largest military establishments. Ireland had no armored vehicles, no artillery, no machine guns, and very few rifles. For Ireland to confront the British Empire directly would be suicidal. The Rising had demonstrated that. The new war was a war of pinpricks. IRA men attacked police barracks and ambushed convoys carrying Crown forces. Police raided homes where they suspected Irish soldiers or government officials were hiding. The war grew in intensity and bitterness, but it remained a "police action."

The Irish government and Sinn Fein organized a boycott of police. The police in Ireland, representatives of the Crown, were never all that popular. Like the police in England, the force had been founded by Sir Robert Peel. But while the English police are "bobbies," those in Ireland were "peelers." Ideally, under the boycott, no one would talk to policemen; no tradesmen or shopkeepers would deal with them. The boycott was never that thorough, but many policemen decided to find another type of work. Few Irishmen now wanted to join the police.

That didn't help Lloyd George's police action, which would require far more than the normal complement of cops. So the British government recruited large numbers of restless, unemployed English veterans of World War I. There weren't enough police uniforms for them, so they wore a com-

bination of black police uniforms and khaki army uniforms. Some wag nicknamed them the Black and Tans, a reference to a famous pack of foxhounds
in Limerick. And the Irish Revolutionary War came to be called the Black
and Tan War.

The Black and Tans specialized in what were called "unauthorized
reprisals"—actions that would not be officially ordered, but which would not
be punished. The British military objected to unauthorized reprisals and did
not carry out any, but Lloyd George liked them, and the "Tans"spent much
of their time performing them. They burned homes of persons suspected of
helping the Republicans, sometimes of merely sympathizing with them. If
any of them were attacked, they burned businesses, usually creameries, the
most important businesses in most rural Irish towns. At times, they burned
whole villages. They rode through towns in lorries (pickup trucks) shooting
people on the street. They tortured prisoners. They, or regular members of
the RIC, assassinated the lord mayor of Cork.

On June 16, 1920, a Lt. Col. Smyth told the Black and Tans he commanded, "The more you shoot, the better I will like it, and I assure you, no
policeman will get in trouble for shooting any man."[4]

For all their ruthlessness, the Tans were not able to dampen the fires of
rebellion in Ireland. Winston Churchill thought another force was needed.
He proposed "a special force of 8,000 men" to train the police in counterinsurgency and add muscle to the Black and Tans.[5] They were recruited from
former army officers, men who had once been responsible for the lives of
tens or hundreds of men but were now jobless. They were bitter and frustrated, and they took out their frustrations on the Irish. They were called the
Auxiliary Police. Each carried a rifle and a revolver, sometimes two revolvers.
Training rapidly became a minor part of their work. They formed a separate
unit, elected their own officers and engaged in their own operations, especially unauthorized reprisals. In one of these operations, they burned down
the center of Cork City. The British government said this massive arson was
the work of the IRA, but the Auxiliaries boasted of it by wearing burned
corks on their Glengarry bonnets.

The British press referred to these newly minted "policemen" as
"cadets." It annoyed Tom Barry, an IRA commandant, that these "battle-
hardened captains and majors" were described as cadets after his column
ambushed a convoy of them.[6]

The IRA of the Black and Tan war was somewhat better organized and
trained than its counterpart in the Rising, but a shortage of weapons was still
a problem. The Volunteers had continued recruiting after the Rising.
Recruits now were investigated before being accepted. They were organized
in squads, sections (equivalent to American platoons), companies, battalions, and brigades. The brigades were based on counties. The Volunteers

practiced close-order drill and bayonet fighting with broomsticks. They got some training in squad tactics—learning how to lay an ambush, for example, or rehearsing an attack on a police barracks. To achieve this, training officers like Ernie O'Malley, a young medical student who did some unofficial (and ineffective) sniping during the Rising and joined the Volunteers immediately after it, traveled from county to county to drill the Volunteers in hidden locations. The Volunteers didn't get much marksmanship practice because weapons and ammunition were scarce. Volunteers were able to buy some rifles from British soldiers, and they obtained others from commercial sources until the government forbade possession of guns. They managed to have other weapons smuggled in, but there were never enough.

When the fighting began, the Volunteers—now the army of the Irish Republic—stole explosives from mines and tried to capture rifles and pistols from the police. One of the main motives for raiding police barracks and ambushing Black and Tans and Auxiliaries was to capture their weapons. All of these operations were small-scale, and executed on local initiative and directed by local officers. Headquarters in Dublin was mainly concerned with getting troops the supplies and training they needed, encouraging their officers to take action and—very occasionally—replacing those who didn't. The problem of weapons shortages was met by the establishment of "flying columns." Most of the troops in an IRA battalion lived at home and trained surreptitiously. They took turns at campaigning with the flying columns, in which every man was armed. Members of a flying column traveled from place to place in their counties, living in the houses of supporters or in the open in the mountains. Sometimes they lived in dugouts with camouflaged entrances. They raided barracks, ambushed enemy convoys, tried to defend towns against raids by the Tans or "Auxies," and performed other military actions.

This pinprick war was anything but decisive. It could have continued for years. The British tried to end it by capturing the Irish leaders. The reason they failed is why Michael Collins became a national hero.

Collins's contributions to the Irish struggle for independence were legion. As minister of finance, he organized the national loan and raised an enormous amount of money—all of which was paid back. He was director of operations for the IRA. But most important, he was chief of the army's intelligence.

Collins was a genius at winning people and persuading them to take action. He managed to recruit spies in all the agencies of British rule, including Dublin Castle and the police. He knew most of the moves the police and detectives would make before they made them. Because of him, the Dail Eireann and its agencies continued to function. Toward the end of the war, Ernie O'Malley wrote:

The enemy controlled the cities and the larger towns but English departments of government did not function as before. Taxes were not collected, their courts were empty, local administration was often handled by Republican county councils which interpreted the orders and decrees issued by Dail Eireann. Dail Eireann was the virtual *de jure* and *de facto* government, and even where the English strength was great, as in Dublin or Cork, they lived a garrison life.[7]

If Collins and his agents had been less effective, that never would have happened. Collins himself was the most wanted man in Ireland, but he bicycled all over the city performing his multiple duties. The police didn't recognize him because they didn't know what he looked like. The British authorities became disgusted at the incompetence of the agents they had in Dublin and brought in a group of top English intelligence officers. They were called the Cairo Gang, both because they hung out at the Cairo Café in Dublin and because they were old Middle East hands. Their mission was not only to locate the Irish leaders, but to kill them, if possible.

On September 23, 1920, they entered the hotel room of John Lynch at 2 A.M. and shot him while he was in his bed. Lynch was not an IRA intelligence agent or a major Irish leader. He was one of Collins's loan organizers and was in town to give Collins 23,000 pounds sterling. The British did catch three of Collins's agents, but they didn't know whom they had. They released the men after torture and interrogation. Collins, on the other hand, learned the identity of Lynch's killer and the rest of the Cairo Gang. He obtained the keys to where they were staying and enlisted the help of porters in their hotels. On November 21, 1920, his agents shot nineteen of the Cairo Gang. The British reaction was to send Black and Tans and Auxiliaries to a Gaelic football game and fire into the crowd with rifles and machine guns. Fourteen people were killed and hundreds wounded. None had anything to do with what the British called "Bloody Sunday."

Frank O'Connor got his first experience as a professional writer in the IRA's public information department, assisting Erskine Childers during the Civil War that followed the revolution. He summed up what was perhaps the most important operation of the war—intelligence and counterintelligence: "Though the Volunteers ambushed lorries and attacked barracks, and the military initiated vast roundups, thousands of men on both sides never fired a shot in anger at them; the real fighters were postmen, telephone operators, hotel porters, cipher experts; the only real weapon, the revolver."[8]

O'Connor later joined an IRA branch that was probably as vital in the revolution as the intelligence service. The IRA's intelligence and counterintelligence operations prevented the revolution from being snuffed out. But the public information department made the British sue for peace.

When the Black and Tan War began, newspapers in Britain and Ireland, as well as international correspondents, got only the war news the Lloyd George government released. The Dail and its agents were a small group of conspirators who did not represent the people of Ireland. The IRA was a collection of "well paid murderers" who spent their time shooting police, soldiers, and loyal civilians in the back from behind hedges. The Black and Tans and Auxiliaries were embattled police trying desperately to restore order. The government news releases reinforced all the ancient English prejudices about the Irish. The Irish were childlike, quarrelsome, and incapable of self-government. Only a strong military rule could keep order on that island.

The IRA included a publicity department. During most of the war it was headed by Erskine Childers, a man O'Connor described as "one of the great romantic figures of the period."[9] He was born in England but had been raised in Ireland. He had fought in the British Army during the Boer War, and during World War I he served in the Royal Navy as commander of a torpedo boat squadron, an aerial observer, and an intelligence officer. In 1914, he took his yacht across the North Sea and picked up a load of rifles for the Irish Volunteers, navigating his overloaded boat through a horrendous storm that had driven all other small boats off the Irish Sea. In appearance, though, he looked like anything but "a great romantic figure." He had an English accent and the manner of a fussbudget, reminding O'Connor of an English country parson.

Childers had rapidly developed from a Liberal Party home-ruler to a rabid Republican. When World War I ended, he went to IRA headquarters and volunteered his service. The IRA leaders considered his experience. He had been in the horse artillery in the Boer War, but Ireland had no artillery. He had been in the navy, but Ireland had no navy, either. He had been an aviator, but there was no Irish air force. But he had also been a writer. He had written a best-selling spy novel, *The Riddle of the Sands,* and a number of pieces on military history and military analysis. So he went to the publicity department. When Desmond Fitzgerald, the chief of the department, was arrested, Childers took his place. Childers was not particularly happy about the assignment.

"I had thought I was going off to a bloody combat," he told O'Connor, "and instead, I found myself in Mick Sullivan's feather bed in Kilnamartyr."[10]

He saw his task as countering the British propaganda by letting the world know what was really going on in Ireland. His first medium was the *Irish Bulletin,* a few mimeographed sheets distributed to Dublin newspapers and foreign reporters. It came out five times a week. Friday's edition contained "The Weekly Summary of Acts of Aggression Committed in Ireland by the Military and Police of the Usurping English Government." It listed all the murders, arsons, floggings, cases of torture, beatings, and other atrocities committed by Crown forces. It also described killings and other acts the British had attributed to Republican forces. Within a year, it had attained a circulation of 600 in Ireland, Britain, Europe, and the United States. Childers became one of the British government's most-wanted and had to keep moving his office. The search for him intensified after he was elected to the Dail. In the U.S. Senate, Senator Robert LaFollette delivered a series of speeches in favor of Irish independence. He used material gathered by Erskine Childers.

Childers was able to address the British public directly when the *London Daily News* commissioned him to write a series of articles on "Military Rule in Ireland." The eight articles were reprinted in a pamphlet, thousands of copies of which were distributed in Britain and the United States. Another pamphlet—*Who Burnt Cork City?*—created a sensation in Britain. Although the Auxiliaries openly boasted of their arson in Ireland, the British public had been told that the great fire was started by the IRA.

Childers's work produced results in England. Members of the British establishment began to demand an end to the atrocities in Ireland. Those demanding peace included former Prime Minister Herbert Asquith; the authors G. K. Chesterton, G. B. Shaw, and H. G. Wells; Lord Bryce, Lord Grey, Lady Frances Balfour, Lady Robert Cecil, the Archbishop of Canterbury; and two generals, Sir Hubert Gough and Sir Frederick Maurice. Even King George V complained about the war in Ireland.

The pressure on Lloyd George became unbearable. Three days after the king gave a speech in Ireland calling for peace, the prime minister proposed a truce and released all Irish political prisoners.

De Valera and a number of Irish notables went to London to talk with Lloyd George and other British leaders. The British insisted that six counties of Ulster be excluded from the rest of Ireland and that all Irish officials take an oath of loyalty to the Crown. Arthur Griffith, the old monarchist, was most agreeable to the British proposal; de Valera and Childers the most opposed. When de Valera presented the British proposal to the Dail, it was unanimously rejected. The most opposed was diminutive Cathal Brugha, who during the Rising, it was said, had received enough wounds to kill six other men. Brugha (originally Charles Burgess) was, like de Valera and Childers, only half Irish, but he was a ferocious Republican. At one point, he wanted to go to London and shoot all the members of the British cabinet if peace negotiations broke down entirely.

De Valera did not like the exclusion of the Ulster counties, and he did not want to take an oath of loyalty to the British Crown. He proposed that Ireland be "externally associated with the British Empire." Although that was the current situation of India, Pakistan, and South Africa, to Lloyd George and his group, it was unthinkable. De Valera knew that in further talks, he could do no more than get the British backs up. Further, he felt that he had to stay in Dublin to restrain the likes of Brugha. He also felt that he would be able to act as a brake on the delegation he sent to England for further talks. They were supposed to check with him on any potential agreement. For the delegation, he appointed men he thought most likely to achieve a compromise acceptable to both sides.

Griffith, who would lead the delegation, was a skilled negotiator and had already shown himself most likely to see the British side. His deputy was Michael Collins, a strong Republican, but a man of immense charm who was most likely to get the British to see the Irish side. Gavin Duffy and Eamonn Duggan, two other members, were lawyers who could make sure all *i*'s were dotted and *t*'s crossed. Robert Barton, Childers's cousin, was an ardent Republican, but as he had been in prison until the truce, he was still somewhat out of the political mainstream. Childers himself was a nonvoting secretary of the delegation. He was no more likely to compromise than de Valera himself, which was probably why he had no vote.

The delegation was probably the best de Valera could put together. It represented all sides of Irish political thought, but left out diamond-hard hard-liners like Brugha and gave no vote to hard-liners like Childers. As for himself, de Valera would have agreed with what Sean McEoin, later a high-ranking Free Stater, said: "Mr. de Valera knew that he personally could not get any more than he had been offered by Lloyd George. . . . He thought that Collins with his personality and Griffith with his sagacity might do better—and indeed, they did." [11]

The selection of the delegation and the talks themselves are still highly controversial in Ireland. Fans of de Valera and Collins, although both champions are long dead, are still vociferous. Each claims that the other leader betrayed his man. The Collins people say de Valera knew no delegation could have got a republic from the British, so he sent Collins to London instead of going there himself so "the Big Fellow" could take the heat when he failed. This argument skips the fact that Griffith, not Collins, was the leader of the delegation. The de Valera people say that Collins, who, regardless of title, had the most clout in the delegation, should have checked with their man before he gave away the six counties and agreed to an oath of loyalty. At any rate, it is no secret that de Valera and Collins were rivals and little love was lost between them.

Collins, like de Valera, was a wily politician. But so was Lloyd George. Collins knew the situation in Ireland intimately, especially the supplies available to the IRA. That situation was not good. In his mind, it overbalanced the success of Ireland's shadow government noted by Ernie O'Malley. The trouble was that he didn't understand the situation in England. Lloyd

George had not proposed a peace out of the goodness of his heart. He was under heavy pressure to make peace. But when discussions reached an impasse, the Welsh Wizard pulled a rabbit out of his hat. The Irish must agree to his terms, he said, "or face instant and terrible war." Lloyd George could not have brought "instant and terrible war" down on the Irish when the Dail first met. He certainly could not do so now. But his bluff succeeded.

The treaty that the delegation brought back would recognize an "Irish Free State" in Ireland minus the six counties. It could have its own army and custom services, but the British navy would be based in some of its ports. And all of its officials would swear loyalty to the British monarch.

The debate in the Dail was bitter and personal. The strain of revolution was beginning to take its toll of Arthur Griffith. The once-brilliant journalist was losing it. Because of Childers's English accent, Griffith conceived the strange notion that Childers was a British agent trying to wreck the revolution. He even accused him of deliberately starting World War I with his novel, *The Riddle of the Sands*.[12] He argued with Childers in the Dail, finally shouting, "I will not reply to any damned Englishman in this assembly!"

In the end, the Dail voted for the treaty sixty-four to fifty-seven. What swung the vote for the treaty—and against a republic—was the Irish Republican Brotherhood. Collins was president of the IRB, and the Dail members who belonged to the IRB recognized him as president of Ireland and were oath-bound to support him.

The outcome of the debate was known before the vote. Just before it, Barton had seen Collins and Childers, once fast friends, arguing in a corridor.

"Does this mean we're going to part?" Collins asked.

"I'm afraid so," Childers said.

Then "Collins crushed his fist into his eyes, and all at once Barton saw the flood of tears as he tossed his head in misery."[13]

The antitreaty delegates walked out of the Dail. The army split up. De Valera joined the republican military—not as a commander or even an officer, but as a private. No other private ever had so much clout. Childers became a captain, again in charge of propaganda. The Republican troops were now the IRA. The government troops were called the Free Staters. Shooting began when IRA troops under Rory O'Connor seized the Four Courts building in the heart of Dublin. Collins desperately tried to get them to leave. Churchill was threatening to send British troops in to quell the disorder. Collins finally borrowed some artillery from the British and shelled the building. Most of the IRA troops managed to escape the burning building; most of the rest surrendered. One who did not surrender was Cathal Brugha. He appeared on the street with a Mauser pistol in each hand, firing at the Staters. A machine gun burst finally ended the career of as brave and committed a Republican as ever put on a green uniform. The war raged for months with the IRA gradually losing. The Irish people had limited independence now, and they were tired of endless war. They were proving Mao's maxim about the fish and the sea long before Mao said it. (See chapter 11.)

Collins, now commander-in-chief of the army as well as President of Ireland, wanted to see how the fight was going in his native County Cork. He ran into an IRA ambush and was killed. Shortly before that, Arthur Griffith had a stroke and died.

The Revolution in Ireland now followed a pattern found in many revolutions. In Mexico, for instance, after all the revolutionary lions, Villa, Zapata, and Obregón had died, the jackal, Plutarco Elias Calles, stepped in. Calles was an organizer. He aimed to restore order (and in his case, do himself some good). In Russia, Lenin and Trotsky were followed by Stalin. In Ireland, the organizer was Kevin O'Higgins—not the president of the republic but a talented politician. O'Higgins wanted to bring order and unity to Ireland.

To bring order, he introduced a draconian criminal code that included flogging, the death penalty for ownership of a gun, and provision for executing Republican prisoners in retaliation for killings by the IRA. In carrying out this last provision, he had the best man at his wedding executed.

To bring unity, he set up a scapegoat, Erskine Childers. Childers, with his background in British intelligence and his English accent, made a perfect scapegoat. O'Higgins accused him of destroying bridges and other parts of the Irish infrastructure so the Free State would fail and the British would step in.

"The newspapers continued to appear with bloodier stories of the fights and ambushes Childers is supposed to have led," Frank O'Connor wrote. "Hendrick [Childers's other assistant] and I only laughed at them. We, who didn't even know how to redraft and slant an agency message, couldn't be expected to know how clever men prepare the way for someone's execution."

De Valera decided to set up a new shadow government, and he sent word to Childers to meet him. The Staters caught Childers at his cousin's house where he had stopped on his way to meet de Valera. He was carrying a tiny Colt .25 automatic that Michael Collins had given him years before. He didn't carry it because he depended on that little gun for protection, but because Collins had given it to him. Carrying that gun gave O'Higgins grounds to have him shot by a firing squad. That was on November 24, 1922. Five years later, O'Higgins was assassinated. The murder was never solved.

Twenty days before Childers was killed, Ernie O'Malley was shot seventeen times when Staters raided the house where he was staying. In the course of the Black and Tan War O'Malley had been shot several times, almost blown apart by a hand grenade, burned attacking a police barracks, tortured by the Black and Tans, and finally riddled with bullets by the Irish

Free State Army. But he lived and was sent to prison, where, in 1924, he was the last Republican political prisoner to be released. He left the Free State and went to Europe, then to the United States. He didn't return to Ireland until 1935, after de Valera had returned to power, abolished the oath of loyalty, and made Ireland a real republic.

In their revolution, the Irish provided a formula for how a small, weak nation could gain its independence from a large, powerful one—a working, shadow government, combined with low-level, guerrilla fighting by an army that disappeared into the population, and a powerful propaganda campaign aimed at the outside world and the population of the "mother country." One man who observed the process closely was a photographer's assistant in Paris, who later returned to his own country and took the name Ho Chi Minh. A generation later, the leaders of the Algerian Revolution listed among their heroes the leaders of the Irish Revolution.

The civil war that followed proved another maxim of guerrilla warfare. Guerrillas are to the people as fish are to the sea. If the temperature of the sea becomes unhealthy, the fish disappear. In Ireland, the population cooled for the Republican guerrillas because four years of warfare had caused great suffering, and the people already had a measure of independence. That measure wasn't entirely satisfactory, but the people finally achieved true independence through the slower and less painful process of politics.

CHAPTER 9

Stirrings in the Arab World: The Rif War, 1921–1926

By the early years of the twentieth century, almost all of Africa had been staked out by the European powers. But the portion of the continent closest to Europe, Morocco, was independent. The French had been in Algeria since 1830, and they had since added Tunisia to their empire. If they could grab Morocco, they'd have the whole Maghreb (the West, in Arabic). The Ottoman Empire still owned what is now Libya, but Britain had ousted it as the dominant power in Egypt. Britain was strongly against any commercial rival, like France or Germany, sharing domination of the strategic Strait of Gibraltar with its fortress on "the Rock" across the strait. Spain, also across the Strait, was by no means in a class with the other European nations, but it had African colonies and was strong enough to worry the sultan. Spain and Morocco had ancient ties, most of them unfriendly. Germany had no colonies near Morocco, but its bumptious monarch, Kaiser Wilhelm II, was hungry for colonies.

While in 1900, Morocco was, as Douglas Porch put it, "still nominally independent, it was as independent as a mouse surrounded by several hungry cats warily disputing who would carry off the dinner."[1]

A situation like this would seem to call for caution on the part of Morocco's ruler. Things were dangerous enough without giving the "cats" an excuse to act. But the Sultan had little control over his subjects. That was especially true of his subjects in the Rif—the steep mountains arising from the Mediterranean shore of northern Morocco. The Riffi were tribal Berbers, the fair-complexioned aboriginal inhabitants of North Africa who spoke, not Arabic, but Shilha. They stayed in their mountains during the great Arab invasion of the Middle Ages and since had as little to do with the surrounding Arabs and Arabic-speaking Berbers as possible. The Arabs reciprocated the feelings of the Riffi. "Berber," in fact, is Arabic for "barbarian." An Arab proverb states that "Honey is not grease, durra [a grain of sorghum] is not food, Shilha is not a language."[2] At the beginning of the last century, the most notorious Riffi was Sherif Moulai Ahmed ben Muhammad el Raisuni, a descendant of the Prophet whose father hoped that he would become a religious leader. Raisuni had other ideas. He became a bandit. Among other crimes, he kidnapped a man named Ion Perdicaris, leading to Theodore Roosevelt's demand that the Sultan produce "Perdicaris alive or Raisuli [*sic*] dead."[3] Raisuni eventually got a handsome ransom for Perdicaris and appointment as Caid of Tangier, and Perdicaris got his freedom, after which he moved to Tunbridge Wells, England. Raisuni later kidnapped Sir Harry Maclean, a Scottish mercenary who was commander of the sultan's army.

More than any other man, Raisuni demonstrated to the world that Morocco had no government. He convinced the Europeans that something must be done. The French had already been crossing the border from Algeria in pursuit of southern Moroccan raiders. Britain still wouldn't agree to the French occupying the Mediterranean coast opposite Gibraltar, but it would not object to Spain having a presence there. (After all, Spain was already on the north shore of the strait.) So, in 1904, France and Spain signed an agreement giving Spain a "sphere of influence" on the north shore and France one in the rest of Morocco.

In 1909, six European railroad workers were killed by Riffi tribesmen. Spain increased its forces in the city of Melilla from 5,000 to 22,000 men and pushed into the countryside. By 1910, the Spanish had subdued a few tribes but suffered 2,517 casualties. The Spanish troops were poorly trained, lacked maps, and had few cannons or machine guns. The war continued until 1912, leaving most of the Rif untamed. That year, the French and Spanish signed a treaty making Morocco a protectorate.

While this slow-motion Spanish offensive was going on, Spain began studying the French military establishment in Algeria. This led to first, the establishment of native troops under European officers, the *Regulares,* like similar French forces, and, second, to organize the *Tercio de Extranjeros* (Regiment of Foreigners) usually called the Spanish Foreign Legion, although three-quarters of them were Spanish.

Moulai Ahmed ben Muhammad el Raisuni called up his gang when Spanish troops got too close. After a few skirmishes, he and the Spanish opened negotiations. Fighting continued on other fronts. In one action, a twenty-three-year-old captain of the Regulares was hit in the stomach, but continued to direct his troops. That action brought Capt. Francisco Franco a promotion to major. In 1919, el Raisuni opened guerrilla war against the Spanish by attacking their supply convoys.

On October 14, 1920, the Spanish scored a major coup by taking Xauen. Xauen, the "holy city of the Berbers," was Raisuni's main base and was considered impregnable. The key man in the Spanish attack was Col. Alberto Castro Girona, a Spanish Arabist, who entered the city disguised as a charcoal burner and bribed the town's notables to surrender.

While all this was going on, there were developments well behind the Spanish lines that would not only affect this war, but which would have an impact on European history. Muhammad ben Abd el Karim Khattabi, who was to become better known as Abd el-Krim, took a job at the Spanish Bureau of Native Affairs in Melillo. He rose from clerk to interpreter and was appointed a judge in 1913. After what one writer calls "some ill-advised comments to a Captain of the Indigenous Office at Alhucemas," he was imprisoned for eleven months.[4] That was a sentence that the Spanish military court would come to regret. Abd el-Krim was reinstated May 1917, but he left the Spanish service in December 1918, and began organizing resistance to an expected Spanish move deeper into the Rif. He managed to unite the Rif tribes into a single military force.

Back in Spain, the army was not happy. There were too many officers and too little equipment. Training was poor, pay was low, and morale was lower. Civilians were just as unhappy. The Cortes (parliament) was not really representative, and the government was full of corruption. King Alfonso thought a big victory in Africa would distract both the soldiers and the civilians from their troubles. Gen. Manuel Fernández Silvestre was aware of the king's wishes. In Silvestre's opinion, all other Spanish generals were too cautious. Early in 1920, Silvestre took command of Spanish forces in Morocco. Silvestre was reputed "to rely more on *cojones* than military acumen."[5] He laughed on February 17, 1921, when he received Abd el-Krim's warning that if he crossed the Amekran River, the tribes of the Rif would resist in force.

Early in 1921, Silvestre launched a major offensive. Spanish troops pushed deep into the mountains without taking measures to secure their lines of communication and supply and without establishing control over the areas they passed through. They were dispersed through the mountains without adequate communications or means of coordination. Abd el-Krim's men gobbled up Spanish outposts and cut off all supplies to the main body. They took more than twenty Spanish posts and massacred their garrisons. At the seaside town of Afrau, the garrison was picked up by Spanish warships, and at Zoco el Telata de Metalsa, the Spanish escaped to French territory.

Some writers have said the Riffi had little more than flintlocks when they attacked the Spanish. That's not true, the mountaineers were always in the market for modern rifles, but they were soon much better equipped than when they began. They took all of the Spanish artillery and machine guns as well as all the rifles they could lay their hands on. They besieged Silvestre's headquarters at Anual for five days before Silvestre ordered a retreat on July 22, 1921. The retreat became a rout. Silvestre committed suicide, and the remaining Spanish troops fled eighty kilometers to Monte Arruit, where Abd el-Krim's forces surrounded them. Gen. Dámaso Berenguer

Fuste, the high commissioner of the protectorate, authorized the Monte Arruit garrison, under Gen. Felipe Navarro, to surrender August 9, 1921. In spite of the surrender, the Riffi massacred a large part of the garrison and took 600 others, including General Navarro, prisoner.

Of the 25,700 Spanish troops and 5,100 Regulares, 13,192 were killed and 1,100 captured.[6] Abd el-Krim had only about 3,000 fighters, but by scattering his army through the mountains, Silvestre made it possible for the Riffi to destroy one part at a time. Riffi losses came to about 1,000. In Spain, the campaign was called the Disaster of Anual.

Much of the blame fell on King Alfonso. Gen. Miguel Primo de Rivera proclaimed himself dictator and took over the government, while Alfonso remained head of state. Primo then declared a state of war throughout Spain. The other generals supported Primo de Rivera. They hoped by this to prevent condemnation of the army and the monarchy. Primo's dictatorship was not as brutal as most other European and Latin American dictatorships. He attempted to end the industrial strife in Catalonia by involving labor unions in the process and controlling the employers, an idea he may have picked up from the recently established dictatorship of Benito Mussolini. But Spain had taken a long step toward the Spanish Civil War—a dress rehearsal for World War II.

Back in Morocco, fighting continued between the Spanish and the Riffi. Francisco Franco, leading Spanish Foreign Legionnaires, built up a reputation as a brave and sagacious combat leader, and Riffian artillery made short work of the wooden blockhouses Silvestre's troops had built. By September, the Spanish had more artillery in the field and—in coastal areas—considerable help from the guns of the Spanish Navy.

The rest of 1921 and 1922 was spent in vicious back-and-forth fighting between Spanish troops and their Moroccan auxiliaries on one side and the Riffi of Abd el Krim on the other. In this, the Spanish Foreign Legion distinguished itself for both bravery and ferocity. The Legionnaires' battle cry was *Viva la Muerte!* (Long Live Death).

The Spanish belatedly started to modernize their army. They purchased a dozen French Renault FT 17 tanks, small (6.5 tons) machine-gun-armed tanks that were also a standard armored vehicle in the United States and several other countries in addition to France. On March 18, 1922, they used them against the Beni Said tribe. The tankers had only two months' training, and that did not include weapons testing, driving in wet weather, or coordination with infantry. The tanks could do only four miles per hour, but that was faster than the infantry, which was slogging through rain and mud. The tanks had outrun the infantry by the time they contacted the Berbers. The Beni Said fired at the tanks with everything they had, but nothing would penetrate the armor. The frustrated Berbers climbed up on the tanks and poked their daggers into the vision slits of the drivers and gunners. After troubles with ignition and jammed guns, the tankers had to withdraw, leaving two tanks dead on the battlefield.

El Raisuni had joined his fellow Riffians in the struggle against the Spanish, although he was still running his own show. On May 12, 1922, the Spanish took another of Raisuni's strongholds, Tazarut, but they didn't take the wily bandit. In the fall, the Spanish took a fortified hilltop south of Anual called Tizzi Azza. But Abd el-Krim put artillery on a higher hilltop and forced the Spanish to dig in for the winter. Tizzi Azza was to remain under siege for the next two years.

On January 27, 1923, the Spanish government paid Abd el-Krim 4.27 million pesetas ransom for the prisoners taken in the Anual campaign. General Navarro and 44 other officers, 245 enlisted men, and 40 civilians were returned. On June 8, Lt. Colonel Franco, age thirty, was appointed commander of the Spanish Foreign Legion. About the same time, Abd el-Krim, age forty-two, appointed himself emir (prince) of the Rif. He was acclaimed not only in his native eastern mountains, but in the western zone, which had been dominated by Moulai Ahmed ben Muhammad el Raisuni. By this time, Abd el-Krim had 80,000 fighters and 200 pieces of artillery.

Beginning in 1923, the Spanish, later joined by the French, are alleged to have begun aerial bombing of villages in the Rif, using mustard gas and other poison gases. A Spanish writer, Juan Pando, has cited written sources, including letters from Spanish soldiers who were themselves injured by the gas. A Berber organization, the Association of Toxic Gas Victims (the ATGV), claims that the present population of the Rif has a much higher than normal rate of cancer because of the gas. Pando, however, points out that areas of France and Belgium, which were gassed far more heavily during World War I, do not have abnormal cancer rates.

The ATGV has been trying to organize an international conference to be held in Morocco on the use of gas in the Rif War. Not surprisingly, the governments of Spain and France are opposed to such a conference. More surprisingly, so is the government of Morocco. The Riffian Berbers, like their cousins in Algeria, usually called Kabyles (Shilha for "tribes"), are separatists. The king's government, bent on recovering all lands, like Western Sahara, once part of Morocco, wants to give no aid or comfort to separatists.

In spite of tanks, planes, and poison gas, the war was not going well for Spain in 1924. In August, Spanish troops began withdrawing to defensible positions near the coast. In September, 10,000 Spanish soldiers were surrounded in the city of Xauen. Two Spanish columns, one led by Alberto Castro Girona, the "charcoal burner" who arranged the surrender of Xauen back in 1920, tried to break the siege. Instead, they were also besieged. In October, Primo de Rivera appointed himself high commissioner of

Morocco. Nothing changed. In November, the Spanish began the evacuation of Xauen, leaving five battalions of the Foreign Legion as a rear guard. On November 17, Franco led his rear guard out of the city at night after doing something that inspired a similar scene in the novel *Beau Geste*: he stuffed uniforms with straw and propped them up behind the defenses of Xauen.[7]

When he entered Xauen, Abd el Krim captured his only rival for power in the Rif—el Raisuni.

In April 1925, Abd el-Krim let success go to his head. He attacked the French. The French army was an altogether different proposition than the Spanish army. The French army was fully equipped, highly trained, and hardened by four sanguinary years on the Western Front of World War I. In addition, it was huge. Nevertheless, between April and June of 1925, Abd el-Krim took two-thirds of the French frontier posts, killed 3,000 Frenchmen, and advanced to within twenty miles of Fez, the capital of French Morocco.

On August 28, the French struck back. Marshal Henri Philippe Pétain, the hero of Verdun, launched an offensive from the south with 160,000 men. About a week later, a Spanish army landed on the shore of the Rif while Spanish and French warships pounded Riffian positions. In October, Spanish and French troops met. Four months later, Francisco Franco, who spearheaded the Spanish landing, became the youngest general in all Europe.

In the spring of 1926, the French and Spanish began their spring offensive. There were 325,000 French troops and 140,000 Spanish. By May, Abd el-Krim had only about 12,000 men, mostly members of his own tribe, the Beni Urriagel. On May 27, 1926, Abd el-Krim surrendered and was exiled to the French island of Réunion. In 1947, the French allowed him to live in France, but he stopped at Egypt, where he was granted asylum and spent the rest of his life plotting ways to free the Maghreb from European domination.

Abd el-Krim was a nationalist, not an Islamic fanatic, but his success showed a younger generation that conflict with the Occident was not hopeless. And many of them were extreme Islamists. As a guerrilla, Abd el-Krim was a sound strategist who knew how to use a smaller force to destroy a large one that was scattered and lacked coordination. He was a leader who was able to unite usually suspicious tribes and who could achieve enthusiastic support from the civilian population. He was to inspire a future generation of revolutionary leaders, including Mao Zedong.

The Rif War caused a breakdown in the Spanish monarchy, which was abolished completely five years after the war. Five years after that, the new Spanish republic was attacked by Spain's leading hero of the Rif War. Francisco Franco led an army from Morocco, the core of which was the Spanish Foreign Legion and the Moroccan Regulares. That war provided a proving

Abd el-Krim (center) after his surrender to the French Army. The Berber leader's Riffian tribesmen almost drove the Spanish out of Morocco, but the battle-hardened French were too numerous and too well equipped.
LIBRARY OF CONGRESS

ground for the three greatest European dictators—Hitler, Mussolini, and Stalin—to try out their weapons. Franco, in spite of his tremendous debt to Germany and Italy, managed to keep his nation neutral during World War II. He had developed political skills during the Rif War as a leader of troops as diverse as the native Regulares, Foreign Legionnaires, and Moroccan militia. Then he honed those skills as a dictator by playing the three rival pillars of his administration—the Falange Party, the Acción Católica, and the army—against each other.

CHAPTER 10

Holy Warriors in the Holy Places: Ibn Sa'ud in the Hejaz, 1925

In the eighteenth century, a certain Muslim named Muhammad ibn Abd al Wahab was preaching in the city of Medina. He held that all additions to Muslim culture since AD 950 were spurious and should be expunged. That included the veneration of saints, widespread among the Shi'a; ostentation in worship (Wahhabi mosques did not even have minarets); luxurious living; and a host of other practices. Drinking alcohol, of course, had always been seen as sinful, but al Wahab also denounced card playing, smoking, and most types of music and dancing.[1]

The people of Medina didn't agree, and al Wahab was forced to flee to the Nejd, a scattering of desert oases in central Arabia. In the Nejd, the Muslim reformer converted the sheik of the powerful Sa'ud tribe. Desert Muslims, in both Arabia and North Africa, have always been receptive to puritanical reformers. They themselves have almost no luxuries, so it's been easy for them to see that luxuries distract people from the will of God. The rise of puritanical sects has been a recurrent phenomenon in the Muslim world. In the medieval Sahara, for instance, there were the Tuareg Almoravids. One of the characteristics of these reform movements has been a desire to conquer "unbelievers," especially other Muslims. The Almoravids made war on the black Muslim empires of West Africa and the Moorish caliphate in Spain. (They made war on the Spanish Christians, too, but that was almost incidental at first.) In Arabia, the Sa'ud tribe set out to conquer its neighbors in 1763. By 1811, they ruled all of Arabia except Yemen.

The sultan of Turkey claimed to be the ruler of Arabia, but the Wahhabis, desert guerrillas striking seemingly out of nowhere on camels and horses, defeated all his expeditions. The sultan had to call on his viceroy in Egypt, Muhammad Ali, who had built a modern army. In 1818, Muhammad Ali drove the Wahhabis out of the cities of the Hejaz, including the holy cities of Medina and Mecca. The desert tribesmen retired to the Nejd and their capital, Riyadh, where they rebuilt their forces. The Bedouin guerrillas were far more mobile than the Egyptian regulars. They were safe in their desert fastness.

In 1821, they struck east instead of west, and by 1833, they controlled all of Arabia's Persian Gulf coast. Over the years, the Sa'udis' religious fervor declined, and their domain shrank. In 1884, the Rashid tribe, the Sa'udis' ancient rivals in central Arabia, took Riyadh, and the Sa'udi emir and his family fled to Kuwait.

In 1901, the Sa'udi emir, Abd al-Rahman ibn Faisal, was succeeded by his twenty-one-year-old son, Abdul Aziz bin Abdul Rhamanibn Faisal al Sa'ud. Ibn Sa'ud (as he was to be commonly known in the West)was an imposing figure—six feet, four inches tall and powerfully built. Other Arabs said he was strong as an elephant and brave as a lion. In 1902, he rounded up a few fellow tribesmen and drove the Rashidis out of Riyadh. He continually led his Bedouin raiders against the other clans and tribes of the Nejd, especially the ibn Rashid. He picked up more followers after each victory and by 1912, he controlled most of the Nejd.

By that time, Europe seemed to be drifting toward a major war. Britain had long been interested in the sheikdoms of the Persian Gulf both because of the oil known to be there and because the Gulf statelets were on the route to the "jewel of the crown," India. Further, Turkey, the nominal sovereign of the Persian Gulf emirates, was drifting into the German orbit. And the Rashid tribe was strongly pro-Turkish. To the court of Ibn Sa'ud came an English Arabist who helped the desert warrior organize an army and obtain modern weapons. The Englishman was more than just a student of Arabic and Arab culture. He became a Muslim and married a slave girl. His name was Harold St. John Philby, and his fame—or infamy—was to be vastly outweighed by that of his son, whom he nicknamed Kim.

The British helped ibn Sa'ud finally conquer the Rashidis, but they gave more help to one of the desert emir's rivals, Sherif Hussein ibn Ali, the ruler of the Hejaz. Hussein was the father of T. E. Lawrence's companion, Feisal. (See Chapter 2.) Hussein, with Lawrence's encouragement, dreamed of a vast Arab kingdom, stretching from the Indian Ocean to Anatolia, bounded on the west by Egypt and the Mediterranean and on the east by Persia. Hussein began calling himself "King of Arabia." That did not improve his relations with the British, and British support for Hussein quickly evaporated. With the Sykes-Picot agreement, Britain and France had divided up the Arab portion of the Ottoman Empire. France would be paramount in Syria and Lebanon; Britain in Palestine and Mesopotamia. Whatever Hussein became, it would not be king of all the Arabs. It would not even be king of all the Arabian Peninsula.

Hussein's claim to be the monarch of the peninsula did not please Ibn Sa'ud. To the desert emir, Hussein was a westernized decadent, and it was outrageous that he controlled both the holy cities, Mecca and Medina. Conflict between these two ambitious Arabs was inevitable.

Hussein, because of his cooperation with Lawrence, had more modern equipment, but when his army, led by his son, Abdullah, clashed with the followers of Ibn Sa'ud in 1925, the Hejaz army was destroyed. Both armies were basically guerrilla outfits, and in guerrilla warfare, public support is vital. And in Arabia, leadership is the key to public support. Lawrence had theorized that Semites tend to follow a prophet, so he searched for an Arab leader who could play the role of a secular prophet. He picked Feisal after deciding that both Hussein and Abdullah had the charisma of a pair of clams. But in the prophet business, Feisal himself was no match for Ibn Sa'ud—the giant desert warrior, strong as an elephant and brave as a lion. And Ibn Sa'ud was driven by much more than a mere desire for power. He thought he was fighting for God.

So did his Bedouin. Hussein's people, on the other hand were fighting only for Hussein—a small-time leader who decided he should be a great king. Motivation is probably the most underrated factor in warfare. Time after time, forces of highly motivated men have defeated better trained and better equipped enemies who were less well motivated. In the seventh century, the primitive Arabs—desert warriors, equipped with only light weapons and hardly any discernible organization—defeated the superbly trained and equipped Romans and crushed the equally well trained and equipped

Abd el Aziz Ibn Sa'ud, the desert warrior who founded Sa'udi Arabia, poses for a picture with Sir Percy Cox, a British diplomat.
LIBRARY OF CONGRESS

Persians because they were fired by religious zeal. Four centuries later, the first Crusaders, fired by similar zeal, knifed through the far more numerous, but internally squabbling, Muslims to take Jerusalem. Then the Muslims, united by religious zeal and the desire to free their country from the invaders, drove the Crusaders back to Europe. In our own time, the much better trained and equipped official Iraqi Army, most of whose members joined merely to have a steady job, seems unable to cope with the zealots of the Mahdi Army of Moqtada al Sadr. Training is no substitute for motivation. Motivation may be underrated as a factor because, unlike training, it is so hard to instill. Motives may be noble, like the desire for independence, as in the American Revolution, or ignoble, like hatred for followers of a different religion, as in Germany's Thirty Years War, but we ignore it at our peril.

Ibn Sa'ud became ruler of the holy cities, although he continued to rule from his capital, Riyadh—in those days, about as far from a fleshpot as you could get. Sa'udi Arabia, as he called his kingdom, became a puritan state. The principles of Muhammad ibn Abd al Wahab ruled the land.

Then oil was discovered beneath the sere surface of the Sa'udi Arabian desert. Sa'udi Arabia became a financial power. Ibn Sa'ud passed away, and the power and wealth passed into the hands of the old king's descendants, an increasingly unpuritanical clan.

The puritan Wahhabis did not disappear, however. They became even more extreme. Mecca had always been forbidden to non-Muslims. But the new puritans believed that prohibition should apply to all of the "sacred land" of Arabia. One of Osama bin Laden's greatest complaints was the presence of Western troops on that "sacred land." Wahhabi teachers opened schools in all Muslim lands. Extremist societies like the Muslim Brotherhood of Egypt were influenced by Wahhabism. The Taliban ("Students") of Afghanistan are products of Muslim schools located in Pakistan but run by Wahhabi scholars.

The Wahhabi movement began in the eighteenth century, but it was not until Wahhabis from the bleak heart of Arabia captured Mecca and Medina—Muhammad's birthplace and the city that first gave him support—that the ideas we now call "Islamist" began to sweep over the Muslim world.

CHAPTER 11

The "Protracted War" of Mao Zedong: Chinese Civil War, 1927–1950

Just eighty years ago, a ragtag crowd of soldiers and civilians began one of history's longest retreats. It was a horrible trip, through some of the world's most inhospitable places, inhabited by some of the world's most inhospitable people. But they had no choice. It was retreat or be massacred. That retreat began a process that changed the world's largest country from an anarchic land, which foreign nations had already started to divide up, to one of the greatest powers on earth. It also revolutionized guerrilla warfare and helped spawn revolutions on four continents.

To understand what happened, we have to go back a few years, to the end of the Manchu Dynasty in China.

In 1911, a revolution ended 2,000 years of imperial rule in China. In 1912, an English-speaking, Christian physician who had been educated in the Kingdom of Hawaii became president of the Provisional Government of the Republic of China and founded a new party, the Kuomintang (KMT), or Nationalist Party. The new president, Dr. Sun Yat-sen, had inherited a mess. Most of the southern provinces had declared their independence of the Manchu Dynasty, but many of the northern provinces did not. Japan, Russia, Britain, France, and the United States controlled much of China's commerce and maintained autonomous settlements on Chinese soil with their own military, police, and justice systems. They even patrolled China's rivers and owned some of its railroads.

Army generals, who became known as "warlords," controlled much of the rest of China, and Sun's provisional government had no army. Sun gained the allegiance of the most powerful warlord, Yuan Shi-k'ai, by promising to make him president. But as soon as he became president, Yuan proclaimed himself emperor. The result was another revolution, which quickly turned into chaos, with the warlords exercising what government there was.

Sun sought help from Western powers, but they had other things on their minds. In 1921, he went to the Soviet Union (the Union of Soviet

Socialist Republics). Although the Chinese Communist Party (CCP) had recently been founded, the Soviet Union agreed to help the Kuomintang. In 1923, the two parties formed the First United Front. The Comintern (Communist International, the headquarters of the worldwide Communist Party) encouraged CCP members to join the Kuomintang.

One who did was one of the founders of the CCP, a librarian and teacher from the central province of Hunan. At one time, he was known in English-speaking countries as Mao Tse-tung, but with the new Chinese transliteration system, he is now Mao Zedong. Mao had served in the revolutionary army that overthrew the Manchu Dynasty. After helping to found the Communist Party, Mao devoted himself to organizing the peasants to oppose both the landlords and the rapacious warlords.

The warlords were still China's biggest problem. Sun Yat-sen planned a major expedition into the north to eliminate the warlords, but he died before it could get under way. Command of the Northern Expedition fell to a professional soldier named Jiang Jieshi, better known to English speakers as Chiang Kai-shek. Like Mao and Sun, Chiang was a dedicated revolutionist, but he was also a professional soldier with an interesting history. He was a former member of the Japanese Army and a former gangster.[1]

Mao and Chiang both became leading figures in the Kuomintang, and they quickly became rivals. Mao became a member of the KMT's Shanghai Executive Committee and the party's propaganda chief. Chiang became commander of the Nationalist Army. In his campaigns, Chiang had received a considerable amount of aid from the Russians, including airpower, but he complained that they were meddling in Chinese affairs. In March 1926, Chiang dismissed his Soviet advisers and banned Communist Party members from participating in the top leadership of the Kuomintang. He charged that Communists were behind a plot to kidnap him. The Comintern, however, still hoped to take over the KMT from within, so it urged the Chinese Communist Party to support Chiang's Northern Expedition against the warlords.

That expedition moved in three columns. In the west, Wang Jingwei advanced on Wuhan; in the east, Bai Chongxi drove toward Shanghai; and in the center, Chiang aimed for Nanjing. Wang Jingwei, Chiang's rival for the top position in the KMT, took Wuhan and proclaimed it the national capital of China. He was supported by the Communists. After Chiang took Nanjing and his close associate, Bai, took Shanghai, he turned on the Communists. The results of that campaign ultimately made Mao, formerly only one of several Communist leaders, the supreme Communist in China.

The Russian Communists followed the Marxist gospel that Communism must be based on the urban, industrial proletariat. (It didn't bother them that in 1917, the industrial proletariat in their own country was a distinct minority.) Mao, son of peasants, had an almost mystical faith in the peasantry, who made up the overwhelming majority of all Chinese. When Chiang began his purge of Communists on April 12, 1927, China's urban Communists were sitting ducks. Thousands were shot or beheaded.

Back in his home province, Hunan, Mao led the peasants against Chiang's Kuomintang troops in what was known as the "Autumn Harvest Uprising." The peasants were defeated, and Mao led them into the mountains. After Mao's defeat, the Communist Poliburo denounced him for "military adventurism" and expelled him from the party. That didn't bother Mao. He devoted himself to training a Communist army in the mountains. He recognized that Chiang had overwhelming firepower, so his new Red Army would not battle the KMT in the traditional way. He devised a basic guide for his army in six Chinese characters: "Enemy advances, we retreat. Enemy halts, we harass. Enemy tires, we attack. Enemy retreats, we pursue." Sun Tzu, the ancient Chinese military philosopher, would have heartily endorsed that policy.

Meanwhile, in Wuhan, Wang Jingwei's KMT government was defeated by a local warlord, and, deprived of his Communist support, Wang was forced to join Chiang in Nanjing. Chiang waged a kind of half-hearted war against the Communists in southern China while he continued his campaign against the warlords. In June 1928, he took Beijing, the warlord capital, and six months later, the last major warlord, Zhang Xueliang of Manchuria, submitted. Chiang again focused on the Communists. But there was another distraction.

In 1931, the Japanese invaded Manchuria. Chiang Kai-shek decided the Japanese were too powerful to meet with the Communists in his rear. He wanted to crush the Communists first. He launched four "anti-bandit wars" against them, but he never eliminated the "bandits." For the fifth "anti-bandit" war, in 1934, he consulted German advisers and moved against Mao's people the way the British had moved against the Boers. He surrounded the "Jiangxi Soviet" in the mountains with blockhouses and barbed wire.

The Communists managed to break through the Kuomintang lines, but they suffered horrible losses. About 80,000 soldiers and 50,000 civilians began what became known as the Long March. In January 1935, at a conference of top Communist officials, Mao denounced Otto Braun, the adviser the Soviet Union had sent to help the Jiangxi Soviet. Braun had advised fortifying their mountain base. As a result, Mao said, Chiang had been able to concentrate on one part of the Jiangxi Soviet's territory, pulverize it with aerial bombs and artillery, then launch a massive infantry assault to destroy that portion of the Communists' territory. He then struck another portion. Following Braun's advice was madness, Mao said.

Because of his previous rejection of Comintern advice, Mao was something of a maverick. But this time, he was backed up by Zhou Enlai, the Red

Army's political commissar. Braun went back to Russia, and Mao became the undisputed leader of the CCP and the Red Army.

The problem now was to get out of the reach of Chiang's KMT and find a secure base. Mao and his people marched west across mountains and deserts, and then turned north and northeast to stop at the isolated town of Yan An in northern Shaanxi Province. The 6,000-mile march was a nightmare. Of the 130,000 who began the march, only about 20,000 survived. Marchers froze to death in the mountains, died of hunger or thirst in the deserts, and were slain in innumerable skirmishes.

Yan An was honeycombed with caves in the yellow loess soil. Mao's people connected the caves with tunnels, dug tunnels under houses, and ran tunnels to camouflaged exits. If they were forced to defend their base area, it would be a very mobile defense.

When he was in Hunan, Mao had proposed to Chiang that the CCP and the KMT unite to fight the Japanese invaders of Manchuria. Chiang had rejected the proposal. But his proposal to concentrate on the Communists instead of the Japanese was not popular in China—especially with Manchurians. In 1936, Zhang Xueliang, the former Manchurian warlord, and another general kidnapped Chiang Kai-shek and forced him to make a truce with the Communists. The Second United Front was established.

In 1937, the Japanese began an all-out war. They aimed to conquer all of China. Japanese planes bombed Chinese cities, and Japanese troops flooded into northern China and cities along the coast. They pushed along China's great rivers and defeated KMT troops in a series of battles.

China, though, is a huge country with millions of square miles and, to the Japanese, a seemingly inexhaustible supply of manpower. The Japanese army bogged down. The Japanese army, being a modern organization, began experiencing shortages of oil. Oil was available in the Dutch East Indies. Japan had signed the Tripartite Pact with Germany and Italy, so the Netherlands, which was an enemy of Germany, was also its enemy. The same was true of France. The only obstacle to sweeping through French Indochina and into the Dutch East Indies was the United States, which had recently stopped exporting oil to Japan. So Japan attacked Pearl Harbor, and its war expanded enormously. Japan could no longer concentrate on China.

The position of the Japanese in China, practically immobile and scattered over thousands of miles of coastline and river valley, made them ideal targets for guerrillas, and Mao took advantage of that. He conducted a war of raids and ambushes, with his troops appearing suddenly and disappearing equally fast. Convoys and small outposts were his targets, and his bases were hidden from the Japanese. Villagers in the area would give the invaders no information.

That silence was due to a policy Mao instituted. In the past, warlord troops routinely pillaged the villages, although they never committed atrocities that compared to those of the Japanese. Mao's treatment of civilians was diametrically opposed to the methods of the warlords and the Japanese.

"Many people," he said, "think it impossible for guerrillas to exist for long in the enemy's rear. Such a belief reveals a lack of comprehension of the relationship that should exist between the people and the troops. The former may be likened to water and the latter to the fish who inhabit it. How can it be said that these two cannot exist together? It is only undisciplined troops who make the people their enemies and who, like the fish out of its native element, cannot live."[2]

Mao laid down eight rules for his men when living among civilians. The first, "Replace the door when you leave the house," requires some explanation. In Chinese villages, during the summer, doors were often removed and used as beds. The other rules were: "2. Roll up the bedding on which you have slept. 3. Be courteous. 4. Be honest in your transactions. 5. Return what you borrow. 6. Replace what you break. 7. Do not bathe in the presence of women. 8. Do not without authority search the pocketbooks of those you arrest."[3] Such sensitivity to the feelings of civilians is rare among occupying troops, but Mao conclusively proved that it works.

Mao's guerrillas depended on the people for more than just cover. Villagers kept them informed of enemy movements and provided food and shelter. The Japanese provided weapons and ammunition, as the Spanish had for Abd el-Krim's Riffi. (See Chapter 9.) Gathering guns and ammunition was the prime objective of many of the guerrillas' raids and ambushes. The villagers were also the source of recruits, so they had to be converted to Mao's cause.

"All our strength must be used to spread the doctrine of armed resistance to Japan, to arm the people, to organize self-defense units, and to train guerrilla bands," he said.[4]

The "self-defense units" were a kind of home guard, people armed with swords, spears, shotguns, and antique rifles. They would fight the Japanese only in the most desperate emergencies. Their more usual duties were collecting information, eliminating spies, and collecting "contributions" from local citizens. These contributions were part of what Mao called "reasonable protection" of commerce. "We interpret 'reasonable protection' to mean that people must contribute money in proportion to the money they have. Farmers will be required to furnish a certain share of their crops to guerrilla troops. Confiscation, except in the case of businesses run by traitors, is prohibited."[5]

The "guerrilla bands" were Mao's striking force. They had rifles, machine guns, and mortars. They operated in small groups so that they could quickly appear and disappear.

Bodies of Communist soldiers lay on a Chinese street after Chiang Kai-shek of the Kuomintang turned on his erstwhile allies. LIBRARY OF CONGRESS

"The movement of guerrilla troops must be secret and of supernatural rapidity; the enemy must be taken unaware and the action entered speedily. There can be no procrastination in the execution of plans; no assumption of a negative or passive defense; no great dispersion of forces in many local engagements. The basic method is the attack in a violent and deceptive form."[6] In another place, Mao said guerrilla bands must "move with the fluidity of water and the ease of the blowing wind."[7]

Some 2,500 years earlier, Sun Tzu, the ancient Chinese strategist, said: "All warfare is based on deception. Therefore, when capable, feign incapacity; when active, inactivity. When near, make it appear that you are far away; when far away, that you are near. Offer the enemy a bait to lure him; feign disorder and strike him."[8]

Sun Tzu had no more ardent disciple than Mao Zedong. But Mao did not merely adopt the ideas of the ancient master. He added something new and original in his writings. Previously, all military theorists who put their thoughts on pages held that guerrillas were useful only when they coordinated their efforts with regular field armies. Mao, too, believed in the coordination of guerrillas and regulars. But he said the regular field armies could grow out of guerrilla bands. The field armies would conduct what he called "mobile warfare." They would move almost constantly, but they would hold ground—temporarily at first, later permanently. They would not disappear like guerrillas, but they would retain the initiative.

"The development of mobile warfare is not only possible but essential," he wrote. "This is because our current war is a desperate and protracted struggle."[9]

When he wrote these words, Mao was probably thinking of a much more protracted struggle than the current war with Japan. Both he and Chiang were conserving their strength in the war with Japan, knowing that the United States was going to defeat Japan and that they would soon be fighting each other. Gen. Joseph "Vinegar Joe" Stilwell, the U.S. adviser to Chiang Kai-shek, complained bitterly about the Generalissimo's holding back—so bitterly that the "China Lobby" eventually had him replaced by Patrick Hurley. The United States had no equivalent to Stilwell at Mao's headquarters.

Mao's guerrillas gradually expanded their areas of control. They advertised each successful ambush and raid. News of victories brought in new recruits. As Germany was staggering out of Russia, Mao got new weapons and supplies from the Soviet Union. His people proselytized tirelessly. Guerrilla platoons and companies grew into battalions and regiments, eventually into divisions and even armies. They fought as regulars, with artillery and armor as well as rifles and machine guns. But they had not forgotten how to be guerrillas. Squads were detached to organize guerrilla warfare in enemy rear areas. When he fought Chiang, Mao's strategy was based on the close cooperation of regulars and guerrillas. As always, the guerrillas bonded with the people in their areas and recruited new fighters for what now called itself the People's Liberation Army (PLA).[10] Mao's regulars fought like guerrillas. They lured the Nationalists into their territory and ambushed them. Nationalists fighting the PLA at the front had their supply lines severed by guerrillas in the rear. If the PLA truly represented the masses, Mao said, and if it appeared to be winning, the enemy troops would desert and join it. KMT morale dropped lower and lower, and the rate of desertions rose higher and higher. The climax of the war came when the PLA was about to cross the Yangtze. Instead of organizing defense behind this enormous river, Chiang fled to Taiwan.

Before World War II, China was, as Mao put it, semicolonialized by foreigners holding "concessions," even real colonies like the British-occupied Hong Kong. Mao turned China into a world power. His example also inspired a host of revolutionists in colonies like Vietnam and semicolonies like Cuba.

PART III

World War II, Cold War, and the Rise of Nationalism and Islamism

CHAPTER 12

Crazy Orde: Mad Master of Guerrilla War, 1936–1944

Because he ate onions as if they were apples, seldom shaved, dressed in shabby, out-of-date uniforms, and rebuked generals, his contemporaries called Lt. Col. Orde Wingate "Crazy Orde."

They didn't know the half of it.

All his life, Wingate suffered from depression. In 1942, after his greatest triumph—defeating a much larger Italian army in Ethiopia with less than 2,000 irregulars and any tribal fighters he could find—Wingate cut his throat. When he revived after receiving seventeen pints of blood, he thought he had died and gone to hell. A priest told him he definitely was not in hell, and the fact that he recovered from his suicide attempt may have meant that God had work for him. That greatly encouraged Wingate.

Son of a martinet officer in Britain's Indian Army and a Bible-thumping mother, Wingate had always taken religion seriously. That was how he got involved in his first notable accomplishment—that, combined with a desire for adventure and a most unmilitary brashness. It happened this way:

Wingate had studied Arabic at the suggestion of his cousin, Sir Reginald Wingate, who once commanded all British forces in what was then the Anglo-Egyptian Sudan. That got him command of a Sudanese company. He became bored with chasing Ethiopian bandits and slavers, so when he got leave, he went into the Libyan Desert with three Arab camel drivers to look for a lost oasis. He didn't find the oasis, but he learned a lot about survival in the desert, and he wrote a report on the trip.

Wingate avidly sought promotion. "Only rank gives you the power to do what you know should be done," he once said. Wingate was always sure he knew what should be done: he never lacked self-confidence. When he failed to get appointed to staff officers' school, he went to the general in charge of selection and complained that his search for the oasis and his report on the expedition had not been considered. Witnesses braced for the sight of an exploding general. Instead, the general told the young officer that there were no vacancies at the school, but that he would be considered for a staff job as soon as one appeared.

114

One appeared soon. Captain Wingate learned that he would be the intelligence officer for the 1st Division in Palestine. At that time, 1936, Zionist Jews were buying land and settling in Palestine. Arab landlords were selling the land, which meant that Arab tenant farmers were being displaced. Arabs were attacking Jewish settlements. Few Britons at the time knew many Jews; hardly any knew an Arab. But they had their stereotypes—the conniving Jew, personified by Shylock, and the noble Arab, the image of Rudolph Valentino in *The Sheik*. Wingate, on the other hand, looked at the Jews and saw God's Chosen People trying to recover the land the Almighty had given them. He decided that God had spared him so he could turn these Zionists into modern Hebrew warriors.

His views of the antagonists didn't jibe with those of his fellow officers. He favored the Jews not only because of their place in the Old Testament, but because as most of them came from Russia and Central Europe, they were steeped in European culture and understood modern technology. They were easier to talk to. It was not only Wingate's views that didn't jibe with those of his messmates. Nothing about Wingate jibed with them. He shaved infrequently and usually wore a ragged sweater and the type of sun helmet that had not been regulation since the end of World War I. But while the other British soldiers in Palestine were natty enough, they weren't very effective. Arab terrorists were blowing up pipelines and bridges and murdering Jewish farmers in kibbutzim. The British had not been able to stop them. Wingate explained why:

Owing to the number of roads in Palestine, to the high degree of mechanization of the troops, and to the presence of an air arm, engagements with the rebels tended to take on a very definite form. A rebel gang would carefully choose a site commanding a road with a covered retreat and very good air cover at hand. It would then lie up and shoot up the first body of troops, police, or Jews, which it considered strong enough to engage with impunity. In the case of troops, the following would occur: The troops, invariably caught at a ground disadvantage, would jump out of their vehicles and take cover. Then they would open fire. Meanwhile, an XX call [a call for reinforcements] would be sent for aircraft, which would arrive within 20 minutes, and often sooner. On the appearance of the aircraft, the gang would retire to its covered position usually among rocks and scrub, and, in spite of claims, very seldom suffered casualties from the subsequent air action.[1]

Because the army and police couldn't protect them, the Jews had to organize a self-defense force, *Haganah* (from the Hebrew word for defense).

Wingate began studying Hebrew and visiting kibbutzim. He decided that the Jewish strategy of waiting behind barbed wire for the Arabs to attack was all wrong. He visited Emmanuel Wilenski, Haganah's chief of intelligence.

"I have a scheme by which the British Army, with the help of your people, can put down these marauders. But I need information about Arab methods and plans before I contact my headquarters. So I have come to request your help." [2]

He arranged to lead a scouting party into Arab territory. He spent some time training the men, who included a youth named Moshe Dayan, later the famous one-eyed commander of the Israeli Army. Then he led them on a thirty-mile hike, mostly in the dark, to an Arab village he believed to be a terrorist base. Just outside the village, Wingate positioned his men for an ambush.

"I shall go forward and reconnoiter," he told Zvi Brenner, his second in command. "If I don't come back, the decisions will be in your hands, Zvi. But don't attack unless you are sure of success." [3]

The men in the ambush position heard shots, screams in Arabic, and then saw a crowd of Arabs run past them. They opened fire. They killed five Arabs and captured four. Then Wingate appeared, holding a captured rifle. He asked one of the captured Arabs where they had hidden their weapons. The Arab denied that there were hidden weapons. Wingate stooped down, grabbed a handful of dirt, and shoved it in the Arab's mouth. He repeated his question. The Arab refused to tell him. Wingate turned to one of the Jewish soldiers.

"Shoot this man," he said.

The soldier hesitated.

"Did you hear? Shoot him."

The soldier shot the Arab. Wingate looked at the other Arabs.

"Now speak."

They spoke.[4] Hugh Foot, a British diplomat, charged that by using tactics like this, Wingate "forfeited our reputation for fair fighting," [5] as if murdering unarmed civilians was fair fighting.

News of Wingate's expedition caused consternation in British headquarters. The British Army was supposed to be neutral, but one of its officers had actually led a raid on an Arab village. Wingate was called before Sir Archibald Wavell, the commanding general in Palestine.

Wingate explained that the Jews, Europeans familiar with modern war and modern technology, had far more military potential than the Arabs. He proposed mixing Jewish settlers with British volunteers to form "Special Night Squads" who could guard strategic locations and root out terrorists. These squads, he said, would allow Britain to decrease the number of troops it had to keep in Palestine.

Wavell liked the idea.

Wingate began organizing and equipping his squads. British soldiers and Haganah members served together. They had their own uniform—broad-brimmed Australian hats, blue police shirts, shorts, and tennis shoes. Wingate's training emphasized use of the bayonet and the hand grenade. At night, targets become invisible a short distance away, so the rifle loses much of its value, he said. The hand grenade on the other hand, is invaluable. Unlike a gun, it does not give away the user's position; it does not require pinpoint accuracy, and it can eliminate several enemies at a time. Wingate emphasized surprise. His squads would leave by truck, then the troops would dismount in some desolate location and march in a new direction.

The Special Night Squads put the Arab terrorists on the defensive and taught the Haganah much about guerrilla warfare. Moshe Dayan was greatly impressed by Wingate.

"I never knew him to lose an engagement," Dayan later wrote. "He was never worried about odds. If we were 20 and the Arabs were 200, or if we were at the bottom of a hill and they were at the top, he would say, 'All right, there's a way to beat them.'. . . [I]n some sense, every leader of the Israeli Army even today is a disciple of Wingate."[6]

Then Wavell was transferred out of Palestine. The new commander did not like the Special Night Squads. British officers were murmuring that Wingate was training men they might have to fight. But before he, too, was transferred, Wingate and his squads demonstrated their value. On October 8, 1938, a large group of Arabs sneaked into Tiberias and massacred nineteen Jews, ten of them children. Another group of Arabs, armed with machine guns, surrounded a British fort and kept the battalion garrisoning it immobile while their comrades were murdering civilians. Wingate was leading two squads ten miles away. When he heard of the massacre, he headed for Tiberias. His squads killed fifty of the terrorists—about twice their own number. Fourteen of the Arabs got away, but Wingate and his men caught up with them and killed them all the next day. In spite of that, the British chief of intelligence got the army to bar Wingate from ever again entering Palestine.[7]

Back in England, Major Wingate commanded an antiaircraft battalion during the "Blitz," but Wavell, now in command of British forces in the Middle East, asked for Wingate, who was to participate in a campaign to take Ethiopia from the Italians. A South African army under Sir Alan Cunningham was to invade Ethiopia from Kenya; a British army under Gen. William Platt was to attack from the Sudan, and inside Ethiopia, Col. Daniel Sandford was to act as a "Lawrence of Ethiopia" and preach rebellion to the Ethiopians. Wingate was to join the Ethiopian army under the exiled emperor Haile Selassie. The emperor had 800 refugee Ethiopian troops,

800 Sudanese militia, 50 British officers and 20 British NCOs. When a British general sneered at the idea of this force invading Ethiopia, held by a quarter of a million Italians, Wingate said, "You are an ignorant fool, General. It is men like you who lose wars."[8]

In spite of that, Wavell made Wingate a lieutenant colonel and Sandford, the would-be "Lawrence of Ethiopia," a brigadier. Wingate hoped to work closely with Sandford, and at one point flew into Sanford's hidden headquarters in the Ethiopian mountains. The airstrip they landed on was short and ended in a chasm. When they were leaving, Wingate's pilot said it was too short for the plane to take off with both of them aboard.

"Don't worry me with such nonsense," Wingate said. "You understand aerodynamics. I understand the will of God. Let's take off."

The pilot managed to take off safely—a feat that earned him the Distinguished Flying Cross.[9]

The cooperation between Wingate and Sandford could have been smoother. Wingate's arrogance didn't help. And, unlike Sandford, he was not impressed with the efforts of his cousin, T. E. Lawrence, in the last war.

Ethiopian emperor Haile Selassie on a horse surrounded by royal attendants before the Italian invasion. Orde Wingate later restored him his throne. LIBRARY OF CONGRESS

He wrote "The Right and Wrong Methods of Dealing with a Fifth Column Population," which he sent to Wavell and his subordinate commanders:

The wrong (or Lawrence) method:
On entering the occupied area, the invading commander gets in touch with the local patriot leader and after an exhortation suggests that the leader can do something to help carry out the operation. The patriot replies that he wants nothing better, but has no arms, money, or ammunition. The commander asks how much he wants. He names some impracticable figure. The commander promises a fraction, which he hands over and waits for results. They are nil. . . .

The right method:
The commander enters an area with a small but highly efficient column with modern equipment and armament, but none to give away. On meeting the patriot he says he has come to fight for the common cause but preserves an air of secrecy and confidence regarding the action he intends to take. The patriot asks what he can do. The commander replies: "Give me supplies which I will purchase at a fair price and pass me information." . . . The following night the commander carries out a successful operation. Next day comes the patriot saying: "Why didn't you tell me you intended to attack. I could have been a great help to you." Says the commander: "Oh well, you have no arms and are not a soldier. And after all, why should you get killed. That is our job." Says the patriot: "But I am a soldier and have been fighting the enemy for years. Only tell me what you want me to do and I will show you we can do it." "But you have no arms or ammunition and I have none to spare." "It is true," says the patriot, "that I have very little ammunition but what I have I want to use in support of my flag." So the commander agrees: "Very well, come along with me this afternoon. I am making a reconnaissance and can probably find some useful job for your followers. But I shall judge by results and if you make a mess of it I shan't be able to use you again." Result: the patriot rushes to the fray with keenness and devotion. He regards the commander as his leader. It is a privilege to follow him.[10]

Wingate used the second method to recruit tribal warriors after he entered Ethiopia commanding Haile Selassie's army. It worked. He had plenty of men for the kind of war he planned. "Given a population favorable to penetration, a thousand resolute and well armed men can paralyze, for an indefinite period, the operations of a hundred thousand," Wingate once wrote.[11] His army, which he dubbed Gideon Force, had no supply lines. It lived off the country. One of its main objectives was to cut the Italian supply lines. The Italians, like most regular soldiers, could not imagine fighting without supply lines. Wingate divided Gideon Force into two main columns. One column surrounded 14,000 Italian soldiers at Bahardar. Instead of trying to hold a fixed circle of entrenchments, Gideon Force kept them in place with a dizzying series of raids and ambushes. The second column attacked an Italian force of 17,000. First, they blew up the bridge over the Nile chasm, cutting off retreat. They made the Italians think there were many thousands of native warriors all around them, so the Italians holed up in a series of fortified outposts.

The Italians had native troops, but Wingate ordered his men to fire only at the white soldiers. Many of the Italians' native auxiliaries deserted to join the Emperor's army. So convinced were the Italians that they were vastly outnumbered that in some outposts, the garrisons retreated before they were attacked. When he entered one town, Wingate got Edmund Stevens, an Italian-speaking reporter for the *Christian Science Monitor,* to call ahead to a string of garrisons to say he and other Italians were hiding from the native rebels who were wreaking havoc in the town. To each garrison, he had the same advice—"Get out!" Most of them did.

Meanwhile, the British force under Platt had bogged down, but the Italians were not prepared for the South Africans marching up from Kenya. The South Africans had no opposition but the terrain. Wingate's troops, like Platt's, were fighting enemy troops. Unlike Platt's they were moving ahead. Nevertheless, Wingate's black troops were not British headquarters' highest priority. In spite of his pleas, Wingate got no air support and precious little motor transport.

Because they had no opposition, the South Africans got to Addis Ababa first. Their commander, Alan Cunningham, ordered Wingate not to bring the emperor to his capital until Cunningham was ready to receive him. But Wingate knew that the British brass could not be seen to be pushing around an exiled emperor that the whole world, except Italy and Germany, regarded as a martyr. He brought Haile Selassie into the city at the head of a triumphal parade.

Then he took Gideon Force out to mop up the Italian remnants. He used the Italian fear of the natives to make the job easier. One Italian commander said he would surrender, but only to British troops. Wingate met the Italian colonel with his second-in-command, a Palestinian Jew. He said the rest of the British were "in position." The Italian never knew that he had seen the only two Allied white men in the area.

Wingate was ordered back to Cairo before he could even say good-bye to the emperor whose throne he had restored. It seemed nobody gave him credit for his accomplishment—his force of fewer than 2,000 Africans had captured more than 20,000 Italians and destroyed an Italian army. The old depression returned, worse than ever before, and he tried to kill himself. It turned out that Wingate not only had depression but cerebral malaria, which can cause insanity and death. Wingate had to pull many strings to convince the authorities he was sane enough for active duty.[12]

And then, Sir Archibald Wavell called for him again. Wavell had been transferred to a quiet area, India. And then Japan entered the war and invaded Burma. Although outnumbered, the Japanese seemed able to run circles around the British. Wavell hoped that Wingate could perform as well in the jungle as he had in the desert.

Wingate proposed forming long-range penetration teams to get at the rear of the Japanese troops. The Japanese had practiced short-range penetration. They packed the supplies they would need for several days, infiltrated the British lines, and attacked them from the rear. Wingate's plan was to train picked men in infiltration and resupply them with airdrops. They could then strike deep in the Japanese rear. They would train with RAF (Royal Air Force) pilots, because the infiltration teams could take no artillery. Dive bombers would take the place of cannons.

As with the Special Night Squads, Wingate's penetrators got their own uniforms—green, instead of khaki, and Australian hats. Wingate wanted to arm them with distinctive weapons, including American rifles and carbines, but foreign weapons were not available. They also had their own unit badge, an image of a Burmese monster called a chinthe. The troops called it a "chindit," and Wingate's guerrillas became the Chindits.

The 3,000 Chindits did penetrate the Japanese lines and cut some Japanese supply lines, but the Japanese were able to concentrate on them and drive them back. But of the 3,000 who began the campaign, 2,200 got out. And Lt. Gen. Mutaguchi Renya, the Japanese commander, began to think more of improving the defense of his position in Burma than of invading India.

The next year, Wingate reorganized the Chindits and formed a partnership with Cols. Philip Cochran and John Allison, two American airmen who had formed the Number 1 Air Commando in China. The first Chindit operation was a kind of trial run. The new one would be the real thing. It would be part of a combined operation. The Chindits' mobile light infantry were to mess up Japanese rear areas while the British moved east from India and the Chinese moved south.

The Chindits would operate from what Wingate, now a major general, called "strongholds." Strongholds were clearings in the jungle where gliders and light planes could land and take off. They would be places where the Chindit columns could be resupplied, and they would be lures that could attract Japanese troops into ambushes. They would all be inaccessible to wheeled vehicles, so the Japanese could bring in no armor or artillery. The Chindits, on the other hand, would have 40mm antiaircraft guns and 25-pounder (88mm) fieldpieces flown in.

Chindit II fly-in was the largest airborne operation in history at that time (March 1944). It would be surpassed only by the D-Day operation. The planes dropped off 9,052 soldiers, 1,359 tons of pack animals, and 254.5 tons of supplies. Mutaguchi, concentrating on a planned offensive, tried to ignore it. His commander ordered him to send two infantry regiments and an artillery battery to take care of the Chindits. All Mutaguchi got were casualties. One trouble with the Allied offensive was that neither the Chinese nor the regular British infantry started their offensive on time. But Wingate's operation was proceeding well. Then, on March 24, 1944, Wingate was flying back from one of his strongholds when his B-25 crashed and ended the career of one of the Second World War's most spectacular commanders. He was forty-one.

Wingate is considered one of the founding fathers of the Israeli Army; he demonstrated—to the dismay of the South African Army—that black soldiers could beat white soldiers, and he pioneered in what, with the addition of helicopters, became air mobile tactics. Still, he is probably the most unappreciated soldier of World War II.

One who did understand his importance was General Mutaguchi. He wrote:

> The advance into Burma of General Wingate's forces at the time of the Imphal campaign brought about serious failures in the strategy of the Japanese Army. . . .
>
> General Wingate's airborne campaign spread more and more widely, and the Area Army Commander picked out the 24th Mixed Independent Brigade and part of the 2nd Division to confront Wingate's forces. The counterattack by these units on the 24th and 25th of March ended in failure. . . . Further the fact that we had no alternative but to use our feeble air force against these airborne forces was a very great obstacle to the execution of the Imphal campaign . . . and were an important reason for its failure.
>
> On 26th March I heard on Delhi radio that General Wingate had been killed in an aeroplane crash. I realized what a loss this was to the British Army and said a prayer for the soul of this man in whom I had met my match.[13]

CHAPTER 13

The Ustaše, the Četniks, and Tito, 1941–1980

Adolf Hitler was preparing to invade the Soviet Union when a coup d'état in Yugoslavia caused a delay in his plans. He had thoroughly intimidated the Yugoslav regent, Prince Paul, and forced him to make Yugoslavia part of the Axis, as Germany, Italy, Japan, and their client states were called. The nations comprising what was once called the Rome-Berlin-Tokyo Axis now included Bulgaria, Hungary, and Romania. Until the coup, Yugoslavia had been part of the Axis, securing Germany's southern flank. That was important, because the British were now in Greece, supporting that country against Italian invaders.

What happened was that some Yugoslavian officers decided that the pact with Germany was dishonorable and sent Prince Paul into exile. They seem not to have calculated what Hitler's reaction to the coup would be. They thought they could appease Hitler by refusing to help the British and the Greeks.

"I have decided to destroy Yugoslavia," he told Hermann Goering and other members of his inner circle.[1]

He planned to invade Yugoslavia, then continue on to Greece and help out the Italians. He didn't think his trip through the Balkans would take too much time. Most Allied strategists disagreed. In fact, Hitler's decision to invade Yugoslavia led to some minor rejoicing in the Allied camp (Britain, Greece, and various governments-in-exile) and in the United States. Yugoslavia had a million-man army. It had few tanks, but mountainous land with few good roads—actually few roads of any kind—was hardly blitzkrieg country. Allied pundits predicted that Hitler's mighty war machine would bog down in the Balkan mountains.

As it turned out, the conquest of Yugoslavia took the Germans just eleven days.

Yugoslavia's mountains certainly did not help Hitler's panzers. But they got a lot of help from the generals who organized the coup. The coup leaders proved to be as dull militarily as they were politically. Instead of analyzing likely invasion routes, they distributed their troops evenly around Yugoslavia's thousand-mile border. That was one factor in blitzkrieg's success. A much more important factor, though, was the ethnic composition of Yugoslavia and how its diverse peoples came to be combined into one country.

Yugoslavia was created after World War I by combining parts of the old Austro-Hungarian Empire with the Kingdom of Serbia. The King of Serbia acquired Bosnia and Herzegovina, Croatia, and Slovenia, and the new state was called the Kingdom of the Serbs, Croats, and Slovenes. They weren't the only ethnic groups. There were also Bosnians, Slavonians, and smaller Slavic groups. And there were pockets of Germans and Hungarians, but these former enemies were not considered by the victorious Allies.

Many of the Bosnians were Muslims. They were not beloved by the Christian Slavs, who referred to them as "Turks," even though all Bosnians, Muslim or Christian, spoke Serbo-Croatian, the common language of most Yugo (South) Slavs. But the Christians didn't get along, either. The Croats, Slovenes, Slavonians, and other groups were Catholic and had long and generally friendly ties with the Austrians and Italians. The Serbs and Macedonians were Orthodox and looked to Russia as their great power protector. The Kingdom of Serbs, Croats, and Slovenes changed its name to Yugoslavia. That was more accurate, and it gave the impression that Yugoslavia was a unified nation. The impression was false.

The "Kingdom of the Serbs, etc." was a gift to Serbia, which had been ravaged during World War I, losing 10 percent of its entire population. The king was a Serb; Serbs dominated the government; Serbian officers ran the army. Non-Serbs were unhappy—especially the Croats. In 1928, a Croat leader, Stjepan Radić, was assassinated, and a Croatian nationalist party was organized. In 1929, the king banned all nationalist parties. Croatian nationalist leaders went into exile and formed a revolutionary organization called Ustaše from the Serbo-Croatian word *ustasi* ("to rise"). In 1932, some Ustaše members rose in rebellion but were driven out of the country. They established a camp in Italy. The great majority of the Croats stayed home, but a huge majority of them were waiting for a better opportunity to rebel.

In 1934, King Alexander visited Marseilles. Vlada Gheorghieff, a Macedonian revolutionist, jumped up on the running board of the royal car and fired two machine pistols into the king's abdomen.[2] Alexander had forgotten to put on his armor vest that day. The king's cavalry escort chopped down Gheorghieff with their unsharpened sabers, and he rolled around the crowd firing both guns on full automatic. It was a pretty bloody scene. The Ustaše did not assassinate Alexander (although members probably wished they had) but they were blamed for it anyhow.

In 1937, Italy and Yugoslavia signed a peace treaty, and the Ustaše exiles were sent back home. The former exiles not imprisoned continued to agitate for independence.

They saw their chance to get it on April 6, 1941, when German, Italian, and Hungarian armies swept into Yugoslavia and the German Luftwaffe annihilated Yugoslavia's air force, much of it caught on the ground. Croatian and Slovenian army units deserted en masse; some of them attacked their Serbian countrymen. The Germans set up a puppet state, "The Independent State of Croatia," under a Ustaše government and gave it Bosnia and Herzegovina as well as Croatia. A greatly reduced Serbia got another puppet government; the Italians occupied western Slovenia, Dalmatia, Montenegro, and Kosovo; while Germany annexed eastern Slovenia to the Third Reich. Bulgaria annexed Macedonia; Hungary took a slice of Vojvodina.

Much of the Yugoslavian army fled into the mountains. Serbian soldiers gathered around Col. Dragoljub "Draza" Mihajlović, an ardent nationalist and royalist who wanted to keep part of Yugoslavia free, so the king would have a country to come back to. Mihajlović's men took the name Četniks, originally the term for the Serb guerrillas who fought the Ottoman Turks in the nineteenth and early twentieth centuries. Mihajlović began raiding German outposts and ambushing supply columns, but the Germans began massacring civilians in reprisals for attacks by resistance forces. German general Wilhelm Keitel wrote, "In reprisal for the life of a German soldier, the general rule should be capital punishment for 50 to 100 Communists."[3] By "Communists" Keitel meant any Yugoslavian. In the town of Kragujevac, for instance, to avenge a few casualties, the Germans attempted to kill every male inhabitant over the age of fifteen, and they actually did kill some 5,000, shooting them in batches of 100 in one day. Mihajlović refrained from major attacks on the Axis after reprisals began. Both he and the Germans expected the Allies to land in the Balkans, especially after the United States entered the war. When that happened, the Četniks would take the Axis forces in the rear.

When Germany invaded the Soviet Union, a new force appeared in Yugoslavia. This was the Partisans led by Josip Broz, better known by his code name, Tito. Tito was a Croat and a leading Communist. His Partisans included all ethnic groups, which made it easy to recruit followers. He ordered his troops not to enforce Communist ideology in areas they occupied. That, too, helped him recruit troops. He didn't worry about German reprisals. He guessed—correctly, it turned out—that slaughtering civilians would only enrage the population, thus increasing the strength of the resistance movement.

For a while, the Partisans and the Četniks cooperated in fighting the Axis. But Mihajlović and Tito had such different outlooks that cooperation became impossible. The Yugoslavian government in exile appointed Mihajlović minister of war, while Tito was as opposed to the royal government as he was to the Axis. Mihajlović saw Communism as great a danger to the

Josip Broz, better known as
Tito, pores over maps in
Yugoslavian wilderness. Tito
was by far the most successful
resistance leader in Europe.

monarchy as Nazism. Nor did his patriotism extend beyond the borders
of Serbia proper. To Tito, Mihajlović was a reactionary advocate of the feudal past.

Before long, there were no clear lines of conflict in Yugoslavia. Both Partisans and Četniks fought Axis troops; at times, each cooperated with Axis
troops. Partisans and Četniks fought each other. Partisans and Četniks
fought Ustaše troops. Četniks fought the Ustaše more often, because to the
Ustaše, all Serbs were the enemy. Ustaše atrocities against the Serbs
exceeded even those of the Germans. To add to the confusion, the troops of
the puppet Serbian government were also called Četniks, so reports of
Četniks fighting Partisans did not always mean the followers of Mihajlović
and Tito were warring with each other. Then there were the ancient feuds—
Christians versus Muslims, Orthodox versus Catholics, Albanians versus
Macedonians, and others—now made more deadly because hatred was reinforced with rifle bullets. Much of this internecine warfare was in areas occupied by the Italians, who did not try to maintain order. Atrocities were
common to all sides in Yugoslavia. The Italians did not commit atrocities on
anything like the scale of the Germans or the Ustaše, but there is a picture
in David Mountfield's *The Partisans* showing some twenty Yugoslavian civilian

men lined up against a wall while an Italian machine gunner prepared to mow them down.[4]

Both Tito and Mihajlović ordered their troops not to confront superior numbers of the enemy. The fighting was the classic guerrilla strategy of pin-pricks. But because the top German divisions were needed in Russia, the resistance forces in Yugoslavia achieved amazing success early in the war. On September 24, 1941, the Partisans captured the town of Užice, which had a rifle factory, and proclaimed the foundation of the "Republic of Užice." By that time, the Partisans controlled much of western Serbia.

Then the Germans shifted more troops to Yugoslavia and launched the first of their seven offensives against the guerillas. That operation lasted from late September to November 1941. In January 1942, the Germans and other Axis troops renewed their attack. After a pause for the ferocious mountain winter, the Germans and their satellites resumed the offensive in the spring of 1942. The Axis troops drove the Partisans into the mountains in what turned into a kind of mini-version of the Chinese "Long March." Tito lost twenty high-ranking officers and 3,000 soldiers from enemy fire, exposure, and starvation.

Tito's campaigns had many resemblances to those of Mao Zedong. Like Mao, he strove to maintain good relations with the civilian population.

"It is essential," ran one order, "to build up close relations between the army and civilians so that the people feel itself one with the military."[5]

Partisans not only paid for food they got from civilians, they provided reparation for accidental damage. When some Partisan horses got into a wheat field and made inroads into a woman's crop, the Partisans gave her fifty pounds of corn to make up for the damage. They did that although it was only on rare occasions that the Partisans had enough food for themselves. A British liaison officer with the Partisans learned to use young beech leaves with sorrel and wild garlic to make a salad and to eat nettles for vegetables. Another wrote of "quenching our thirst from the dew on the fir cones, and boiling clover and wild spinach in our mess tins."[6] Tito used the "Great March," as he called it, to turn his troops into a more effective force. They had been originally local guerrillas, attached to the towns and valleys where they had always lived. After they had been driven out of their homes, Tito turned them into a national force. Although Tito himself was a Croat, his first Partisan force was mostly Serbian. Now he began to attract Croats, Macedonians, Bosnians, and others. He got his homeless troops to bury their ancient feuds based on nationality and religion. By November 1942, Tito had 100,000 men and women under arms. This "People's Liberation Army" even had its own military academy.

Axis forces continued to launch offensives against the guerrillas, but these operations were something like trying to gather smoke. In May and

June of 1943, they actually encircled the Partisans, with the aid of Mihajlović's Četniks, but Tito's troops slipped through their lines. For most of the war the Partisans were moving from place to place, hitting Axis troops whenever they had a local advantage. Finally, Tito set up a permanent base near the industrial town of Drvar in Bosnia. Located in a cavern and surrounded by Partisan fortifications on steep mountains, it seemed impregnable. Then German paratroopers and glider troops descended on it. Tito barely escaped. Hiding in the woods, he managed to contact the British, who flew him across the Adriatic to the Allied base in Bari, Italy. He later returned to Yugoslavia and set up headquarters on the island of Vis, which was protected by Allied ships and airplanes.

By this time, the future was looking bleak for the Axis. The German 6th Army surrendered at Stalingrad in February. At Kursk, in July, the Germans lost the greatest tank battle of the war, and the German army was now retreating across the Russian plains. The Allies had invaded Italy, which had deposed Benito Mussolini and switched sides. Italy's surrender meant loads of new weapons for Partisans and a huge decrease of enemy occupation troops. By this time, too, the British and Americans had decided that Tito's Partisans were the main Yugoslavian resistance force and directed their aid to Tito instead of Mihajlović.

Tito's support from the Soviet Union during the war was mostly verbal. Consequently, that once-loyal apparatchik became independent. Surprisingly, Joseph Stalin didn't try to strong-arm him. Stalin asked Tito's permission to send troops into Yugoslavia in pursuit of the Germans.

The end of the war was payback time for the victors. One of the victors was Tito. One of the victims was Mihajlović. He was captured, tried for treason, and executed. In the postwar period, Tito ran a Communist dictatorship that managed to stay nonaligned with either the Soviet Union or the United States. He was, of course, Yugoslavia's greatest war hero, he had all the propaganda facilities of the state, and he was able to put down dissent ruthlessly. But his political skill was demonstrated by his death in 1980. The old ethnic rivalries surfaced again in Yugoslavia. In 1983, a Muslim separatist movement began in Bosnia-Herzegovina, Serbs again took total control of the government and the army, and Albanian Kosovars began agitating for an independent Kosovo. Fighting broke out in Bosnia among Muslims, Serbs, and Croats.

Croatia and Slovenia declared their independence in 1991. Serbia tried to enforce Yugoslavian unity. Slovenia was farther away than Croatia, so Serbs concentrated on the Croats. Since the Yugoslavian army was mainly Serbian, the Croat militia was defeated, and the Serbs turned on the secessionists in Bosnia-Herzegovina. After a pause, Croatia again took an active part in the war by attacking Serb forces in the Krajina, the section of the

Adriatic coast Serbia had taken from Croatia. Few observers gave the Croats much chance of success. Even with Serbia busy in Bosnia, the reconquest of the Krajina, if possible, would take months, the most optimistic said.

It took a week.

Croatia had purchased new weapons and hired Military Professional Resources Incorporated (MPRI), an American firm composed of retired American military men, many of very high rank, to train the Croatian armed forces. The new Croatian army was no guerrilla force. A British colonel in charge of the UN observer mission reported, "It was a textbook operation, though not a JNA [Yugoslav National Army] textbook. Whoever wrote that plan of attack could have gone to any NATO staff college in North America or Western Europe and scored an A plus."[7] The Croatian attack coordinated air, armor, artillery, and infantry. A new kind of mercenary force—the private military consultant firm—had debuted in what was once Yugoslavia. The Croats then attacked the Serbs in Bosnia, and Serbia was forced to make peace. Yugoslavia continued to break up, and the world gained a new term for the process—ethnic cleansing. The term was new, but the massacres, mass rapes, and dispossession were but a rerun of much of what happened in Yugoslavia in World War II.

CHAPTER 14

The Prince of Tides:
Inside Inch'on, 1950

The United Nations (UN) forces (actually American and South Korean (SK) troops) were crowded into the southern tip of Korea by the North Korean (NK) Army. Korea is a funnel-shaped country, most of it a long, narrow peninsula. The United Nations had almost total control of the land and the sea. The solution to the UN problem seemed obvious—an amphibious landing behind the North Korean forces. During World War II, the Japanese had landed repeatedly behind the British defenders of Malaya, forcing the larger British force to retreat to Singapore.

Douglas MacArthur, commander of all UN forces engaged in Korea, wanted to make such a landing, but he had trouble getting his plan approved. As former army combat historian Bevin Alexander put it, "The remarkable thing about this plan is that it is what the situation practically demanded, and yet MacArthur had to fight a dogged battle with the top American military leadership, the Joint Chiefs of Staff [JCS], to get it approved."[1]

Although the United States had made many successful landings against strong opposition in the Pacific island-hopping campaign of World War II and, with the British, the largest amphibious landing in history at Normandy, the Joint Chiefs were worried. They remembered Anzio, another landing behind enemy lines on a long, narrow peninsula.

The Anzio landing was supposed to cut off the Germans fighting in southern Italy, but it wasn't far enough behind the German lines and it was close to Rome, a major German base. Further, Gen. Mark Wayne Clark, commander of the Italian operation, told the Anzio commander, Maj. Gen. John Lucas, "Don't stick your neck out." Lucas took Clark's advice too seriously, and he did not take advantage of the surprise his landing achieved. The Germans surrounded the Anzio beachhead. Anzio wasn't a disaster, but it was a tremendous waste.

MacArthur finally used his eloquence, prestige, and rank (he outranked all of the chiefs) to convince the JCS that the landing should be made and that it should be at Inch'on. Inch'on was the second largest port in Korea, and it was far behind the enemy lines. It was close to Seoul, the captured South Korean capital, and Seoul was a communications and transportation hub. MacArthur believed that in spite of its importance, Seoul was lightly garrisoned. The biggest problem with Inch'on was its tides. There was about twenty-nine feet between high tide and low tide. When the tide was low, it exposed mudflats extending up to six miles from shore. No boats could cross the mudflats; whether wheeled and tracked vehicles or even men on foot could was unknown. In any case, the mudflats were a horrendous obstacle.

MacArthur had an answer to the tide problem. He was named Eugene Clark.

Clark was a thirty-nine-year-old naval lieutenant, a "mustang" who had enlisted as a seaman and worked his way up to chief petty officer, the highest enlisted rank, before he won a commission. He knew a lot about amphibious operations, having been at the big one on Okinawa and several others. At this time, he was serving on the Geographic Branch of MacArthur's staff, where he had been studying tides and other conditions on the Korean

Douglas MacArthur observes the Inch'on landing, which caused a rout of North Korean forces during the Korean War. Key man in this operation was Eugene Clark, a Navy lieutenant who conducted a guerrilla campaign behind the North Korean lines. NATIONAL ARCHIVES

coasts. Before he got this staff job, he wrote, "I had enjoyed some highly clandestine operations along the China coast, trying to help the Nationalist Chinese in their losing struggle with the Communists."[2]

Clark was told that the information about Inch'on had to be absolutely accurate—not only about tides, but about the size and location of NK forces, fortifications, and the sympathies of the people in the area. The job would involve personal observation on the ground. Clark eagerly accepted the assignment and began making preparations. He recruited two South Korean officers to help him. Youn Joung was an SK naval lieutenant. He spoke Korean, English, Chinese, and Japanese. Ke In-Ju was an SK Army colonel who spoke Korean, Chinese, and Japanese, but no English. Ke had once headed SK counterintelligence before he fell out with President Syngman Rhee. Clark had learned Japanese while on occupation duty after the war, so he was able to talk with Ke. The three intelligence officers tried not to use Japanese around ordinary Koreans. Korean memories of the Japanese occupation were deep and bitter.[3] The Clark expedition was so secret that both Korean officers were given noms de guerre. Youn became Yong Chi Ho and Ke, Kim Nam Sun. Even the British officers on the destroyer that took them to a rendezvous with an SK gunboat did not know their real names. During World War II, both Korean officers had been anti-Japanese guerrillas operating out of Manchuria, where they learned Chinese, among other things. After the war, they served on MacArthur's staff.

Clark hoped to recruit a small fifth column behind the NK lines to help him get information. He was able to get guns, ammunition, and other supplies for such a force. There was one problem with guns. He was able to get hand grenades, pistols, carbines, submachine guns, and even some machine guns but no rifles. All rifles available were needed on the Pusan Perimeter. That ensured that most of any fighting Clark or his team did would be at short range.

Off the coast of Communist-occupied South Korea, Clark's party transferred to an SK gunboat captained by Commander Lee Sung Ho.[4] "I have orders from Admiral Sohn [the commander of the SK Navy] to place my ship under your command, Mr. Clark," Captain Lee said.[5] Lee's ship was a former U.S. Navy subchaser with a three-inch gun and three .50-caliber machine guns. Lee and his ship were to prove invaluable.

The original plan was for Clark, Youn, and Ke to land on Tokshok-do, ["do" is Korean for "island"], the island closest to Inch'on that could be protected by the SK and UN navies. The trouble was that Tokshok-do was fifteen miles from Inch'on harbor. But when they got to Tokshok-do, Clark learned that the troops normally garrisoning one island in the harbor had been pulled off for training. That left only five soldiers on the island, Yonghung-do. A very small minority of the islanders, about twenty persons out of a thousand, favored the Reds, called *Inminkyun* in Korean. The Northerners were not popular because they had imposed a heavy tax, to be paid in rice, on the islanders. The islanders were afraid of starving. In addition, soon after they arrived, the Reds had executed a number of villagers they had decided were reactionary.

Lee took his gunboat up to Yonghung-do and loaned Clark a group of sailors to act as a landing party. The five NK soldiers tried to flee in a small boat. Clark asked one of the machine gunners to sink the boat, but not harm the soldiers. He wanted to question them. But the inexperienced gunner killed all five. Ke and Youn released all the people the Communists had imprisoned in the local jail and replaced them with the Communist sympathizers. Meanwhile, Lee took his ship to the neighboring island of Taebu-do, the base of the NK battalion that had jurisdiction over Yonghung-do. He bombarded the island to discourage any attempt by the Reds to reoccupy Yonghung-do. The North Koreans had no idea that the enemy in their midst consisted of only three men.

There was a shortage of able-bodied young men on Yonghung-do. It seemed that the Communists had drafted them into the army or into labor battalions. But Youn and Ke began talking to the teenagers on the island and soon had more than 100 ready to fight the North Koreans. Clark and his team organized and armed a guard force for Yonghung-do.

The two Korean officers knew that their mission involved reconnaissance behind the enemy lines, but had only a vague idea of its purpose. The next morning Clark outlined the objectives. They were to gather information needed for a possible landing at Inch'on. Clark knew the landing was to be at Inch'on, but to keep it as secret as possible, he said that it could take place at a dozen other places on the Korean coasts. One thing was definite: it was to take place September 15, 1950. They had two weeks to gather the necessary information. The most important information was whether or not the North Koreans had mined the narrow passageways in the harbor that led to the city of Inch'on and whether or not they had heavy guns covering those narrow channels. A ship sunk in one of those channels could bring the landing to a standstill. Another problem was the lack of navigational aids, like lighthouses. At that time, even the most experienced native pilots would not take a ship into Inch'on harbor at night. There were three lighthouses, but the Communists had turned them all off.

That information concerned getting the invasion fleet into the harbor. Other needed information concerned getting the troops ashore. It was necessary to locate the enemy's gun positions and other vital components of his defense. It appeared that MacArthur was right when he assumed the North Koreans had not heavily garrisoned Inch'on, but a few men with machine guns and light artillery could wreak havoc on troops wallowing in mud or trying to climb the high seawalls around Inch'on. Those positions would have to be identified so that they could be located from the air, because much of the covering fire for the landing would be provided by bombers and fighter-bombers.

Then there were the mudflats. If the tide went out while the landing was in progress, could troops walk across them? Could trucks and tanks drive across them? How about the angle of incline on the beach? An LST (landing ship tank) had to be trimmed to the correct angle for the slope of the beach so that the bow would hit the beach first. It should run as far up the beach as possible, so the troops would be exposed to only a minimum of hostile fire while crossing an open beach. If it was not trimmed properly, the ship may hit the bottom in comparatively deep water and broach, that is swing around horizontally, making the anchor and rudder useless and leaving the ship exposed to enemy guns. And troops leaving the ship in deep water carrying heavy loads might drown. Smaller, shallow-draft landing craft had problems, too. The biggest were the high seawalls around Inch'on. The small island of Wolmi-do, connected to Inch'on by a narrow causeway, had beaches without seawalls, but it would be necessary to investigate both those beaches and the seawalls.

This early planning was enlivened by a typhoon and an air attack on Lee's ship. The storm further inhibited any contemplated NK counterattacks, and the SK gunboat sustained little damage.

Colonel Ke interrogated the people who had been identified as Communist sympathizers and concluded that they were merely "opportunists," who had decided life would be easier if they agreed with the occupiers. They had no useful information. He did find one woman, a young widow, who had become the mistress of the NK chief of the island. She might be useful. The NK officer was now on Taebu-do with the NK battalion. Clark had the woman released to join her boyfriend provided she would send reports on what was going on in the enemy battalion. Her two children stayed on Yonghung-do to ensure her loyalty while she was smuggled over to Taebu-do at night before the moon rose. She would periodically meet with couriers at night and give them reports. Clark also sent a boatman named Rhee to Inch'on itself to locate a motor sampan, which would give them a great advantage in a harbor filled with sailing craft. Rhee, like the widow, was smuggled ashore in the darkest part of the night. Later, Ke recruited two more men and a woman to spy on the mainland. The men went to Inch'on, and the woman went all the way into Seoul.

The Communists, too, were smuggling people from island to island in the dark of the night. They were putting infiltrators on Yonghung-do, one or two at a time. Clark worried that they might attempt a full-scale invasion using the junks that were currently beached on Taebu-do. He and the

Korean officers discussed where they could go if the Reds did invade Yonghung-do. They eventually decided on Clark's choice, the tiny island of Palmi-do, site of the most important lighthouse in Inch'on Harbor. Palmi-do, a rocky outcrop in the harbor, had only one place, a narrow sand spit, where anyone could land. That could be covered by a single machine gun.

Clark organized what he called a "junk navy" composed of the junks and sampans the islanders used for fishing and trading. The key man in the junk navy was the head of the local fishermen's association, a man named Chang. Chang, Clark later wrote, "far from looking like a businessman, had all the physical attributes and appearance of a China Coast pirate."[6] The impression was enhanced by the razor-sharp Gurkha *kukri* in his belt. Chang, leading a squadron of armed junks, became a real pirate, or at least a privateer. (Actually, Clark suspected that Chang was not without experience in buccaneering.) He captured NK junks approaching Inch'on. His goal was not gold, but information.

Captain Lee reported that he had destroyed a floating mine west of Tokshok-do. He believed that it had floated down from Haeju in North Korea. He said most of the officers he knew in the NK Navy were not trained in handling mines, but Clark thought they should station junks to watch for enemy mine-laying junks in the two narrow channels, East Channel and Flying Fish Channel. Lee came up with a supplement to the antimine plan: "We can make reasonably certain that they haven't laid a field by running my ship up the channels and into the harbor each day. She draws fifteen feet and will set off any mine at that depth."[7]

"Searching his face carefully," Clark later wrote, "I could see that he wasn't pulling my leg. He meant it."[8]

Lee's trips up the channels would also draw the fire of any guns zeroed on those passageways. He said he would cruise around the harbor and try to draw fire from any other guns.

"What do you suppose Admiral Sohn would say to that proposition, Lee?" Clark asked. "Wouldn't he nail your hide to the mast if he found out about it?"

"Nothing of the kind. Our orders are to seek out and destroy the enemy wherever we can find him. I would go in on them at maximum range, just in case they had a couple of 155s."[9]

Clark grudgingly okayed the plan if Lee would stay within a few hundred yards of Palmi-do and get behind the island if enemy artillery straddled his ship.

Clark's team decided that if Palmi-do was unoccupied, it would make a perfect base for the antimine patrol. So Clark and Youn set out, at night, of course, to visit the island and its lighthouse, taking along a machine gun and some of the teenaged guardsmen. They found nobody on the island and the lighthouse locked from the outside. Clark left three men and a machine gun to guard the island.

When they returned to Yong-hung-do, Captain Lee appeared and told Clark about a boatload of people who had just escaped from Taemuuni-do, an island at the north end of the harbor. They were running away from a particularly barbarous political officer named Yeh. Yeh was a native of Tae-muuni-do who became a Communist and a friend of Kim Il Sung, the North Korean dictator. When he returned to the South, Yeh personally executed his mother and then his grandparents. He confiscated almost all of the islanders' rice and was threatening to put dozens more to death. Those were the people who had escaped. The man who led the escape was a tough old junk captain named Min. He reminded Clark of Chang.

Clark and his party decided to raid Taemuuni-do and capture Yeh. That tyrant should be a gold mine of information.

Before they could start, some of Clark's teenage militiamen caught an infiltrator. They were distressed when he told them not to kill the prisoner but to patch up his wounds and guard him so he could be questioned. Although Colonel Ke was an expert interrogator, he could get no informa-tion from the prisoner. The infiltrator was obviously a hard-boiled North Korean soldier, not an islander. Clark decided that the next day he would make a sweep of Yonghung-do using all the friendly islanders. But as night was falling, it was time to raid Taemuuni-do.

The raiders used Chang's junk and included, besides Chang and his crew, Clark, Youn, Min, some other men from Taemuuni-do who would help Min in guiding the raiders, and some of Clark's teenage warriors. The raiders also included the gunnery officer of Lee's gunboat, Lieutenant Ham, who had previously scouted the island. All told, there were ten raiders, not counting Chang and his crew. This pickup crew would land on an island held by many times their number of NK regulars, intending to kidnap the commanding officer and free the captives he had locked up. Ke had to stay on Yonghung-do to get reports from his spies. Lee and his gunboat stayed in the channel between Younghung-do and Tebu-do to discourage an NK inva-sion attempt.

Chang took his boat around Taemuuni-do to the side of the island opposite the village. The raiders stripped to their undershorts and rubbed themselves with charcoal so they'd be almost invisible in the dark. Each had a knife, some hand grenades, and a pistol or submachine gun. Min took three men to the school that the Reds were using as a jail. The school was located on the left of the village. Most of the others went to the right edge of the village while Clark, Youn, and one of the Taemuuni-do villagers went directly to Yeh's house. Because Min had the longest distance to travel, the

sound of his shooting would be the signal to begin. Clark, Youn and the vil-
lager managed to enter Yeh's house without being seen.

When they heard the sound of Min's guns, the men on the far right
began throwing hand grenades into houses sheltering NK soldiers. Clark
and his party jumped Yeh's guards and killed them with knives. Clark
stunned Yeh with a blow on the head, then he and Youn carried the NK hon-
cho and one of their wounded comrades out on their backs. Two NK soldiers saw them and opened fire. Clark and Youn fell flat, and Clark shot
down the Reds with his pistol. When they met the rest of the raiders, Clark
and Youn discovered that the object of their raid, Yeh, was dead. One of the
North Koreans who fired at them in front of Yeh's house had accidentally
killed the political officer.

Min and his party had succeeded in liberating the captives, who went off
to hide in the hills. The raiders lost four men, but they killed more of the
enemy. Although Yeh was dead, they had captured two more North Koreans
who could be questioned. Clark and Youn fell asleep almost as soon as they
got on Chang's junk. They had been operating on two hours of sleep a night.

When they woke up, Ke told them what the spies had discovered. He
had the location of every defensive position around Inch'on; he learned that
there had been no significant troop movements into Inch'on; there were
1,000 Red soldiers in Inch'on and 100 police. All of that information was
radioed to Tokyo. Ke had also found a man named Chi from Inch'on who
was leading a group of refugees in the Inch'on hills. He begged for supplies
and guns so his people could fight the Reds. And he wanted to see Clark,
because the North Koreans had told them that all Americans had fled
Korea. Clark saw him, gave him weapons and supplies, and was delighted at
having guerrilla allies in the hills behind Inch'on. A few days later, Chi
reported that he had found another resistance group, which also needed
weapons. Clark could now get information from guerrillas in the vicinity of
Seoul and Kimpo Airport.

Then Captain Lee gave a hair-raising demonstration of how to learn the
size and range of enemy guns. He took his gunboat almost up to the beach
of the fortified island of Wolmi-do, connected to Inch'on by a concrete
causeway, and opened fire. As Clark and the others watched, he dodged
incoming rounds until he was out of range of the enemy guns.

Lee then came ashore and gave everybody the bad news: he had been
reassigned to another job. The gunboat that had kept the North Korean
troops from invading Yonghung-do was going away. And there was a fifth column of infiltrators on the island. Conditions were right for an NK invasion
of Yonghung-do that night. Clark ordered the anti-infiltrator search to
begin. His people located some scouts who fled to a defensive position. They
had rifles that outranged any guns Clark's people had. Clark had Youn take

some guardsmen through the brush to a flanking position and fire at the infiltrators. He crawled up the rocky slope until he was above the Reds and then lobbed grenades at them. Clark, Youn, and their men then moved on the main body of infiltrators. There were about twenty of them hidden in a rocky maze with both flanks and rear protected by cliffs. Clark built a fire in the crevices of rock and smoked them out. The Reds ran down to the beach and into the fire of the other guardsmen. All were killed or captured.

Clark considered the infiltrators a "pest." The big threat was the battalion on Taebu-do. There were no NK naval ships on Taebu-do, but the North Koreans on Taebu-do had several junks. Clark was so sure the Communists would attack as soon as it was dark he got his junk navy afloat before nightfall and put Chang in charge of fleet movements. He rode on Chang's junk with some guardsmen and the group's heaviest artillery—a .50-caliber machine gun. Youn commanded the gunners on another junk with a .30-caliber machine gun. Altogether there were five junks, and all carried machine guns.

The NK junk fleet appeared as expected. There were six junks, led by an enormous seagoing craft. All were packed with NK regular soldiers, and the big junk had a cannon that outranged anything Clark's fleet carried. The big NK junk began firing and eventually began hitting Chang's junk. Fortunately, the NK cannon was an antitank gun. Antitank ammunition is meant to penetrate armor. It is either solid shot, which never explodes, or shells with a delay fuse that keeps the shell from exploding until it has pierced the armor. The NK rounds punched holes in the junk without exploding. Soon the junk was within range of Clark's .50-caliber. Clark told the gunner to pour fire into the big junk's bow. The enemy junk began to literally disintegrate under the hail of bullets. Enemy soldiers jumped into the sea. Chang's junk continued into the NK array, and the .50-caliber machine gun spread panic through the Communist fleet. The guardsmen from Yonghung-do calmly picked off all the enemy soldiers in the water. Chang inspected the enemy boats and recommended keeping two that were still seaworthy. They sank the rest. Clark's fleet lost two junks and his troops took many casualties. But the enemy fleet had been annihilated.

The battle of the junks didn't end the threat from Taebu-do. From interrogating captured infiltrators, Ke learned that the battalion on the island had been reinforced with "special guns" and a heavy weapons company. If the last attempt failed, they were to try again. The Reds on Taebu-do believed that the South Koreans had three platoons of regulars on Yonghung-do, with a heavy-weapons squad in each platoon. But they also knew that the gunboat was gone.

Just before the battle of the junks, Chang had captured two more junks. One of them was carrying a party of seven *kisaeng* girls (geishas). Ke promptly took charge of them, to the outrage of Chang, who held to the old pirate code that captured cargo belongs to the captor. But now Ke told of all the information he had gotten from the Seoul demimonde. The North Koreans were making no special preparations. They had checkpoints on the roads, but they were only concerned with civilian men of military age. Ke learned of tank hideouts, ammunition dumps, and other points of interest.

Clark and Youn took Benzedrine tables and coffee and left for another scouting trip, this time to the fortified island of Wolmi-do. Before boarding, they stripped and plastered themselves with mud. Youn and a youth named Chae who had spent a lot of time on Wolmi-do took knives. Clark took binoculars. They located some machine-gun nests, but no gunners. They learned that the beach, where there was no seawall, was perfect for landing craft. They watched the guards and were even close enough to eavesdrop on their conversations. Then, literally naked to their enemies, they got back on the sampan and returned to Yonghung-do.

Clark was surprised when one of the islanders shouted that a battleship had entered the harbor. It turned out to be a U.S. destroyer that looked like a battleship to people who had never seen a bigger naval ship than Lee's ex-subchaser. Tokyo had heard that the North Koreans were going to attack Yonghung-do and had sent the ship to evacuate Clark. Clark refused to be evacuated, but asked the destroyer's captain for some medical supplies and for a little bombardment of the NK positions on Taebu-do. The captain, Commander Cecil Welte, gladly complied.

That night, Clark and Youn set out to check on the mudflats and the seawalls. Their sampan, a small, shallow-draft boat, grounded a long distance from the shore. Clark poked a pole into the mud and found that it was three feet deep—too deep to walk on. Their boatman backed off and found a channel through the mudflat. The mud there was two feet deep. Clark and Youn roped themselves together on a long rope, a safety measure in case one should step into quicksand. It took them half an hour to travel 500 yards. They continued slopping through the mud and finally discovered a good landing area—good for smaller landing craft, not LSTs, which would be stranded far from the shore even at high tide. At one point a guard challenged them. They remained still and quiet, and the guard eventually went away. They were measuring the height of a seawall when Youn fell into quicksand—actually quick mud. Clark was able to haul him out, but not without difficulty. They finally got safely back to Yonghung-do.

Rhee, the man sent to find a power boat, had finally succeeded. He brought not only the boat, but the boat's owner, who wanted to get away from the Communists. They shifted their heavy machine gun from Chang's junk to the diesel-powered junk. Captain Lee and the gunboat returned to Inch'on harbor, greatly adding to Clark's naval strength. Clark asked him to check a couple of new channels for mines in case the landing fleet opted for a two-pronged approach. Clark visited his guerrilla allies on the mainland, and while there, he, Youn, and Chae joined ten guerrillas to ambush an NK patrol. A short time later, four cruisers, two U.S. and two British, entered the harbor and began bombarding Wolmi-do. From the mountainside, where they were, Clark and the guerrillas had a perfect place for spotting enemy guns as they tried to return fire. Unfortunately they had no direct communication with the ships. They could reach only headquarters in Tokyo. Chi, the guerrilla leader, agreed to note those enemy gun positions in the days ahead as the "softening up" of Inch'on continued.

The last days before the landing were full of action. Lee's gunboat had left to join the invasion fleet. Clark's people continued attacking NK junks, but the North Koreans began blowing some of them up in hopes of taking the attackers with them. Red commandos were raiding Yonghung-do, and some of them were staying on the island, hiding like the previous infiltrators. On the last day before the UN attack, Clark's people had another battle with infiltrators. Then the North Koreans launched a serious invasion. Clark instructed his junk navy to stay out of East Channel and Flying Fish Channel. The UN warships and troopships would be using them.

The Reds landed with overwhelming numbers and, after a hard fight, Clark, Ke, Youn, and their guardsmen got on the powered junk and went to Palmi-do. At 3:00 A.M. they turned on the lighthouse light, and the invasion fleet steamed into Inch'on Harbor. Troops of the 5th Marine Regiment took Wolmi-do without one death and only seventeen wounded. The machine guns and artillery that Clark and Youn had spotted had all been wiped out before the landing craft touched the beach. The sea walls were no problem; the landing craft that approached them all had ladders of the right height. Ten days after the Inch'on landing, American troops were in Seoul. The NK Army around Pusan collapsed.

Clark received the Silver Star for his exploit. He won an oak-leaf cluster for his Silver Star for a series of commando raids he and Youn later led against islands off North Korea. While in North Korea, he observed Chinese troops massing along the Yalu River. He warned Tokyo, but his warning was ignored. The Silver Star is a good medal, but it's not the highest, or even the second highest, a sailor can earn. He was not put in for anything higher. In contrast, his supreme commander, General MacArthur, was awarded the Medal of Honor, the nation's highest award, after he left Corregidor for Australia, leaving his subordinate, Jonathan "Skinny" Wainwright, to surrender to the Japanese.[10]

CHAPTER 15

Spooks and Huks: The "Ugly American" in Action, 1945–1951

The Philippine "People's Anti-Japanese Army," in Tagalog, *Hukbo ng Bayan Laban Sa Hapan,* or Hukbalahap for short and simply "the Huks" for shorter, was bad news. The Huks had been one of a number of guerrilla groups who had fought the Japanese occupiers during World War II. Unfortunately, the Huk leadership, including the Huk "El Supremo," Luis Taruc, was Communist.

When the war ended, the Huks controlled a large part of central Luzon (the largest of the Philippine Islands and the location of Manila, the capital). The Philippines became an independent nation in 1946, with a government modeled on that of the United States. At first, the Hukbalahaps tried to gain control of the nation by political means, but that proved too slow. So they went back to waging guerrilla war, this time against fellow Filipinos. Huk agents traveled all over the islands denouncing the current government as lackeys of the United States, which had been occupying the Philippines since the Spanish-American war in 1898. The Hukbalahap movement became increasingly strong, but not because Filipinos hated Americans. After half a century, Filipinos had adopted much of American culture, and English, rather than Spanish, was the second language of most Filipinos. The Huks gained strength because the government of the Philippines was horribly corrupt, with a few rich and powerful families lording it over most Filipinos as if they were medieval nobles and the others were serfs. The first postwar president of the Philippines, Manuel Roxas, had served in the Japanese puppet government, but he was a friend of Douglas MacArthur, former field marshal of the Philippine Army.[1] So instead of being imprisoned like other collaborators, he was elected president. Roxas was one of the Filipino aristocracy—the types called *los oligarcos* in Latin America—and became as much of an American puppet as he had been a Japanese puppet.

At one village in Luzon, a Huk speaker was busily denouncing "American imperialism" as the cause of all the ills afflicting the nation. A car passing through the village stopped, and a tall man with a mustache got out.

There was no doubt about his nationality. He wore the uniform of an American army officer. He walked up to the speaker.

"What's the matter?" he asked. "Didn't you ever have an American friend?"

Obviously, many in the crowd did have American friends, and they remembered the Americans as the people who, a short time before, had driven out the hated Japanese. They crowded around the officer and talked about Americans they had known. None, it seemed, had any bad memories. The Huk agitator slipped away, but the officer later said, "It was a long time before I could get away from the gossipy friendliness" of the crowd.[2]

The officer was not just any passing tourist. Edward Lansdale may have been the most effective CIA (Central Intelligence Agency) agent in "the company's" history as well as America's most remarkable counterguerrilla leader. During World War II, Lansdale had joined the Office of Strategic Services, the ancestor of the CIA. Although jokers said OSS stood for "Oh So Social," Lansdale was no socialite. He held an Army Reserve commission before the war, but during the Depression, he had to work so hard to make ends meet that he didn't have time for his military duties. He resigned his commission. When the war began, he applied for reinstatement, but his commission was not restored immediately. While he was waiting, he joined the OSS. He was finally commissioned as an army intelligence officer, but he continued to work for the OSS.

When the war ended, the OSS disappeared, but Lansdale stayed in the army. He was sent to the Philippines, where the United States was helping its former colony become an independent nation. Lansdale's brother, Ben, had served in the Philippines during the war. Before he left the States, Lansdale quizzed his brother on all things Filipino—social structure, family life, holidays and occasions for celebration, even songs. He memorized the songs and learned to play them on his harmonica. Ben asked him why he was interested in Filipino songs. Ed said he wanted to communicate with the people, and it would help to know "their songs, something they hold dear to their hearts."[3]

His job was chief of the Analysis Branch of the Intelligence Division in the headquarters of Armed Forces Western Pacific. One of his assignments was to report on the economic, political, and military situation in the Ryukyus, a string of Japanese islands stretching from Japan to Taiwan. The United States had not yet established a military government in the islands. When he got there, Lansdale saw that the people were starving. Japan had shipped food to the islands, but the Japanese governor had taken control of it and had been selling it for his personal profit. Lansdale confiscated the food stocks and distributed the food to the hungry islanders. He then called for a public meeting and accused the governor of theft. His interpreter,

Matsue Yagawa, a Nisei soldier, warned Lansdale that the governor had a gun in his desk drawer and was inching toward it.

Lansdale had a .45 automatic in a shoulder holster. He said to Yagawa, "Tell him I know he's got a gun, and I'm waiting for him to get it. Tell him I want him to take a shot at me so I can kill him in front of all the people."

The governor, who had pretended he didn't understand English, jumped up and yelled, "I don't have a gun!" Lansdale arrested him and had him sent off to Japan for trial.

Yagawa was disappointed. He had thought Lansdale was a latter-day Wyatt Earp.

"How fast are you on the draw?" he asked. Lansdale admitted he didn't know. He'd never tried to draw from a shoulder holster. He tried to draw the pistol, and he couldn't get it out of the holster.

"Jeez," Yagawa said, "you would have been creamed."[4]

Most of Lansdale's work was in the Philippines. In his first few weeks, he wrote twenty-three staff studies on political, economic, and social conditions in the Philippines. He published a weekly analysis of the Philippine press, and he studied every report his agents sent him, especially those concerned with the Hukbalahaps. The Huks fascinated him. He wanted to know what attracted Juan de la Cruz—the Filipino John Doe—to the Communists. He decided to find out personally. He studied maps and predicted what trails the Huk guerrillas would take after being attacked by government troops. Then he camped on those trails and waited for the Huks to appear. His main weapon was his harmonica. He insisted this approach was not as dangerous as it seems.

"I was one person and they were an armed group. I would smile. . . . I would ask if they needed cigarettes or some food or did anybody want a drink? They would come up and say 'Yeah, I'd like a cigarette' instead of shooting me. You don't kill a guy laughing, being nice to you."[5]

Lansdale met the Huks often enough to become close to some of the leaders. He longed to meet Luis Taruc. One day, a Filipino friend introduced him to a woman who knew Taruc. The woman, Patrocinio Yapcinco Kelly, had gone to the same high school as Taruc, and Taruc had married a close friend of hers. Pat Kelly, as everyone called her, was of Chinese descent. She had been married to red-haired James Kelly, a man of mixed Filipino-Irish descent, just before the war. James Kelly had become ill during the Japanese occupation. And as food was scarce and medicine unavailable, he had died. Pat was a journalist and, she told Lansdale, "I used to cover Turuc the Huk."[6]

Pat Kelly's acquaintances with members of the Hukbalahap were extensive, and she introduced Lansdale to many of them. One day Lansdale heard that Taruc's sister was pregnant and was losing teeth because she couldn't get enough calcium-rich food. He went to her house with calcium pills. He took off his shoes before entering, as a polite Filipino would. The front door was ajar, but there was no sign of life in the house. He looked into the house and called, "Anybody home?"

Armed men suddenly surrounded him. One of them motioned for him to come inside. "You're a spy!" he said.

"Don't shoot," Lansdale said. "Look at the floor. You'll get it bloody, and she'll have to clean it up. If you're going to shoot me, do it outside."

The men looked puzzled.

"I didn't say it to be a smart aleck. I was well brought up, too."

The men wanted to know who he was and what he was doing there. It was obvious that El Surpemo was visiting his sister, and these were his bodyguards.

Lansdale told them he was an American intelligence officer, and his job was to learn facts and report them to the president of the United States. He had come to visit Taruc's sister in his search for facts. What he did was similar to what people in their own headquarters did. "You write news releases and get couriers to take them to the Manila papers. They risk their lives going on bus rides through military lines and checkpoints. . . . Your very good stories get picked up by the Associated Press or United Press, translated and sent on to the U.S. . . . The president of the U.S. reads them and you get your story before him in that way." His stories, Lansdale said, went directly to the Pentagon and from there to the president. They got to the president much faster than the news stories. So, he concluded, "What do you want me to tell the President of the United States?"[7]

They had many things they wanted to tell the president of the United States. Lansdale took them all down on his notepad. When the Huks ran out of requests, he visited Taruc's sister. While Lansdale was busy with the bodyguards, it seems, Taruc left from the back of the house.

In Lansdale's excursions into Huk-dominated territory he was not being a khaki-clad Santa Claus. He was no friend of the Hukbalahap movement. MacArthur had once said that the Huks were strong in the "sugar country" of Luzon, but "If I worked in those sugar fields, I'd probably be a Huk myself."[8] But in one of his reports, Lansdale wrote of the Huks, "in the provinces of Pampanga, Nueva Ecija, Tarlac, Bulacon, and Pangasinan, they are . . . establishing a reign of terror."[9] Lansdale cultivated Huks because he was trying to learn how the Huks saw life and discover their weaknesses. After his failure to meet Taruc, he said, "I really would have liked to know the guy—what worried him, what made him happy—to give me some clues [as] to what I did right and what I did wrong. What I thought was brilliant might have been a stupid mistake."[10]

But if Lansdale was no uniformed Santa Claus, neither was he a two-faced cynic. He wanted to know what motivated the Huks so that the powers-that-be could take actions to satisfy the needs of people who might otherwise join the Huks. Not all Lansdale's encounters with the Huks were friendly. When he returned from a business trip with his car riddled with bullet holes, his wife, Helen, became very unhappy about the army and about the Philippines. Lansdale applied for a commission in the newly created U.S. Air Force, because he thought it would be less hidebound than the army. The air force accepted him, and then it took him out of the Philippines and made him an instructor at its Strategic Intelligence School at Lowry Air Force Base. Lansdale didn't forget the Philippines. He told everyone he met about the Philippines' need for aid in the struggle against the Communist rebels. We had aided Greece in a similar fight, he pointed out, so why not help our own protégés, the Filipinos?

Lansdale's interest in the Philippines led the air force to loan him to a new federal agency, which, like the CIA, was an offspring of the OSS. The CIA was originally established to analyze intelligence gathered by other agencies. Even after it got its own field agents, it did not engage in paramilitary operations, like the OSS. To carry out paramilitary work, the government created a new agency, one with a deliberately uninformative name, the Office of Policy Coordination. The OPC sent Lansdale back to the Philippines.

He went back in the uniform of an air force lieutenant colonel, but he was really a full-fledged member of the Black World. His rank in this almost-unknown agency was also unknown, but it was much weightier than anything symbolized by a silver oak leaf. Before he left Washington, Lansdale had begun getting involved in top-level Philippine politics.

A Filipino friend, Maj. Mamerto Montemayor, introduced Lansdale to a young Filipino congressman who had come to Washington to lobby for benefits for Filipino war veterans. The congressman, Ramon Magsaysay (mag SIGH sigh), and Lansdale had a long talk. Magsaysay was an impressive man. He had been an auto mechanic who became a guerrilla leader during the war and then went into politics. He was big—six feet tall and powerfully built—a giant in the Philippines. And he was smart: he seemed to know everything about the Byzantine politics of his country, and his proposed solutions to Philippine problems seemed brilliant.

"I decided he should be the guy to handle [the Huk war] out in the Philippines because of his feeling toward the people and the enemy," Lansdale recalled. "He understood the problem, which very few Filipinos or Americans ever did."[11]

Lansdale introduced Magsaysay to officials at the OPC, the Air Force, the Defense Department and the State Department. The American officials then went to Philippine president Elpidio Quirino, who had succeeded Manuel Roxas, and strongly suggested that he appoint Congressman

Ramon Magsaysay takes the oath of office as President of Philippines. Magsaysay's victory and the defeat of the Communist Hukbalahaps were engineered by Edward Lansdale, a top CIA official who was the model for the title character in Lederer and Burdick's *The Ugly American*. LIBRARY OF CONGRESS

Magsaysay secretary of defense. Lansdale followed Magsaysay back to the Philippines. Officially, he was an intelligence officer with the Joint U.S. Military Advisory Group. That was just a cover. He actually reported directly to the Defense and State Departments through the OPC. His assignment: build up a power base for Magsaysay.

The new secretary of defense was out in the field when Lansdale arrived. (This time, Helen and the children stayed in the States.) Lansdale almost reflexively went back to trying to determine the lay of the land. He learned from journalists and politicians he knew from his previous time in the Philippines that President Quirino was even more corrupt than President Roxas. The President's brother, Tony Quirino, headed a gang of thugs who beat up or murdered any critics of the government. Lansdale's friends told him the government had lost the support of the people.

Lansdale could see how people would find it hard to support Quirino, but would they support the Huks instead? The guerrillas were committing atrocities. They had recently raided a military hospital, for instance, and killed all the doctors and nurses and then hacked up the patients with bolos. Lansdale visited the location of the massacre and asked the townspeople about the Huks. He was shocked to learn that they still liked the Huks. They told him the Huks had politely asked them to get off the streets, because they were going to attack the soldiers and didn't want any innocent people to get hurt. The people thought attacking the soldiers was a good idea. The soldiers stole the people's chickens and pigs and beat up or killed anyone who didn't show them enough respect.

Lansdale learned enough about the Quirino machine to make him worry about Magsaysay. When the defense secretary returned, Lansdale persuaded him to move his family to a safe place in the country and stay with him at Camp Murphy, a military base. Lansdale continued gathering intelligence and having long talks with Magsaysay. He persuaded Magsaysay to run for president against Quirino. But first, they would show that Magsaysay was the answer to the Hukbalahap problem. That meant plenty of work for both of them.

Taruc was planning to spread the Huk movement beyond Luzon. One projected target was the Visayan Islands in the central part of the archipelago. Lansdale visited the farm of a friend on Panay, one of the larger Visayans. As usual, he wandered widely and visited people. A Filipino friend, Frank Zaldarriaga, said of Lansdale, "He used to carry a harmonica in his pocket. . . . He could make a friend of everybody except Satan, I think." Zaldarriaga traveled widely on his own business, but he found that Lansdale was known everywhere he went. People would ask him, "Do you know Lansdale?" and he'd mutter to himself, "This son of his mother got ahead of me again." [12]

Soon after Lansdale returned from his "holiday" on Panay, Huk agents arrived. They asked about an American colonel who had been there. An American had been there, the Visayans told them, but if he were a colonel, it must have been in the Salvation Army. All he did was play his harmonica and tell stories. [13] A few days later, the Huk officer in charge of organizing Panay, Guillermo Capadocia, was killed in an ambush, based on information Lansdale had collected while playing his harmonica and telling stories. Capadocia's assistant didn't know what to do. He asked a couple of trusted islanders what he should do. "Surrender," they told him. Both of them had been converted by Lansdale during his visit.

Magsaysay, at Lansdale's suggestion, detailed a company of soldiers to join the Huks. They went into the swamps, let their hair and beards grow, sang Huk songs, and were accepted by the real Huks. They gave Magsaysay firsthand information about what was going on in the enemy camp. At times, the Huks suspected that there were spies among them, even when there were not. Lansdale capitalized on those suspicions. When he learned the names of Huk officers, he had a light plane with a loudspeaker fly over areas where Huks were believed to be hiding. The plane would call out the names of the officers and tell them they were doomed, because the government knew all about them. It ended the announcement with "Thank you, our friend in your squadron, for all the information." The usual result was a Huk court of inquiry and the execution of some guerrillas who were innocent of any spying.

When Lansdale and Magsaysay learned that someone at a government arsenal was supplying the Huks with weapons, they arranged that the next weapons given to the guerrillas would be doctored. Grenades with zero-delay fuses exploded in users' hands, and rifle bolts flew back as soon as they were fired.

Huks frequently organized demonstrations of citizens in Philippine towns. The government response was usually to send in troops. People got hurt, sometimes killed. And because of that, the Huks got many new members. Lansdale tried another approach. He sent men to the scene with coffee and hot chocolate for the demonstrators. The drinks contained a powerful laxative.

One of his grislier dirty tricks involved the folk belief in the *asuang*, a Philippine vampire. His agents would start the rumor that a particular area was haunted by an asuang. Then soldiers would wait for a Huk patrol. They'd grab the last man in the patrol, punch two holes in his neck, and drain out all the blood. Then they'd leave the body where the next patrol would see it.

Guerrilla wars are not won by dirty tricks alone. Lansdale knew he'd have to wean away the Huks' popular support. To do that, he gave kaffeeklatsches with Magsaysay that were attended by military and civilian officials. "He never ordered but only asked," recalled Medardo Justiano, a Filipino officer. "What do you think of doing it this way?" or "Don't you think this is how we should treat the problem?"[14] He would sit quietly and let you talk," said another friend. Then he would sum up what had been said, emphasizing points he wanted to make. "Suddenly, you are getting revelation. You think, 'Oh my God, why didn't I think of this?' Then I made my own judgment. Where did that come from? From myself! But he helped! That's why I would trust a man like him."[15]

One crying need, Lansdale saw, was to reform the army. Among the ideas to come from Lansdale's bull sessions was to use army doctors to treat civilians wounded in military actions and to use army lawyers to help villagers with legal problems. Until then, poor people who could not afford lawyers were at the mercy of the rich. Then there was the ten-centavo telegram. Anyone with something to tell the secretary of defense could wire him for the nominal fee of ten centavos. Magsaysay complained that soldiers always knew when he was going to inspect them. Lansdale suggested surprise inspections. Magsaysay began leaving for inspections in the middle of the night without telling anyone. As a result, he sacked several commanding officers, and the army stopped treating civilians like serfs.

Magsaysay came up with the blockbuster idea. Any Huk who was not wanted for a civilian crime could get a tract of undeveloped land to farm. Like the U.S. Homestead Act of 1860, if he farmed the land and stayed out of trouble, he got title to the farm.

In the off-year elections of 1951, Lansdale imported a New York politician named Gabriel Kaplan who went to chambers of commerce, veterans' groups, Jaycees, and other civic organizations and showed them how to minimize vote cheating. His listeners formed the National Movement for Free Elections. They sent out volunteers with cameras to watch the polls, and Philippine troops kept Quirino's thugs from making trouble. Lansdale could not resist another dirty trick. He forged Huk leaflets urging voters to boycott the elections. Out of five million voters, four and a half million cast ballots. Quirino's party lost in a landslide. And the Huks lost credibility.

There was little love lost between the CIA and the OPC. At one point someone in the CIA told Quirino that Lansdale was not merely an air force officer but a high-ranking spook. Quirino threatened to declare Lansdale persona non grata, but John Foster Dulles, the U.S. secretary of state and brother of CIA chief Allen Dulles, blocked that move. But Gen. Albert Pierson, head of the Joint U.S. Military Advisory Group, told the press that Lansdale was no longer a member of the group. The result: Lansdale got another cover and Pierson got relieved of his command.

Magsaysay ran for president in 1953 and won in another landslide. A few weeks later, Luis Taruc surrendered. The Huk war was over.

Lansdale was reassigned to Vietnam, where he, in subtle and unsubtle ways, took over the war from the French, directed the defeat of various warlords and gangsters, and established Ngo Dinh Diem as our man in Saigon. He might have done much more if it weren't for interference in Washington.[16]

While in Vietnam, Lansdale, the secret agent, acquired most unwelcome notoriety. The principal characters in three major novels were modeled on him. In the first, *The Ugly American* by William J. Lederer and Eugene Burdick, there was not much effort to disguise him. He was Colonel Hillandale, an ugly, harmonica-playing American who was a model of how Americans *should* conduct themselves in a foreign country. Lansdale wasn't ugly, but otherwise the picture was pretty accurate. Hillandale was a good guy, but Lansdale wasn't pleased. Secrecy is important to a secret agent.

He was even less pleased with the next two books. In one, *The Quiet American* by Graham Greene, the American agent was a young idealist who caused disasters because of his ideals. In the third, *Le Mal Jaune* by Jean Larteguy (published in the United States as *Yellow Fever*), he was Col. Lionel Teryman, a crude, brutal, French-hating U.S. agent.

Lansdale eventually retired from the CIA and from the air force, with the rank of major general. He had an extraordinary career, but his greatest triumph was ending the Huk war.

CHAPTER 16

Showdown at Dien Bien Phu: Indochina War, 1954

On May 7, 1954, what was described as the French "fortress" of Dien Bien Phu was taken by the Vietnamese guerrillas of the Viet Minh Army. The news caused shock not only in France, but in Europe and the Americas. An army of skinny little brown people, primitive guerrillas using hand-me-down weapons from China, had defeated—in a classic set-piece battle—the army of France, for centuries one of the world's leading military powers. The Dutch, of course, had already been ousted from the East Indies, but the Netherlands hadn't been a major military power since the seventeenth century, and the native population of Indonesia was many times that of the "mother country." Even the fools who were later to call the French "cheese-eating surrender monkeys" were surprised by Dien Bien Phu. (Which, incidentally, never surrendered. It was overrun.)

Actually, one of the more surprising things about Dien Bien Phu was that it had been able to hold out so long. Even more surprising was that an army that so prided itself on its professionalism had allowed itself to get into a situation like the defense of Dien Bien Phu.

The French troops in Dien Bien Phu *were* professionals, too. French law prohibited the use of draftees, who made up the bulk of the French Army, from serving in the colonies. All the French soldiers in French Indochina were volunteers. So were the Algerians, Moroccans, and the mixture of mainly Europeans who made up the Foreign Legion. (Ethnic French made up about 30 percent of the French forces, but the Foreign Legion and the Algerian and Moroccan troops were also members of elite regiments.) They were paratroopers, tankers, gunners, and hard-bitten infantrymen. There were also Vietnamese troops of the Colonial Army who had repeatedly demonstrated their fighting ability. They were, of course, of the same race and background as their enemies. In addition, the French Army in Dien Bien Phu included T'ai militia from the hill tribes in northern Vietnam. These would fight ferociously for their homes, but tended to lose interest when moved out of their own areas.

The war had been dragging on since 1946, with the Viet Minh rebels, who got arms and supplies from China, growing increasingly strong. But toward the end of 1953, the French in Indochina received massive American aid in weapons and supplies, while American money made it possible to hire thousands more Vietnamese troops for the Colonial Army. Ho Chi Minh, the Communist leader, for the first time showed signs of uneasiness. In an interview with a reporter from the Swedish newspaper *Expressen* on November 29, 1953, he said that "the government and people of the Democratic Republic of Vietnam are ready to discuss French propositions for an armistice and a settlement of the Indochinese question by negotiations."[1]

The French, too, were preparing for peace talks, but they wanted to do something to improve their rather unimpressive situation before the talks began. The French problem was that they were grossly inferior in numbers to the Viet Minh Army led by Vo Nguyen Giap. They had an air force, and the Viet Minh did not, but the planes they had were far too few for the work they had to do. The Viet Minh, following the recommendations of Mao Zedong (see Chapter 11) had progressed from guerrilla war by scattered bands what Mao called "mobile warfare," conducted by regular and reserve troops organized in units as large as divisions. Besides rifles and machine guns, they had bazookas, 75mm recoilless rifles, 82mm and 120mm mortars, antiaircraft artillery, and 105mm howitzers.

Mobile warfare, Vietnamese style, seldom involved European-style battle lines. The Viet Minh infested an area. You didn't see rows of trenches, bunkers, and barbed wire, but you saw plenty of bullets, shells, and exploding land mines when you entered their territory. The French were afraid the Viet Minh were going to move into Laos, another state in the French Union, the combination of semi-independent states that had replaced the pre–World War II French Empire. The French wanted to block that invasion, and they also wanted to make the Viet Minh worry about their own rear areas. They decided to use their one advantage, control of the air.

They were encouraged by their experience at a place called Na San, an outpost in the jungle that was supplied entirely by air. When the Viet Minh attacked it, they were repulsed with heavy losses. Air-supplied bases like Na San had been pioneered by Gen. Orde Wingate in Burma during World War II, and they seriously discomfited the Japanese Army. (See Chapter 12.) The French commander in chief, Gen. Henri Navarre, thought Dien Bien Phu would be an ideal location for such a base. It was located in a broad river valley that led through the mountains of northwestern Vietnam into Laos. The valley was open enough to allow the construction of a major air base. It could not only cut the Viet Minh off from the Laotian rice they had been eating, it could also block an invasion of Laos, he thought. And if it were turned into an air-supplied fortress in the wilderness, it would be an irresistible magnet for a Viet Minh attack. Giap's troops had never been very successful when they attacked well fortified positions. In fact, the Viet Minh tried to avoid stand-up battles with the better-armed French. Navarre longed to get his elusive foe in such a battle. A French victory in a major battle would greatly strengthen the hand of French negotiators. Navarre's subordinate, Maj. Gen. Rene Cogny, who commanded French forces in Northern Vietnam, was no great fan of a fortress in the wilderness, but he thought a base at Dien Bien Phu could be a useful supply point for T'ai tribesmen who manned some rather ineffective guerrilla bands in the northwestern hills. Navarre also saw possibilities for guerrilla action based on Dien Bien Phu. When French paratroopers took the base and other troops flew in to staff it, Navarre ordered that half of the garrison should at all times be out probing the enemy's rear areas.

On paper, the plan looked good. Many French and foreign dignitaries, including American generals, visited Dien Bien Phu and praised the fortress in the wilderness. The only skeptics, it seemed, were members of General Cogny's staff. Before the base was established, they unanimously signed a memo that they hoped Cogny would read to Navarre:

> It seems that to the general staff, the occupation of Dien Bien Phu will close the road to Luang-Prabang and deprive the Viet-Minh of the rice of the region. In that kind of country, you can't interdict a road. This is a European-type notion without any value here. The Viets can get through anywhere. We can see this right here in the Red River Delta. . . . While a clear-cut threat exists against the Delta [the Red River Delta, the region of Hanoi] which become[s] more evident every day, we will immobilize 300 kilometers from Hanoi the equivalent of three regimental combat teams. They represent all the reinforcements which we have received . . . which will permit us to inflict losses upon the enemy.[2]

A few years later in the same country, William Westmoreland would learn the folly of expecting a fixed fortress (Khe Sanh) to block an enemy who moved along footpaths in the jungle. (See Chapter 20.) The futility of setting up a roadblock in a roadless jungle was only one flaw in the plan. Another was the location of Dien Bien Phu. The valley, where the airstrip and headquarters of the garrison was located, would be flooded during the monsoon rains. The French built outposts on hills around the airstrip to keep the enemy at least eight kilometers from that vital facility. But that meant that the "fortress" would have a perimeter of thirty-one miles. Experience in Vietnam had shown that the longest line a 700-man battalion could hold was 1,500 yards—about one man for every two yards. The garrison was to have about

10,000 men, but Navarre's orders were that "at the very least" half of the garrison was supposed be out patrolling the jungle.[3] So Dien Bien Phu would actually have 5,000 men holding a line of about 50,000 yards—one man for every ten yards. In other words, the garrison would be only one-fifth of the absolute minimum required to hold the line. Dien Bien Phu's garrison was later increased, and patrols, long-range or short-range, became impossible, thus doubling the original garrison. But the garrison never approached the bare minimum needed to hold the line. And although there were not enough men to hold that thirty-one-mile Dien Bien Phu perimeter, the perimeter itself was too short. All the French hilltop outposts were overlooked by higher hills. There were seven of these outposts, each given a woman's name. They were Anne-Marie, Beatrice, Claudine, Dominique, Eliane, Gabrielle, Huguette, and Isabelle. Isabelle, south of Dien Bien Phu, was farther from the main force than the others and guarded a reserve air strip. To hold the hills that overlooked the French outposts would require far more men than were available to French forces in Indochina.

In spite of his shortage of men to hold Dien Bien Phu, Navarre proceeded with another pet project—the destruction of a Viet Minh area in central Vietnam. "Operation Atlante" was to be composed of three phases. The first would require twenty-five infantry, three artillery, and two engineering battalions. Phase two would take thirty-four infantry and five artillery battalions. The third phase would require forty-five infantry and eight artillery battalions. Operation Atlante, which was to be carried out by a high proportion of very green Vietnamese troops, foundered. More men became available for Dien Bien Phu, although not nearly enough.

Navarre's intelligence officers assured him that there was little chance of attack by a strong enemy force at Dien Bien Phu.[4] They quickly learned that there were strong enemy forces in the area, though. The long-range patrols Navarre had wanted proved to be disasters. One was particularly disastrous: an officer carrying a detailed map of the French installation was killed, and the enemy learned the exact location of French batteries, ammunition dumps, and other potential targets. The Viet Minh were masters of camouflage, and the French walked into trap after trap. Long -range patrols had to be abandoned. A little later, as the Viet Minh crept closer and closer, short-range patrols, too, had to end. That did not discourage the commanding general, who became increasingly enamored of the idea of fighting a decisive battle at the wilderness base. He knew that Giap's men had artillery as heavy as 105mm howitzers, and mortars as heavy as 120mm. He ordered Col. Christian de Castries, commander of the base, to prepare accordingly. De Castries then ordered all troops to fortify their positions to resist 105mm howitzer shells. In his *Hell in a Very Small Place,* Bernard B. Fall, who had spent a considerable amount of time in wartime Vietnam, wrote:

The engineering manuals of every modern army have an answer to
this problem: two layers of wood beams at least six inches in diame-
ter, separated by three feet of closely packed earth topped off by
sandbags to absorb splinters. No protecting roof was to cover an
unsupported area more than six feet in width.[5]

There was, of course, an unlimited supply of dirt, but few trees in the
area were suitable for bunker roofs. To use the trees that were suitable
would involve sending woodcutting parties deep into territory held by the
Viet Minh. And after the wood was cut, there was no way to get it out. The
soldiers tore apart all the peasant houses in search of suitable beams. That
didn't get anywhere near the wood needed, but it made all the villagers pro-
Communist. The Dien Bien Phu garrison was able to collect 2,200 tons of
wood. To meet minimal engineering requirements, they would need 34,000
more tons. The C-47s that supplied Dien Bien Phu would have to make
12,000 flights carrying nothing but wood. That would take five months, and
no other supplies, like food, ammunition, and medicine could be brought
in. To provide minimal protection for a single battalion, 500 tons of barbed
wire were also needed.

The result of all this was that Dien Bien Phu had no shellproof bunkers.
When the Viet Minh attack began, a single shell hit the command post of Lt.
Col. Jules Gaucher, commander of outpost "Beatrice," and killed him and all
his staff. There was no solid barbed wire perimeter defense, in fact, no
unbroken perimeter. The strong points were isolated from each other.
Although they knew that they were heavily outnumbered, and most knew
that the Viet Minh had acquired a lot of artillery from the Chinese, the
French appeared optimistic.

Col. Charles Piroth, commander of the artillery in Dien Bien Phu,
happily explained to all visitors why the Viet Minh artillery would be no
problem:

"Firstly, the Viet Minh won't succeed in getting their artillery through
to here.

"Secondly, if they do get here, we'll smash them.

"Thirdly, if they do manage to keep on shooting, they will be unable to
supply their pieces with enough ammunition to do us any real harm."[6]

It didn't work out that way. When it didn't, Piroth, beside himself with
shame, guilt, and despair, committed suicide with a hand grenade.

Piroth, like the French high command, was relying too heavily on the
British experience in Burma and their own at Na San. The Japanese had
been unable to bring artillery through the roadless, watery Burmese jungle,
and the Viet Minh artillery was greatly outclassed by the French at Na San.
Further, the Japanese general, Mutagashi Renya, could not concentrate on

French soldiers on patrol in the thickets around Dien Bien Phu. French leadership underestimated the abilities of the Viet Minh guerrillas, and that led to disaster.
LIBRARY OF CONGRESS

Wingate's "strongholds," because he had to worry about a larger British-Indian army to his west. And at Na San, the French, not the Viet Minh, held the high ground.

Vo Nguyen Giap, nevertheless, accomplished a logistical miracle by moving equipment as heavy as 105mm howitzers through the forests and mountains of northwest Viet Nam. (The 105, the standard U.S. light artillery piece, came from the Chinese Communists, who captured scores of them from the Chinese Nationalists.) He did it by drafting all of the population of the area as unpaid labor to build roads and drag equipment along them. He also frustrated the French aerial observers and bombers by camouflaging what his laborers had built. In thick forests, for instance, the Viet Minh tied the tops of trees together so the road beneath them could not be seen. The 105s were the most unwieldy as well as most powerful of the Viet Minh weapons. They also had a couple of other U.S.-made weapons: the 75mm pack howitzer, which can be broken down and carried by a squad of men, and the 75mm recoilless rifle, which can be carried and fired by a single man. The 120mm mortar, a Russian weapon, is often wheeled. It fires a bigger shell than the 105, but it is much lighter.

At Na San, Giap tried to rush the French defenses with a "human sea" attack and suffered heavy casualties. At Dien Bien Phu, he took his time and prepared carefully. His forced laborers brought up tons of ammunition for his weapons. When they occupied the heights overlooking the French outposts, the Viet Minh dug artillery and machine gun bunkers so well camouflaged that only the firing port was visible. The howitzers on the mountaintops were able to use direct fire—they were aimed like rifles instead of firing from behind slopes and using their high trajectories to drop shells on a target. Direct fire is more accurate, but more dangerous to the gunners unless the guns are, as Giap's were, well protected. A prime target for the Viet Minh was the main airstrip. They zeroed in the airstrip with all their weapons, including automatic Russian 37 mm and 20 mm antiaircraft guns, which could fire down on parked planes as well as up at approaching ones.

The result of Navarre's bad strategic decisions and Giap's brilliance was a foregone conclusion. But it took a while. Outnumbering the French at least five to one and outgunning them by about the same proportion, the Viet Minh, who held all the high ground and controlled all the surrounding land, were finally able to eliminate any help from the air and attacked on March 13, 1954. The French fought back from their flimsy bunkers and spotty barbed wire entanglements. Resistance at Dien Bien Phu didn't end until May 7, 1954.

The Viet Minh attacked and took the outer French outposts one by one. At first, they used heavy bombardments followed by a mass infantry attack. That worked, but it involved many Viet Minh deaths. Giap then switched to infiltration—relatively small groups of infantry taking advantage of all cover—following the bombardment. That was better, but still bloody. Finally, he reverted to the siege tactics of the eighteenth century. The Viet Minh dug zigzag approach trenches, called saps, from their lines to the French positions. They even tunneled under French wire entanglements and bunkers. This reversion to the tactics of the Sieur de Vauban impressed Western observers and would later have an effect on the U.S. troops in Vietnam. (See Chapter 20.)

The French gave the Viet Minh some surprises. One, as the end approached, was a counterattack ordered by de Castries and led by Marcel Bigeard, a paratrooper who would later become famous in Algeria. The French captured seventeen Viet Minh antiaircraft guns and killed 350 Viet Minh gunners.[7] At the time, the Viet Minh were expecting a French surrender. On May 6, the day before the end, the French shattered what Giap expected to be the final assault with an application of TOT (time on target—arranging to have all guns spread over a wide area fire so that all projectiles arrive at the same instant). This technique had been pioneered by the Americans in Korea two or three years earlier.[8]

At the end, the Viet Minh took 10,998 prisoners, 5,195 of whom were wounded. Giap's army suffered 7,950 dead and 15,000 wounded.[9] But they won.

The prisoners who could walk were marched some 500 miles to prison camps while carrying rice rations for the group and many of the wounded on litters. Even the unwounded were exhausted; many were also sick. It was, as much as the aftermath of Bataan, a death march. About a third of those captured at Dien Bien Phu returned to France or French possessions.[10]

In the prison camps, the Viet Minh subjected the prisoners to brainwashing, like the treatment given to American POWs in Korea. The effects on the European prisoners differed from those on the North Africans. The North Africans were ridiculed for fighting for an imperialist power. Why, the Viet Minh asked them, didn't they fight for their own countries? The Moroccans and Algerians thought about that. The French and other Europeans rejected the lessons presented to them in the "group learning" sessions. But they learned not to do so openly, because group learning was enforced by group punishments, such as withholding food or medicine from the whole group. Those who were obviously intractable were transferred to a "reprisal camp" from which no one ever returned.

The survivors did not embrace Communism, but they became convinced that they would have to fight Communism or any other enemy with the same ruthless methods the Communists used. They were about to get a chance to do so in Algeria.

As battles go, Dien Bien Phu wasn't much; as sieges go, it wasn't long. But it sounded the death knell of the old French Empire. The tolling of that bell was heard around the world. Especially in North Africa.

CHAPTER 17

The High Cost of Terror: Algeria, 1954–1962

On May 8, 1945, all of Europe was ready to celebrate. The previous night, the Nazis had surrendered. Europe was again at peace. Parades and celebrations were being planned everywhere. That was true even in the town of Setif in the section of Algeria known as Petite Kabilie. The Kabyles, as Kabilie is called in English, live in the mountain chain that runs diagonally through northern Algeria and Morocco. In Morocco, the Mediterranean portion of this range is known as the Rif, site of the Rif War of the 1920s. (See Chapter 9.) Farther south, the range becomes the massive High Atlas Mountains. The population of all of these mountains is not Arab, but what the Arabs call Berbers—a word that the mountaineers do not like: it means "barbarians." When the Arab tribes swept over North Africa in the early Middle Ages, the Berbers stayed in the mountains and had as little to do with the invaders as possible. Over the centuries, the Berbers adopted Islam, and many spoke Arabic as their first language, but the mountaineers kept their own languages and passed their time feuding with each other, clan against clan.

In 1921, the Berbers in Spanish Morocco rose against Spain and almost drove the Spanish into the sea. Nationalism had come to North Africa. The people in the Rif did not forget that their cousins in Morocco had almost achieved freedom from European rule. The French had been ruling Algeria since 1830, and their rule had become increasingly irritating to the individualistic Berbers. Now, when all the world was proclaiming a new dawn of freedom, seemed a good time to join the victory celebration and at the same time ask for more freedom for Algerians.

The people of Setif asked permission of French authorities to hold a victory parade and lay a wreath at the *monument aux morts* to honor the Algerians who had died in the war just ended. There had been a fair amount of Algerian agitation against French restrictions on their liberty, but the subprefect of Setif could hardly refuse to approve a victory parade. When the paraders displayed banners with mottoes like "Long Live Free and Independent Algeria," though, the police tried to confiscate them. Fighting broke out, which led to killing, which led to massacre. Twenty gendarmes could not control 8,000 Muslims. Some of the marchers had been armed and obviously prepared for trouble. Groups of them in taxicabs and on bicycles and horses dashed into the surrounding communities proclaiming a holy war. The killings went on for five days. A total of 103 Europeans were killed, another hundred were wounded, and dozens of women were raped. At Perigotville, rioters raided an arms magazine and burned down the town. Similar rioting, with murder, rape, and arson, broke out in Guelma, 200 miles away.

The French reaction was ferocious. Troops rampaged through Muslim neighborhoods and towns, executing suspects wholesale. Dive-bombers blasted towns that were hard to reach by land. A French cruiser subjected another town to naval gunfire. Settlers of European descent, called *Colons* or *pieds noirs*, formed vigilante gangs and murdered more Muslims.[1] Estimates of Muslim dead ranged from 1,020 to 45,000. Historians now generally believe that around 6,000 died in what the Colons called *ratonnade* (rat hunt).[2]

War correspondent Edward Behr wrote: "Every one of the 'new wave' of Algerian nationalists prominent in the National Liberation Front today traces his revolutionary determination back to May 1945 . . . each of them felt after May 1945 that some sort of armed uprising would sooner or later become necessary."[3]

A number of revolutionary groups organized—the Movement for the Triumph of Democratic Liberties (MTLD), the Special Organization (OS), and the Revolutionary Committee of Unity and Action (CRUA), which later became the National Liberation Front (FLN). They waited for an opportune time to strike again. The fall of Dien Bien Phu signaled what looked like an opportune time. The mighty French Empire was disappearing.

On the night of October 31, 1954, the FLN announced that it was going to restore a sovereign Algerian state. Berber commandos fanned out from an oak forest in the Aures Mountains to strike simultaneous blows at French installations. Unfortunately for the rebels, some of the raiders were trigger-happy. Not one shot was to be fired before 3 A.M., but the group raiding a police station opened fire two hours early. The French officer in charge notified his headquarters, and French security forces attacked and surprised the rebels who were still waiting for the time to begin the action. At a police barracks in another part of the country, a raid aimed at securing weapons failed when a demolition crew blew up a bridge thirty-five minutes early. In Algiers, bombs intended to spread confusion by blowing up a gasworks were too weak to do anything.

The French reacted predictably: they arrested the usual suspects. But in this case, most of the usual suspects—members of the MTLD, less violent nationalists than members of the rival FLN—were innocent. When they were released, they joined the violent FLN. The French premier, François Mitterrand, forbade any promiscuous bombardments of suspected rebel villages and merged the autonomous Algerian police with the police of metropolitan France to maintain tighter control of them. Local commanders, however, frequently ignored these orders. They were frustrated trying to run down guerrillas who ambushed troop columns or raided outposts and then disappeared into the night. Soldiers wrote home about the "Arab telegraph"—beacon fires on hilltops—that flashed word of their coming far faster than anyone could march.

"We don't take prisoners," a sergeant told a new-coming soldier, "but they don't, either."[4]

At this time, the prime target of the rebels was the French military and French officials. But they also took revenge on informers and collaborators, Muslims they called "Beni Oui Ouis." The rebels grew in strength and organization. They got weapons from Morocco and Tunisia, which the French had allowed to become independent so they could concentrate on keeping Algeria French. Unlike the protectorates of Morocco and Tunisia, Algeria was legally a part of metropolitan France. The French had been there more than a century, and more than a million French and other Europeans had settled there. At first, the rebels fought in squad-size units of a dozen or less. But as the war went on, they frequently appeared in companies of a hundred or more. They took control of territory and issued edicts like those prohibiting smoking or drinking alcoholic beverages. These edicts were said to be aimed at the *"grand colons"* tobacco growers and winemakers. But they were also enforcing the strict Islamic practices of the Wahhabis of Sau'di Arabia and those that would later be adopted by Islamic factions in Iran, Afghanistan, and Iraq. (See Chapter 10.) Extreme Islamism was beginning to mix with nationalism in North Africa.

Jacques Soustelle, a Gaullist politician, came to Algeria as governor general aiming to heal the rift between colons and Muslims. But as the rebels began killing European civilians, he began to agree to harsher treatment of the Muslims. When Soustelle arrived in Algiers, he was no favorite of the pieds noirs. Some said—and a few even believed—he was an Arab and his real name was Ben Soussan. But a year later, when he went back to France, crowds of colons appeared to see him off and mourn his departure. Among the measures the army suggested and Soustelle adopted were "collective responsibility" and "collective punishment." These ideas came from the veterans of Indochina, especially those who had been imprisoned after Dien Bien Phu. If the rebels had knocked down telephone poles, for example, the army forced the residents of the area to replace them. If there were too many incidents in an area, the residents might be moved to concentration camps and the village destroyed. Sometimes the village was destroyed without bothering to remove the residents.

The herding of villagers into concentration camps, called *camps de regroupement* (grouping camps) by the French, closely resembled the concentration camps the Spanish introduced in Cuba, the British built in South Africa, and the Americans established in the Philippines. In 1958, a correspondent for the French newspaper *Figaro* wrote:

> Crammed together in unbroken wretchedness, fifteen to a tent since 1957, this human flotsam lies tangled in an indescribable state. There are 1,800 children living at Bessombourg. . . . At the moment, the entire population is fed on semolina. Each person receives about four ounces of semolina a day. . . . Milk is given out twice a week: one pint per child. No rations of fat have been distributed for eight months. . . . No rations of soap for a year. . . .[5]

In retaliation, Muslim rebels in June 1955 declared war on all French civilians, regardless of age or sex. They knew that this would provoke far more retaliation by the French but that retaliation would also further turn the people against the French. As Mostefa Ben Boulaid, one of the FLN leaders, told Commandant Vincent Monteil, a French officer who could speak several Berber dialects, the French "pacification" efforts were "our best recruiting agents."[6] On August 20, the results of the policy were seen in Constantine and its port, Philippeville (now Skikda). Hundreds of Muslim civilians, men, women, and even children, swarmed through the streets killing colons, while the women shrilled their eerie, traditional "you-you-you" war cry to encourage the men. No one had to encourage the women, who slaughtered people with knives and hatchets, or the little children who kicked in the heads of old people who had been knocked to the ground. And all the time, armed FLN guerrillas egged on the crowd.

Paratroopers finally arrived on the scene and mowed down any Muslims they saw, including those who tried to surrender. Soustelle claimed that the mob killed 123 and that 1,273 Muslims were also killed. Most observers believe that these figures, particularly of Muslim deaths, are too low.[7]

Early in 1957, the French guillotined two FLN members who had been convicted of murder. Ramdane Abane, a leading FLN chief, ordered Saadi Yacef, head of the FLN network in Algiers, to take revenge. "Kill any European between the ages of eighteen and fifty-four. But no women, no children, no old people."[8] What was to become known as the "Battle of Algiers" had begun. Until this time, the capital city had been one of the few quiet spots in northern Algeria. It was to gain worldwide notoriety for ruthlessness and cruelty on both sides.

Yacef had been preparing for an urban guerrilla campaign in the city for months. He had his headquarters in the Casbah, a small, incredibly crowded Muslim slum, a maze of twisting streets, some no wider than many American sidewalks, shadowed by ancient stone buildings. Yacef found masons to construct secret passages from building to building, and hiding places behind false walls for fugitives, weapons, and bomb factories. He had skilled chemists making bombs, and he had enlisted some 1,400 operatives who ranged from gunmen and thugs to attractive young women and teenage girls.

Yacef's gunmen opened the battle. Between June 21 and 24, they shot forty-nine Europeans at random. Colon vigilantes struck back by bombing a house on the Rue de Thebes in the Casbah. According to some colons, it was the home of FLN gunmen. But the explosion destroyed three other houses and killed seventy people, including women and children. Yacef met bombs with bombs. He sent his girls, dressed in western clothes and wearing western hairstyles, out to deliver them. People who looked like colons, especially good-looking young women, were unlikely to be searched or questioned at French checkpoints. They carried bombs in their beach bags, which they left in restaurants, milk bars, airline waiting rooms—anywhere there would be a large number of Europeans. That many of the victims would be children, as at *Le Milk Bar,* a popular ice cream shop, made no difference.

Then the gunmen struck again. This time, the gunman was Ali le Pointe, a pimp and con man who became the hero of Gillo Pontecorvo's classic film, *The Battle of Algiers.* He killed Amedee Froger, the mayor of Algiers.

The French governor-general, Robert Lacoste, who had replaced Jacques Soustelle, took a drastic step. He put Gen. Jacques Massu, commander of the 10th Para Division, in charge of maintaining order in Algiers. Massu was a veteran of Indochina, and his division had recently returned from the disastrous Suez expedition. He and his troopers were bitter over the defeat in Indochina and what they saw as a betrayal by their allies at Suez. They saw the Algerian revolt as another aspect of the growing Communist menace they had fought in Indochina.[9]

Massu divided Algiers into four sections and made each of his four regiments responsible for one. The 3rd Parachute Regiment, commanded by Col. Marcel Bigeard, a hero of Dien Bien Phu, got the Casbah. The fictional Colonel Mathieu of *The Battle of Algiers* was based on the real-life Colonel Bigeard and the real-life Col. Yves Godard. Godard was Massu's chief of staff, an intellectual who had once commanded the 11th Shock battalion, a kind of special ops outfit that reported directly to the prime minister and the SDECE *(Service de Documentation Exterieure et de Contre-Espionnage).* Both were aided by the brilliant and somewhat sinister Colonel Roger Trinquier, a pioneer paratrooper whose cloak-and-dagger background was even more extensive than Godard's.[10]

The first challenge to Massu was the FLN's call for an eight-day general strike. The army broke the strike rapidly by dragging workers out of their homes and trucking them to their jobs. Shopkeepers had closed their shops and locked steel shutters over their storefronts. Paratroopers ripped the shutters off by hitching them to armored cars, and in one case, a French colonel fired a tank's cannon into a store. Soldiers and citizens looted the stores until their owners appeared.

Massu set up checkpoints at every exit from the Casbah. Nobody could get out or in without proper identification papers. Godard recognized that the terrorists would probably have impeccable forged papers, so he sent a major to police headquarters to collect all dossiers the gendarmes had on suspected FLN members. All the suspects were then rounded up and interrogated. Thousands of people were arrested with no semblance of legal process. "Interrogation" meant torture—torture on a scale that boggles the mind. Techniques of torment ranged from a revival of the "water cure" used by American troops in the Philippine War (See Chapter 2) at the beginning of the twentieth century to the use of electric shock. All of the methods used by the Gestapo and the SS during World War II were incorporated into the intelligence-gathering effort. Bottles were pushed into women's vaginas and high-pressure hoses inserted into rectums. Both often caused serious internal injuries. As a matter of fact, the torture caused a lot of fatal injuries. Paul Teitgen, secretary-general of the Algiers prefecture and in charge of the city police—a person in a position to know—estimated that more than 3,000 persons "put to the question" had died. They had been tortured to death.[11]

Tens of thousands more, of course, had been tortured and survived—sort of. The interrogation program produced a huge amount of false information, but the paratroopers followed each lead like bloodhounds. They also got tips from Trinquier's network of spies, and they had some lucky breaks, like capturing both Yacef's bomb transporter and his bomb maker. In the end, they wiped out the terrorist organization in Algiers, although the national FLN leaders who were in the city got out and fled to Tunis.

Conquering Algiers did not end the war, of course. The guerrillas in the mountains were getting more and more competent. They had divided the country into six command areas or "wilayas," each of which had a distinctive character. Wilaya 4, which included the city of Algiers, had a rather loose command structure and worked hard to help the peasants in its area. Its troops repeatedly ambushed and routed French units. They also induced many Algerian natives in French units to defect.

Marcel Bigeard and his paratroopers were rushed from Algiers into the mountains to deal with the guerrillas. Bigeard heard that Si Lakhdar, an

FLN leader, was leading two companies, totaling 300 men, to meet a second FLN officer, Si Azedine, the military commander of Wilaya 4. Bigeard put his command post in Lakhdar's path and spread his troops out in an arc around the CP. One company, 3 Company, was in a rather isolated position. Azedine, marching toward Lakhdar, discovered 3 Company hiding in the rocks. He got word to Lakhdar, and both FLN groups fell on the isolated company. The paratroopers in 3 Company called for help. Bigeard, using helicopters, moved two companies up into battle position in half an hour— a demonstration of phenomenal speed. He called in air support, but the Berbers resisted fiercely and when night came, they infiltrated the French lines, leaving 96 dead out of some 600, but taking almost all of the dead guerrillas' weapons with them. The French claimed a victory in this fight near the mountain village of Agounennda, but it was a disturbing victory. At Agounennda, the French had every advantage—numbers, heavy weapons, helicopters, fighter-bombers, and even superior tactics. They surrounded the guerrillas and should have wiped them out. They didn't come close. In few encounters with guerrillas would the French ever have the advantages they had at Agounennda.

The fighting in the mountains and on the edge of the desert might have gone on forever if it were not for the Battle of Algiers. Urban guerrilla war in a big city attracted the world's press. Previously, the fighting in Algeria had attracted little notice even in France. First, there were the indiscriminate murders by the FLN, then there were rumors of torture by the army. French draftees wrote home about what they had seen. People like Henri Alleg, a French Communist who had been tortured in Algeria, wrote a book, *The Question,* which described the horrible suffering he and others had to undergo. It caused an uproar in France. Reporters descended on Algeria and discovered features of the war like the regroupement camps. A movement to end the war grew like an avalanche in France and among France's allies.

The United States and Britain began pressing the French government to end the suffering of the Algerians. Foreign pressure grew after French bombers attacked and wiped out Sakiet, a Tunisian village that the French charged was a base for Algerian guerrillas and arms smugglers. Among the buildings hit was a school; among the dead, many children. It dawned on the French government that the day of punitive expeditions, like those France and Britain had frequently launched across colonial borders in the previous century, was over. France was forced to go on the defensive. France began building the Morice Line, a belt of electrified barbed wire, motion detectors, and minefields along the Tunisian border. It was quite effective. The FLN lost many men trying to breach it. But there was no such line on Algeria's western border, with Morocco.

Inside France, the antiwar movement was turning the already unstable government of the Fourth Republic into something like chaos. On May 21, 1957, as the battle of Algiers was winding down and reports of torture and other atrocities were appearing in French media, Guy Mollet failed to win a vote of confidence in the National Assembly. His government fell, as did so many postwar French governments. But the French were not able to organize another government for twenty-two days. When they succeeded, they tried again to pass laws that would satisfy most of the Muslims, but the pied noir lobby sank all such efforts. On November 5, 1957, Maurice Bourges-Maunoury was succeeded by Felix Gaillard as prime minister. Gaillard lasted until April 15. Then France went thirty-seven days without a government.

In Algeria, the war seemed endless. About a year after Mollet's fall, there were what one French journalist called *Les 13 Complots du 13 Mai*. Actually, there probably were *more* than thirteen conspiracies leading to the events of May 13, 1958. The army officers were furious about the lack of help they were getting from the national government. (Of course, nobody was getting any help from the national government.) They were afraid the government was planning to abandon Algeria. The rebels, naturally, were furious with the government, too. They feared that the French would never leave. The pieds noirs feared that Paris was going to leave them a minority of Christians

Charles de Gaulle was called out of retirement to solve the problem of Algeria. He did, but in a way nobody expected.

LIBRARY OF CONGRESS

in a Muslim sea. Fury at the government was almost the only thing the rebels and the pieds noirs had in common. The other thing was that they, and everybody else, were looking for a savior. There was only one man in all France who looked like savior material, *Le Grand Charles*. While everybody else was furious with the government, Gaullists, like Jacques Soustelle, were furiously trying to sell their man to all of the various conspiracies. The anti-war French and the moderate nationalists in Algeria were convinced that de Gaulle favored Algerian independence. The army and the pieds noirs knew he was for *Algerie française*. All of these elements mixed together the way charcoal, sulfur, and potassium nitrate mix. Algerian politics in early May 1958 was like a barrel of gunpowder. All that was needed for a great explosion was one match. The FLN provided that when it disclosed on May 9 that it had sentenced to death three French soldiers it had been holding.

That same day, Gen. Raoul Salan, commanding general in Algeria, sent a telegram to Paul Ely, the chief of staff of the French Army. He said, in part:

> The army in Algeria is troubled by recognition of its responsibility towards the men who are fighting and risking a useless sacrifice if the representatives of the nation are not determined to maintain *Algerie française*. . . .
>
> The French army, in its unanimity, would feel outraged by the abandonment of this national patrimony. One cannot predict how it would react in its despair. . . .
>
> I request you bring to the attention of the President of the Republic our anguish, which only a government firmly determined to maintain our flag in Algeria can efface.[12]

For the first time since Napoleon, the French Army was threatening to overthrow the government.

Salan announced in Algeria that there would be a ceremony at the *monument aux morts* to honor the three soldiers killed by the FLN. He then showed his telegram to Ely to Robert Lacoste. The next day, the governor-general sneaked out of Algeria.

On May 13, a huge crowd swarmed around the monument to the war dead. Lest anybody be confused about their sympathies, the streets were full of cars blowing their horns—three short blasts and two long ones: beep-beep-beep (pause) BEEEEP BEEEEP. Al-ge-rie FRAN-ÇAISE—the mechanical war cry of the pieds noirs.

Pierre Lagaillarde, a young pied noir demagogue, led the mob to break into and sack the *gouvernement-genéral* building, the capitol of Algeria. Lagaillarde tried to associate himself with the popular General Massu, a hero of the Battle of Algiers. Massu was no fan of Lagaillarde, but he began organizing a "Committee of Public Safety," which would govern Algeria in the absence of a governor-general. The conspirators then got Salan to send a telegram to the president of the republic, Rene Coty, stating "the responsible military authorities deem it an imperative necessity to appeal to a national arbiter with a view to constituting a government of public safety. A call for calm by this high authority is alone capable of re-establishing the situation."[13] Nobody had any doubt as to who that "national arbiter" might be.

In Paris, the Assembly elected Pierre Pflimlin prime minister. Pflimlin then ordered an embargo of Algeria. In Algiers, Salan, in the course of a speech on May 15, said, "Vive de Gaulle!" The crowd went wild. The next day, the ever-present crowd of colons in the forum outside the *gouvernement-général* building was joined by 30,000 Muslims. On May 23, Massu's paratroopers landed in Corsica and took over the island. Pflimlin decided to retake the island. He tried to call up the navy, but was told all the ships were at sea, and headquarters was unable to contact them. In interviews with Coty and Pflimlin, de Gaulle said he would never use force to gain power in France, but he refused to appeal to the army for restraint. Meanwhile, he called his banker friend, Georges Pompidou, and asked him to think of names for a cabinet.

On May 28, Pflimlin resigned. Coty appointed de Gaulle prime minister. On June 1, the Assembly accepted de Gaulle.

De Gaulle promised a new constitution with equality for all citizens, both men and women, of the French Union and a referendum for all citizens of nations in the union on whether they would wish to be part of the French Commonwealth, independent but associated with France, or completely independent. (This did not apply to Algeria, which was legally a part of France.) The new constitution, which provided, for the first time in French history, a strong president, passed overwhelmingly everywhere. In Algeria, in spite of FLN efforts to prevent a vote, 79.9 percent of the electorate voted, and 96.6 percent of them voted "oui." De Gaulle's margin in the parliamentary elections that followed was lower, but still 65 percent.

Firmly in power, de Gaulle disbanded the "Committee of Public Safety" and transferred most of the army officers who were involved in the disturbances in Algeria to less sensitive posts. The FLN responded to de Gaulle's initiative by setting up a government in exile. De Gaulle appointed Gen. Maurice Challe commander in Algeria and ordered him to launch an offense to crush the FLN once and for all.

Challe's multiple offensives were crushing. The FLN was again reduced to fighting in squad-size units, always short of food and ammunition. Challe greatly accelerated the regroupement program, which greatly reduced the ability of guerrillas to obtain food, shelter, and information. It also greatly increased the suffering of ordinary rural Algerians, and it increased the psychological unease of ordinary French people.

Challe said, "The military phase of the rebellion is terminated." This idea has been picked up by many writers and has provided the French Army with a "stabbed in the back" legend: the soldiers can claim that they didn't lose the war, they were stabbed in the back by the politicians, just as the German Army didn't lose World War I and innumerable other losing armies were betrayed by the home front—in their postwar excuses. De Gaulle knew better. He later recalled visiting a "pacified" villages where schoolchildren had serenaded him with the *Marseillaise*.

> Just as I was leaving, the Muslim town clerk stopped me, bowing and trembling, and murmured: "*Mon General*, don't be taken in! Everyone here wants independence." At Saida, where the heroic Bigeard introduced me to a [Muslim] commando unit who had been won over, I caught sight of a young Arab doctor attached to their group. "Well, Doctor, what do you think of it all?" "What we Arabs want, and what we need," he replied, his eyes filled with tears, "is to be responsible for ourselves instead of others being responsible for us." [14]

De Gaulle knew, as few French generals did, that a guerrilla war is not won until a majority of the enemy people accept defeat. On September 16, 1959, he promised the Algerians an election that would let them decide on independence. "I deem it necessary that recourse to self-determination be here and now proclaimed. . . . As for the time of the election, I will decide upon it in due course, at the latest, four years after the actual restoration of peace, that is to say, once a situation has been established whereby loss of life, be it in ambushes or isolated attempts, does not exceed 200 a year." [15]

The crowd cheered and foreign countries were delighted, but General Challe and many other officers were not happy. The FLN was suspicious. And the pieds noirs were outraged.

Their reaction was to dig up paving stones from the streets and build barricades—a French revolutionary tradition that is more than a little silly in a world of high explosive shells and tanks, not to speak of airplanes and helicopters. Challe and the army in Algeria did not use those tanks, however. They said they did not want to spill blood, although on January 24, 1960, the pieds noirs had spilled plenty of blood. A force of gendarmes, carrying unloaded guns, tried to herd them away from the barricades and back to the residential section of the city where most of them lived. The gendarmes were to be supported by a regiment of paratroopers and one of the Foreign

Legion. Neither regiment showed up, and the policemen were mowed down by a fusillade of machine-gun, rifle, and pistol fire from colon civilians.

The army made no move against the barricades. At Challe's headquarters Col. Antoine Argoud, esteemed as the most intelligent officer in the army, blustered that unless de Gaulle dropped self-determination, he would be replaced by Challe.

De Gaulle just waited. The pieds noirs militiamen began to miss their homes and families. They stood behind their barricades bored, cold, and getting colder. A frigid rain began to fall. The colon women who had appeared with home-cooked food and jugs of wine and coffee stopped arriving. The "patriots" at the barricades slowly evaporated. One of the leaders of the pieds noirs, Joseph Ortiz, disappeared. He turned up in Spain and was never seen in Algiers again. The other, Pierre Lagaillarde, went to jail.

De Gaulle made a speech offering to discuss a cease-fire with the FLN, but the leaders of the FLN misinterpreted his offer for a truce to discuss military and other issues as a call for their surrender. The FLN leaders were concerned with more than the independence of Algeria. They wanted to retain their own positions of power, and at this point, they had Algerian rivals. In addition to the war, the FLN leadership was engaged in vicious political infighting, especially those in Tunisia, who were in little danger from the French.[16] In this kind of political infighting, the losers were not merely dead politically. They were just plain dead. And if nothing else, FLN intransigence showed that the rebel movement was by no means on the brink of defeat.

De Gaulle released thousands of FLN prisoners in batches to appease the rebels, but they just went on building up their organization, particularly in Algiers. Strangely, he did not release Ahmed Ben Bella, a top FLN leader whose flight from Morocco to Tunisia for an FLN summit meeting had been hijacked by the French secret service during the Guy Mollet administration. Instead of landing in Tunisia, the plane landed in Algeria. Ben Bella and his party were immediately flown to France, where they were still imprisoned. De Gaulle moved Challe, who had done almost nothing to oppose the colons at the barricades. He had once told Challe he would make him chief of staff of the French armed forces. But the assignment he got was commander of NATO forces in Central Europe. Challe was bitterly disappointed.

In June 1960, the FLN commanders in Wilaya 4, impatient with the fat cats in Tunis who refused to make peace, asked to meet with de Gaulle. They were flown to France and met the president personally. They wanted an independent Algeria. De Gaulle had promised a referendum to let Algerians decide. They were satisfied with that promise and wanted to discuss terms. De Gaulle said it would be far better to have the whole country agree to peace. He would again approach the FLN, and if they rebuffed him again, he would again talk with the officers from Wilaya 4.

De Gaulle made his offer, and the FLN accepted. But they demanded that he recognize the provisional government they had set up, the GPRA (*Gouvernement Provisoire de la République Algérienne*) before talks began. The French refused, because that would be recognizing Algerian independence before the referendum gave the Algerians a chance to decide. The talks ended, and agents from the FLN headquarters in Tunis murdered the officers from Wilaya 4.

In December, de Gaulle traveled to Algeria. A group of dissident army officers and pied noir leaders made plans to capitalize on that. When the president arrived in Algiers, the officers planned to kidnap him and make him change his policies. The pieds noirs planned to kill him. As it turned out, de Gaulle arrived in Algeria, but he never got to Algiers. In spite of that, the pied noirs made several attempts to assassinate him. Since the trouble in Algeria had begun, there were to be thirty-one attempts to assassinate de Gaulle. He survived them all.

The visit touched off wild rioting by the pied noir population of Algiers. At one point, the militant colons went to a Muslim suburb and tried to force the population to demonstrate against de Gaulle. The Muslims drove them out and burned down a French store. The next day, the Muslims rioted. The FLN had spent months preparing for a demonstration, but what happened was enormously larger than anything they had expected. Huge mobs waving green-and-white Algerian flags and shouting, among other things, "Vive de Gaulle," broke out of the Casbah. Many people were killed, and the Great Synagogue in the Casbah was burned down.[17]

De Gaulle decided the time had come to present his second referendum. The question put to the voters in both France and Algeria was "Do you approve the Bill presented to the French people by the President of the Republic concerning the self-determination of the Algerian population and the organization of the public powers in Algeria prior to self-determination?"

Sixteen distinguished generals urged people to vote against the bill. The FLN begged Algerians to boycott the vote. Nevertheless, in Algeria, 75 percent of the vote was "oui." In the city of Algiers, with its large pied noir population, 72 percent were opposed. Many Muslim voters stayed home. But of the total Algerian electorate, more than 55 percent of the Muslims approved. The FLN boycott failed.

Later that month, the Swiss government informed de Gaulle that the FLN was asking for new peace talks.

Before the talks could get under way, a clique of generals hatched a new conspiracy. Although called "the Generals' Putsch," it was really started by firebrand lieutenants and captains persuading their superiors to save Algeria for France. It finally included such notables as Raoul Salan and Maurice Challe. It did not include Colonels Bigeard and Trinquier, who had had more than enough of Algeria.

For an organization that included such renowned strategists, the putsch was an example of spectacularly poor planning. The conspirators expected the armed forces to rise as one, seize all the strategic spots in Paris, and change the government. The navy was not aboard; neither was the air force. All the navy ships were at sea, along with the ranking admiral in Algeria, the day of the putsch. The air force moved all its cargo planes out of Algeria. There was no way rebels could get to France, and there was no way supplies from France could reach them. The conspirators didn't even include all the generals in Algeria. But the most important missing person was the one generals seldom think of—the ordinary enlisted man.

The overwhelming majority of enlisted men in the French Army were not in the "elite" regiments like those of the Foreign Legion and the paratroopers. They were not volunteers. They were civilians at heart, fulfilling their national service obligations. They did not worship their officers. They did not admire the paratroopers. On their transistor radios, they listened to de Gaulle's speech reacting to reports of an attempted coup.

"In the name of France," he shouted, banging a table with his fist, "I order that all means, I repeat, *all means,* be employed to block the road everywhere to those men. . . . I forbid every Frenchman, and above all, every soldier, to execute any of their orders."[18]

"Don't count on the rank and file," and similar slogans appeared everywhere on army bases. Signal troops refused to send orders to rebel units. Arms depots were raided and sacked. A hand grenade exploded in one colonel's command post.

Dismayed and despairing, Challe saw that "failure was developing with a chain reaction."[19]

Rebellious regiments were disbanded; rebel leaders were imprisoned. One remnant of the putsch, the Secret Army Organization, lingered on for a while, exploding bombs and assassinating people in both France and Algeria.[20] It made one unsuccessful attempt after another to assassinate de Gaulle. Eventually, all were tracked down by French secret agents, called *barbouzes* (a nickname for false beards).

The war lasted almost eight years. It cost the French forces 17,465 dead. European civilian casualties, caused by both the FLN and the OAS, came to 2,788 killed and 500 "disappeared." French estimates of Muslim dead are 141,000 FLN fighters killed by French forces, 12,000 FLN fighters killed in internal purges, 16,000 Muslim civilians killed by the FLN and pied noir vigilantes, and 50,000 Muslim civilians abducted by the FLN and presumed dead.[21] Estimates of enemy casualties, of course, may not be very accurate.

As wars go, Algeria did not produce a huge body count. But much of the killing was random, and almost all of it was personal—there was nothing like the mass bombings of World War II. But some 1.8 million Algerians were driven out of their villages and into concentration camps. The civilian economy, what there was of it, was wrecked, and there was an atmosphere of terror for almost eight years—death could strike anyone at any time. Killing people who were entirely innocent of any crime was accepted. All of this left a scar on Algeria.

Algeria became independent on July 3, 1962. The pieds noirs, more than a million of them, left Algeria, mostly for France, urged on by the FLN slogan, "the suitcase or the coffin." And everybody else did not live happily ever after. Ahmed Ben Bella, finally released from prison, was elected president. About three years later, he was overthrown by another FLN leader, Houari Boumedienne, who ruled a one-party state until he died twelve and a half years later. Algeria, potentially the richest country in *el Maghreb,* is the most poverty-stricken, with a standard of living far below that of Tunisia and Morocco. There was a brief period of freedom after Boumedienne's death, and then Islamic fundamentalists began to appear. They were often called Afghans because many of them were Algerians who had gone to Afghanistan to fight the Russians who had invaded that country. They apparently picked up fundamentalism from Sa'udi Arabians and other foreign *mujahideen.* That, combined with the callousness acquired by spending half their lives in an environment of promiscuous murder, made them a dangerous force. They called themselves the *Front Islamique du Salut* (Islamic Salvation Front) or FIS. In 1989, Algeria ended one-party rule. The FIS organized a party to take advantage of this move toward democracy. Fearful of democracy, the Algerian military canceled the elections and took over the country. The FIS revolted. The result was worse than the war of independence. Gangs roamed the countryside, attacking villages for no discernible reason and cutting the throats of men, women, and children. Some of these atrocities were committed by rebels—others, according to rumor, by the military, who blamed their own murders on the rebels. Things got even worse when the FIS was displaced by a harder-line group, the GIA (Armed Islamic Group). Killings became more common and more atrocious. No one was sure who was killing or why they were. Then the killings began to wind down from sheer exhaustion.

But Algeria has yet to recover from those years of terrorism.

CHAPTER 18

The Restless Life of Che Guevara, 1956–1967

Peace and prosperity had no attraction for Ernesto Guevara de la Serna. The young Argentine physician had dedicated his life to revolution. After playing a key role in the Cuban Revolution, Guevara found himself one of the most powerful men in the country. But he wasn't happy. He knew that in much of the world, especially in Latin America and Africa, people lived in grinding poverty. That situation could only be corrected, he believed, by armed revolution.

Guevara was born into an aristocratic Argentine family that had had financial problems but still had enough money to let young Ernesto go to college and medical school. His parents were delighted at the prospect of having a doctor in the family, but Ernesto seemed more interested in wandering than in work. One summer he took a tour with his motorbike through all the northern provinces of Argentina, becoming, he proudly admitted, an expert scrounger. In 1951, he took a year off from medical school to travel all around South America with a friend. They began the trip on the friend's motorcycle, but less than halfway through the tour, the motorcycle broke down, and they went on by walking, hitchhiking, and riding freight trains. The result of the trip was Ernesto's first book, *The Motorcycle Diaries*.[1]

The *Diaries* is a mostly picaresque tale of a well-to-do, rather spoiled youth, taking in the sights and meeting girls in strange countries, but there's a hint of the Che to come in his observations of poverty and his anger at what he saw as U.S. imperialism. Less than a month after graduating from medical school, Guevara was back on the road.[2] With another companion, Guevara scrounged his way through Bolivia, Peru, Ecuador, Panama, Costa Rica, Nicaragua, Honduras, El Salvador, and Guatemala. His diary entries and letters back home show that he was becoming increasingly sympathetic to the Communist point of view.[3] He was not a Communist. In fact, he failed to get a medical job in Guatemala because he was not a member of the party. At one point, he admitted that what kept him from joining the party was that he did not want to submit himself to rigid discipline. The party might object to the trip to Europe he planned to take. But he was attracted to Guatemala because of its "revolution." In Guatemala, President Jacobo Arbenz Guzman was engaged in a program of land reform that was causing loud complaints from the big landowners, many of whom had close ties with the United States.[4] Guevara expected some sort of intervention by the United States. It soon came. A retired colonel named Carlos Castillo Armas led an insurrection against Arbenz. The rebel forces included airplanes that turned out to have been supplied by the U.S. CIA. Even with that aid, the rebels made little progress at first. Guevara joined a militia unit and asked to serve at the front, but the ministry of health sent him to a hospital. Suddenly, the top officers of the Guatemalan Army turned against Arbenz, and he had to resign. It appears that Arbenz was overthrown not by military force but by money slipped to the right hands combined with threats of a U.S. invasion. Arbenz left the country and the "liberators" began arresting all known or suspected leftists. Guevara sought asylum in the Argentine embassy, and his girlfriend, Hilda Gadea (whom he later married), was jailed for a while.

Ernesto and Hilda eventually went to Mexico. While there Guevara treated a Cuban, one of a group who, on July 26, 1953, had taken part in a revolt against Fugencio Batista, the dictator of Cuba. The leaders of the ill-fated Cuban revolt were Fidel Castro and his brother Raúl. Many of their followers were executed; the Castros and some others were imprisoned. But this group had managed to escape from Cuba and find refuge in Mexico. A short time later, the Castros were released from prison and came to Mexico. Around this time, Guevara acquired a nickname—"Che." It was a Guarani Indian word, variously translated as "hey you" or "pal." Among native Spanish speakers it is used only by residents of northern Argentina or Uruguay. Guevara used it a lot.

Fidel Castro and Che Guevara met, and each greatly impressed the other. Castro revealed that he was organizing an invasion force to continue fighting Batista and invited Guevara to join him. The expedition needed a doctor. Che accepted enthusiastically.

The expedition began with a disaster. Castro loaded his people aboard an old yacht, *Granma,* and headed for eastern Cuba. The trip took seven days instead of the expected five. Members of Castro's "fifth column," the July 26 Movement, mostly sympathizers who had not taken part in the original revolt, were going to greet him and were also going to start a disturbance in Santiago de Cuba to distract the government troops. The disturbance erupted and was quelled while Castro and company were at sea. Then the reception committee got tired of waiting and went home. When *Granma* reached the Cuban coast, the helmsman couldn't find the agreed-upon landing spot. Castro told him to head straight for the coast. He did, and the boat struck a sandbar and began to sink. The rebel "army" scrambled out, leaving most of the weapons, ammunition, and medical supplies on the boat.

Meanwhile, the rebels had been spotted by a Cuban coast guard cutter, which notified the armed forces. Castro's forces split into two groups and wandered blindly through the jungle while government planes tried to locate them, firing machine-gun bursts into the forest at random. After two days, the two groups of rebels were reunited and found a native guide. They stopped to rest in a sugarcane field and their guide disappeared. A few minutes later, the Cuban army attacked. Most of Castro's expedition was killed or captured. Of the eighty-two men aboard *Granma,* twenty-two made it to the comparatively safe wilds of the Sierra Maestra.

As Batista had thousands of men under arms, Castro's rebellion seemed as promising as Pancho Villa's when he and four companions left El Paso to overthrow the government of Mexico (see Chapter 3). Of course, Villa built up his army much more rapidly, and he didn't have an underground organization, either. But Villa was a legendary bandit, a Mexican Robin Hood, one of the hero-villains who abound in Mexican history. Castro was only a lawyer. He was, however, a politically savvy lawyer. That was one of the biggest differences between Guevara and Castro.

Although he wasn't a Communist Party member, Che was a hard-line Marxist. He continually complained to Fidel about making compromises, but Castro continually made compromises, and the revolution prospered. Guevara distrusted members of the July 26 Movement who were not in the mountains, the so-called *Llanos* (Spanish for plains or lowlands). But Castro was able to get their cooperation. He talked with other anti-Batista groups that were not part of the Movement. He even (gasp) got covert help from the U.S. State Department and CIA.[5] Some of the help was not so covert. On March 14, 1958, the United States imposed an arms embargo on Cuba. This hurt Batista far more than Castro. Batista depended on the United States for *matériel.* Without spare parts, for example, Batista's air force gradually became useless.

Guevara was a strict disciplinarian. When the guerrillas found it necessary to execute spies and traitors, Guevara frequently volunteered to do the killing. Castro usually went somewhere else. But once, when he was in a bad mood, Castro ordered the execution of a guerrilla for firing his rifle when silence was necessary. Guevara talked *El Jefe* out of that sentence. Unlike the mercurial Castro, Guevara was always the same. He executed not only spies, traitors, and deserters, but also any rebels who abused civilians. He knew that it is suicidal for guerrillas to lose the support of the population.

Another difference between the Argentine physician and the Cuban lawyer was charisma. Castro had it by the carload. There seems to be no case on record that anyone Castro wanted to win over came away with an unfavorable impression. Guevara could be a warm companion to his friends, but he was an Argentine aristocrat from a nation renowned in Latin America for haughtiness. When, after the war, an admirer called him "Che," Guevara fixed him with an icy stare and said, "To you, I am Commandant Guevara."

One great advantage Castro, Guevara, and the rest of the rebel army had was that Batista was widely and thoroughly disliked. He was totally corrupt and enriched himself with bribes from the big landowners and the North American crime syndicate figures who had flocked to Havana. Rich Cubans found him useful but offensive, a crude mulatto who had risen from army sergeant to supreme power. To middle-class intellectuals, he was a dictator, a suppressor of civil liberties. To the peasants, he was the leader of all the tyrants who made their lives miserable. Volunteers for Castro's army appeared in the mountains in a steady and increasing stream. Few guerrilla campaigns have demonstrated the importance of popular support more convincingly than Castro's revolt. Historian Ramon Eduardo Ruiz wrote: "The guerrilla phase of the revolution lasted a short two years, and fighting was sporadic and limited in territorial scope. Castro's militants alone did not vanquish Batista; the caudillo fell because he had lost the support of the politically aware segments of the population."[6]

At first the rebels consisted of small bands in the forested, rugged Sierra Maestra. Peasant sympathizers helped them select targets, lied to the government about their whereabouts, and supplied them with food. Sympathizers at the U.S. naval base at Guantánamo Bay smuggled out arms and ammunition. And the people of the United States openly favored Castro over Batista. Although still outnumbered in total strength, Castro waged a one-sided war in the eastern mountains. He would pick out small outposts, attack them by surprise with overwhelming strength, and then disappear into the trackless mountains. Eventually, the government withdrew the small outposts. Transportation facilities in the Sierra made large outposts impossible. So Castro, like Mao, achieved that great goal of guerrillas, a safe area, in his own country. In the safe area, or *tierra libre*, Che Guevara started enterprises to help take care of the guerrillas' needs. He built a rudimentary hospital and a bakery, and he organized a guerrilla-owned farm. There was a shoe factory, using the hides of local cattle. Another "factory" supplied weapons. One of the oddest (and least successful) was a gadget Che called a "sputnik." It was a condensed milk can containing an explosive and propelled by the rubber band of an underwater speargun. It made a big bang, but tin can fragments aren't very lethal, and it contained no shrapnel. The "armory" also made land mines from unexploded bombs dropped by Batista's planes. And it produced Molotov cocktails that could be launched by shotguns, a weapon detailed in Che's book, *Guerrilla Warfare*.[7] The rebel armories even armored tractors to produce a homemade tank. In time, Castro got real tanks—better than Batista's—from the CIA.[8]

Castro waged successful psychological war on enemy troops. When he captured prisoners, he would release them, demonstrating his contempt for these "slave soldiers." If his men captured them again, he told them, he'd release them again, because, fighting as they were for an unjust tyrant who would never do anything for them, they could never be a formidable enemy, as they would be if they were fighting for an ideal like freedom.

Many of the enemy later enlisted in the rebel army.

Castro's army was organized for guerrilla warfare. There were lieutenants and captains. (But no corporals or sergeants. Castro called all non-commissioned officer positions "slave ranks"—a not-illogical position given the Cuban Army's old world distinction between officers and enlisted personnel.) Castro himself took the rank of *commandante*, equivalent of major. At first, their numbers didn't require any higher rank. When their numbers did increase, the guerrillas operated in a decentralized fashion, seldom massing for a major offensive. Che Guevara became the second commandante of the rebel army, achieving that rank even before Raúl Castro. Raúl and two others became commandantes soon after. Castro's army was grow-

Che Guevara loved cigars and girls, but most of all, he loved revolution. His biggest problem was finding a suitable location. Africa wasn't one, and neither was Bolivia.
LIBRARY OF CONGRESS

ing rapidly. Guevara was ordered to create a military school for recruits and officers. Day-to-day operation of the school was left to Evelio Lafferte, who had recently been a lieutenant in Batista's army.

In addition to running the school and raiding government outposts, convoys, and commercial trucks and buses, Guevara found time for intra-Movement politics. He managed to get Fidel acknowledged as the supreme leader of all the July 26 Movement, eliminating friction between the Llano and the Sierra groups. He had little time for his wife, Hilda. They agreed to a fairly amicable divorce. At the time, Che's life was, as Jon Lee Anderson put it, "a blur of battle."[9] He led attack after attack, even when his right arm was in a cast because of a broken elbow. But during that time, he met pretty blond Aleida March, a revolutionary courier. She became his second wife.

Batista tried to eliminate the rebels once and for all. He sent thousands of soldiers into the mountains. Their object was to surround the rebels and squeeze them into a small area and then destroy them. But high mountains and steep ravines make it hard to maintain unbroken lines. The government soldiers were forced to operate as small groups. And the guerrillas, with their superior intelligence (thanks to popular support) managed to surround and destroy those groups. The Batista offensive was a failure. It was followed by a Castro offensive. Fidel Castro led part of his army in a sweep of eastern Cuba, while Che Guevara led the other part as senior commandante, and defeated the government forces at Santa Clara. That opened the way to Havana, and Batista fled to the Dominican Republic on January 1, 1959.

The end of the revolution saw Che Guevara as the number two man in Cuba. He became chief prosecutor in the postrevolution war crimes trials. With hundred of executions and long prison sentences, he played a major part in eliminating any anti-Castro elements. Later, he became the economic czar of Cuba, and he was an unofficial foreign minister. He traveled around the world visiting sympathetic countries like the Soviet Union and China, unsympathetic countries like the United States, and genuine allies like Ben Bella's Algeria (see Chapter 17).[10]

It seems that Cuba's revolutionary government decided to get involved in Africa after Che's visit to Ahmed Ben Bella in 1964. Although Cuban operations in Africa have often been portrayed as the actions of a Soviet puppet, there is no evidence of Moscow having anything to do with the decision to send Cuban troops to Africa. And why would the Russians pick the Cubans to go to places like the Congo, Angola, and Mozambique when Poles, Czechs, and Bulgarians were closer and more completely under control? There is plenty of evidence, though, that both Castro and Guevara thought Africa was the most promising field for "exporting revolution." The less imaginative Russians thought Cuban efforts should be confined to Latin America, in cooperation with existing Communist parties.[11]

A few months later, Guevara was in Cairo, where he told Gamal Abdel Nasser of his decision to get involved in the Congo. Nasser was shocked.

"Don't try to become another Tarzan, a white man among black men, leading them and protecting them," said the Egyptian colonel, himself a white African. "It can't be done."[12]

Guevara went to Africa with 120 black Cubans to train the revolutionary forces of Laurent Kabila who were trying to overthrow the government of Moise Tshombe, who a few years before was an insurrectionist himself, trying to separate his province, Katanga, from the rest of the Congo.[13] Guevara had scoffed—correctly—at Nasser's warning. Cubans, white and black, had been working and fighting together for a century.[14] But the skin color of Che's troops was the only thing they had in common with their Congolese allies.

Few of the Africans could read or write. They had absolutely no experience in self-government. Not one of them had ever held a commission in a regular army, and in the Belgian colonial army an NCO really was a "slave rank." They were officially the "Popular Army of Liberation," but they called themselves "Simbas"—Swahili for Lions. Many of them believed that a spell cast by a witch doctor would turn all enemy bullets to water. One group, members of the Tutsi Nation, were refugees from Rwanda and had little interest in fighting for the Congo. And, of course, none of the Cubans spoke any Congolese language nor did any Congolese speak Spanish. A few of the Cubans could speak French, as could many of the Congolese.

Che's little force was matched against another small body of exotic troops, Col. "Mad Mike" Hoare's "Wild Geese." (See Chapter 19.) Neither Guevara's Cubans nor Hoare's white mercenaries had any support from the population, of course, but Guevara's Congolese allies were a negative factor. The Wild Geese advanced and forced the Cubans to withdraw. Che noticed that the only thing that seemed to motivate the Congolese was magic, so he enrolled a witch doctor into his force and let him go to work on his African allies. Convinced that the potion the witch doctor had given them would make their enemies' bullets harmless, the Congolese charged the mercenaries wildly while the Cubans retired. Hoare's men let the Congolese get so close they couldn't miss, then mowed them down in heaps. The Wild Geese moved against the Cubans by land and water and overran their positions. Che's men fled, leaving weapons, ammunition, food, and medical supplies behind. For all practical purposes, the Simba Rebellion was over.

Joseph Kasavubu, the president of the Congo, dismissed Prime Minister Moise Tshombe, who had become his most powerful rival in the next presidential election. Kasavubu then reached an agreement with the Organization of African Unity to send the white mercenaries home. Hoare called on General Mobutu, who overruled the order. As Mobutu was later to demonstrate, he was the real strongman in the Congo.

The Cubans were not expelled, but they saw no use in trying to continue a hopeless struggle. Except for Che and twenty hand-picked men, they left Africa.

Che stayed for a while in Tanzania, where he was reunited with Aleida for a time. Then he went to Prague, where he lived incognito for a while, and then for a very brief time, was hiding in Cuba. While in Cuba, he saw neither his family nor his great friend, Fidel Castro.[15] He was preparing for his next adventure, which would be his last. He was training troops for an expedition to Bolivia.

Bolivia was attractive to Che because the leftist government he remembered from his *Motorcycle Diaries* days had been overthrown by a military dictatorship. It was one of the poorest countries in South America. It was also one of the most racially divided. About 30 percent of the population were Quechua Indians, 25 percent Aymara Indians, 30 percent *mestizo* (mixed Indian and European descent), and 5–15 percent European descent.[16] Most of the Indians were illiterate, and in isolated areas few could speak Spanish. Some of the whites were fabulously wealthy. Most of the Indians were desperately poor.

Guevara knew that language would be a problem, so he made some attempt to give his people a smattering of Quechua. Unfortunately, he ended up in a part of the country where the predominant language was Tupí-Guaraní. He had fifty members of his "revolutionary army" in Bolivia. Twenty-nine were Bolivians, sixteen were Cubans, three were Peruvians, he was from Argentina, and the fiftieth was a German woman, Tamara Bunke, known as "Tania." Tania, unknown to Guevara, was an agent of the KGB. While she was unquestionably loyal to Che, there is some suspicion that some of the information she gave to Moscow may have been relayed to Bolivia and led to Guevara's downfall. Che's expedition to Bolivia was not applauded in Moscow. Soviet prime minister Aleksey Kosygin accused Castro of "harming the Communist cause through his sponsorship of guerrilla activity. . . . And through providing support for various anti-government groups, which, although they claimed to be 'Socialist' or Communist, were engaged in disputes with the 'legitimate' Communist parties. . . . Favored by the U.S.S.R."[17]

Guevara certainly had trouble with old-line Communists. Mario Monje, leader of the Bolivian Communist Party, refused to help him. Another problem was the active participation in the Bolivian antiguerrilla movement by the United States. The United States sent a detachment of Special Forces troops to train the Bolivian 2nd Ranger Battalion in counterinsurgency tactics and some CIA agents, notably Felix Rodriguez. Rodriguez was a Cuban exile with a lot of experience in CIA cloak-and-dagger work (with emphasis on the dagger). But the biggest problem for Guevara was that support from the Bolivian peasantry was practically nil. The local Indians were not going to help a small band of foreigners and Spanish-speaking Bolivians who were trying to fight the 20,000-man government army.

For a while, Guevara and his little band trained quietly in the mountains. In the spring, government troops discovered them. The Guevaristas drove the troops away, then conducted a series of raids and ambushes that left thirty soldiers dead, but only one guerrilla.

But the lack of popular support turned the tide. When Che's followers entered a village, they often found either everybody or all of the men were absent. They got little information or food from the villagers. After their few supporters were tortured by the army they got even less. On September 26, 1967, they were surprised near the village of La Higuera and suffered heavy losses. On September 29, Rodriguez persuaded the commander of the 2nd Ranger Battalion to move his 650 U.S.-trained men to Vallegrande. The next day, they trapped Guevara and his men, some of whom managed to break out. On October 8, a peasant woman told the army, that she had heard voices along the banks of the Yuro River. The soldiers attacked, and Che Guevara was severely wounded. The soldiers brought Guevara and the other prisoners to La Higuera and sent word that they had captured the famous Che.

Felix Rodriguez arrived by helicopter with instructions to keep Guevara alive "at all costs." But Col. Joaquin Zenteno Anaya said his orders were to kill Guevara. A trial, the Bolivian government thought, might arouse sympathy for the physician-revolutionist. Rodriguez promised to deliver Che's last messages to his wife and to Fidel Castro. They embraced, and a Bolivian soldier shot Che Guevara to death. Rodriguez kept Guevara's Rolex watch and showed it off proudly for years later. One wonders if he would have saved it if were a Timex instead of a Rolex.

For years many in the United States worried because "a Communist country is only ninety miles from our shores" and would export revolution to the Western Hemisphere. It somehow escaped them that a vastly larger and more powerful Communist country—the Soviet Union—had been only *fifty miles* off our shores for a much longer time and had little luck selling its philosophy in the Americas.

If nothing else, Che Guevara's adventures in the Congo and Bolivia proved that revolution, unlike sugar or rice, is not easily exported.

CHAPTER 19

Mad Mike and the Mercs: First Congo War, 1960–1965

It was to be an amphibious operation in the middle of Africa. The assault team would take motorboats up Lake Tanganyika, one of the enormous lakes in Africa's Great Rift Valley, and hit enemy positions in Albertville, Republic of the Congo. But as he approached the troops who should be boarding the boats, the major knew something was wrong.

"They don't want to go, sir," a lieutenant said. "It's that Belgian. He's been filling the men with stories of the lake and how rough it gets. He reckons we will all drown."

The major knew that someone had deliberately punched a hole in one of the four boats. He suspected it was the Belgian who had joined his mercenary group. He approached the troublemaker. The man said he had lived on the lake shore all his life, and he knew the lake and its storms. He also knew that they would all drown.

"You can go if you want to, but I'm staying," he said. "And most of the men will stay with me."

"I whipped out my heavy 9 mm Browning pistol and clouted him on the side of the head," the major wrote later. "He collapsed like a pricked balloon.

"It was all over in a second, but it was a watershed in my life. The leadership of mercenary troops by force of personality alone demands a hardness of character and a conviction in one's own invincibility which I did not possess. I was obliged to assume those qualities then and there."[1] The major knew that a mercenary leader, unlike a regular officer, has no national authority to back him up.

And that's how Thomas Michael Bernard Hoare, born in Dublin and trained as an accountant, became "Mad Mike" Hoare, African mercenary extraordinaire.

The years following World War II saw the rise of many new nation-states, most of them with no regular military establishment. The world was filled with surplus war matériel and surplus warriors. The stage was set for the

183

rebirth of a medieval institution, the "free company." The heyday of the new "free companies" was the 1960s, and the theater was sub-Saharan Africa.

There were several reasons.

One was that it was around this time that European colonies in Africa were gaining their independence. Some had fairly stable institutions and were more or less self-governing at the time of independence. But others were not. The most notorious example was the former Belgian Congo. Belgian rule, after control of the Congo was taken away from the notorious King Leopold, was good in some ways. In the post–World War II years, the Belgian Congo had one of the highest standards of living in sub-Sahara Africa. The Belgian government provided more schools, clinics, and social welfare organizations than any other government in Africa. But the government was convinced that black Africans were children who needed a firm guiding hand and simple, physical work that would not tax their intellects. It never allowed a Congolese to hold a responsible civil or military position; there were no leaders to take over the country, and the mass of the people had absolutely no schooling. In a nation of 14 million, there were only 16 university graduates and 136 high school graduates.[2]

Another reason for the mercenary revival was that following the "Generals' Putsch" in Algeria, several French regiments, including part of the French Foreign Legion, were disbanded, putting large numbers of professional soldiers into the job market.

Still another reason was that the 1960s were the height of the Cold War, when U.S. and other Western leaders saw a Russian conspiracy behind every disturbance to world peace, and Soviet leaders saw shadowy Americans behind the same disturbances. National governments wanted to take a hand in events that they believed threatened their interests, but they didn't want to do it overtly. Thus the French government asked Col. Roger Trinquier, who played important parts in Indochina and Algeria, to resign from the army and lead a "mercenary" force of other retired French soldiers to help Moise Tshombe in his attempt to free Katanga from the rest of the Congo.[3]

Racial tensions in South Africa and Southern Rhodesia were approaching their peak, and whites there saw the whole clamor for black independence as part of an enormous Communist plot to take over the world. For them, fighting in the Congo was part of an anti-Communist crusade.

On top of all this was the perception that most of the fighting in central Africa was being done by untrained mobs whose savagery was matched only by their ignorance of modern war and modern weapons. It looked like a great opportunity for veterans of World War II and soldier wannabes who had been too young for the big show. The big war had ended some fifteen years before, but there were plenty of veterans still young enough, especially if they were to play leadership roles. For a short time, some of these mercenary leaders became world famous. They included Rolf Steiner, a German; Jean "Black Jacques" Schramme, a Belgian; Bob Denard, a Frenchman; and "Mad Mike" Hoare, who was undoubtedly the most famous of this crew in the English-speaking world.

Mad Mike had been a captain in the British Army, serving with an armor unit in Burma, where he grew to admire that eccentric guerrilla, Orde Wingate, who may have really been mad. (See Chapter 12.) After the war, Hoare moved to South Africa and ran safaris. All this time and for the rest of his life, Hoare remained an Irishman who carried an Irish passport. He called his guerrilla army the "Wild Geese," the nickname of the Irish soldiers who enlisted in Continental armies after the victory of King William in the Battle of the Boyne in 1690. An amusing sidelight on this is that while Hoare was going from triumph to triumph he was identified in the news as "a former British officer." After the comedy of errors that was his Seychelles campaign, he became "an Irish mercenary."

The Seychelles fiasco was far in the future when Hoare first became involved in African wars. The Republic of the Congo achieved independence June 30, 1960. That came as something of a surprise to the Belgian government. All over Africa, former colonies were becoming independent, but in 1959, a Belgian government advisory committee reported that limited self-government would be possible in the Congo *in about thirty years*. Ten days after the commission's report, rioting broke out in Leopoldville. The colonial army, the *Force Publique,* was not able to control the disturbances, some of the soldiers even went on strike, and the population in Belgium opposed sending troops to the Congo. The Belgian government convened a congress of Belgian, foreign, and Congolese leaders to find a solution. For the first time in history, representatives of all Congolese factions spoke with one voice. The Congolese wanted only one thing—independence. Belgium had to give in.

In a hastily organized election, the Congolese elected Joseph Kasavubu, a longtime agitator for independence, president and Patrice Lumumba, fiery young leftist orator, prime minister. That was not exactly a national consensus. Two southern provinces wanted nothing to do with the national government—Kasai, which had rich diamond mines, and Katanga, which had almost all of the rest of the Congo's mineral wealth, especially copper, cobalt, and uranium.[4] On July 11, 1960, Moise Tshombe, a leading Katanga politician, declared Katanga an independent nation.[5] If they left the Congo, Katanga and Kasai would take away most of the new country's national revenue. Kasavubu and Lumumba were sure to take action.

A Belgian corporation, the *Union Minière du Haut Katanga,* controlled most of the mineral wealth of Katanga. It naturally favored Tshombe over the leftist Lumumba and hired large numbers of mercenaries to aid him.

Congolese man points to a banner proclaiming June 30, 1960 the date for the independence of what had been the Belgian Congo. Congolese looked forward to the
date joyfully, but it turned into a disaster. It was, however, a great opportunity for
mercenaries like "Mad Mike" Hoare. LIBRARY OF CONGRESS

Belgium sent "peacekeeping" troops to the Congo, most of whom went to
Katanga and disarmed the Congolese Army there. Those troops then theoretically left the Belgian Army and became part of the Katanga gendarmerie.
Belgium also gave Katanga a number of trainer aircraft that could be armed
to function as fighter-bombers.

In spite of his anti-West, antiwhite, anti-America speeches, Lumumba
sought help from the United Nations. The United States was not about to let
the United Nations send help to a man it considered a raving Communist.
Not getting help from the West, Lumumba turned to the East. He got Russian equipment and Czech advisers for his army and invaded Kasai, where
his troops massacred hundreds of Kasai citizens. Then Katanga counterattacked, and stopped the Congo offensive dead.

The Katanga gendarmerie had been greatly stiffened by former members of the Belgian Army, former French Foreign Legionnaires, and a motley crew of South Africans hoping to find adventure and to bash the
"worldwide Communist conspiracy." It was around this time that Hoare

became involved in the Congo fighting. According to author Anthony Mockler, Hoare was not hired by the Katanga government but by a South African millionaire named Anderson. His mission was to find Anderson's son, who was missing in northern Katanga. He hired some men into what he called "4 Commando" and set out. Mockler says he found that Anderson's son and a Scotsman had been ritually murdered by Baluba tribesmen, who had been at war with Tshombe's Katangans. Hoare then burned the village where the murders occurred, Mockler reports.

"This seems to have been his only major exploit," Mockler wrote, "and he apparently left Katanga before the major battle that marked the end of the year 1961, the second battle of Katanga."[6] Hoare's own memoirs and his record, however, show that he was well known to other mercenaries, including Gerry Puren and Alastair Wicks, who had seen a great deal of action in the Katanga war and who convinced Tshombe that Hoare should command a new mercenary unit.

The Katanga war was not decided on the battlefield but by a political move in Leopoldville. Lumumba had grown too wild and radical for Kasavubu, who, as president, dismissed him. Lumumba then said he was dismissing Kasavubu. But Kasavubu had the army, under Joseph Mobutu, on his side. Eventually, Lumumba was arrested, and Mobutu sent all the Russians and Czechs home. He sent Lumumba to Katanga, where he was assassinated. With Lumumba's death, the Congo split into four warring segments—the central government under Kasavubu and Mobutu; Orientale Province, ruled by Lumumba's successor, Antoine Gizenga; Kasai, under Albert Kalonji; and Moise Tshombe's Katanga. The Soviet bloc recognized Gizenga's regime, and the United States favored Tshombe's. Worried that the Congo might lead to World War III, the United Nations sent peacekeepers to the Congo. The UN troops tried to oust Tshombe, but they were roughly handled by the Katanga gendarmes. Some Ethiopian troops in the UN force did capture Hoare and expel him from the Congo. The Central Congo army invaded Katanga, but it was routed, and it dissolved as a fighting force. The United Nations then dispatched a much stronger force that finally drove Tshombe out of Africa and into exile in Spain. By this time, Hoare had gone back to leading safaris.

The peace that followed the Katanga trouble was short and bitter. With most of the technicians of government gone, the economy was a shambles. Life was harder with independence than it had been under Belgium. In northeastern Congo, Patrice Lumumba's home territory, a new rabble-rouser, Pierre Mulele, appeared and led his followers in rebellion. Mulele's followers were poorly armed, but he was able to use a powerful new weapon—witchcraft. What made witchcraft so powerful was that almost everybody in the Congo believed it.

Mulele convinced his people that the magic, or *dawa,* of a potion he gave them, would turn enemy bullets to water and give its users supernatural powers. They would be "Simbas" (Swahili for lions). They could render opponents powerless by a gesture called "throwing the eyes" at them. If they shouted *"mai Mulele"* (water of Mulele) as they charged, enemies would be seized with an overwhelming panic. The dawa didn't turn any bullets to water, but Mulele's other promises turned out to be correct. Because both sides believed the witchcraft, the shout of "Mai Mulele" did panic enemies. And the targets of "thrown eyes" were often paralyzed with fear. As a matter of fact, a telephone call to Congolese army garrisons saying the Simbas were approaching often caused the soldiers to flee. In a short time, the Simbas had conquered about half of the Congo while spilling little of their own blood.

They spilled a lot of other people's blood, however. The Katanga war had been a very bloody affair, filled with atrocities—rape, murder, torture, cannibalism, and other crimes. But compared with the Simba War, it was conducted with the purest chivalry.

The Simbas killed thousands upon thousands of Congolese because they could read and write, which made them intelligentsia and therefore enemies of the common people, or because they dressed too well, or because they criticized Mulele, or for dozens of other equally weighty reasons. They were usually slaughtered in front of the Lumumba monuments, which were found everywhere in rebel-controlled territory. When the rebellion began, white people were killed and raped for being white. Later, though, the Simbas decided they'd be more useful as hostages. They also thought that church people, priests, nuns, and ministers, whether white or black, also made good hostages.

As the Simbas took town after town, the central government took a desperate measure. It recalled Tshombe from his exile in Spain to become prime minister. The former rebel chief of Katanga was the only Congolese leader who had been successful in war.

With the Simbas approaching Leopoldville, it wasn't hard to convince Tshombe that he again needed white mercenaries. The whites didn't believe in witchcraft, and most of them were better marksmen than the Simbas. Gerry Puren, a South African pilot, told Tshombe that his white hunter friend, Hoare, was the ideal man to lead a mercenary force. Hoare had an excellent record as a combat leader in Burma, a rather unorthodox theater in World War II, and he knew Katanga from leading safaris into that province. Tshombe gave Hoare a contract that called for him to recruit 1,000 fighting men in South Africa, to organize them into a commando, and to use them as a spearhead for the *Armée Nationale Congolaise* (ANC for short). Puren became chief of the Congo Air Force, which had acquired a number of additional planes.

Hoare's was not the only foreign commando attached to the ANC. Bob Denard, a flamboyant Frenchman who had fought with Free French forces in Indochina and later in Morocco, led another commando. Like Hoare, he began his mercenary career in Katanga, where he was part of the group that followed Trinquier to Africa. His career later took him to Zimbabwe, Yemen, Iran, Nigeria, Benin, Gabon, Angola, Zaire (as the Congo had been renamed), and the Comoros Islands. In the Congo, Hoare found Denard to be a too-cautious commander. As with Trinquier, most of Denard's activities were secretly sponsored by the French government. Denard's commando was largely French. There were also Belgian mecenaries. Hoare's unit, although recruited in South Africa, was more polyglot. In addition to English- and Afrikaans-speaking South Africans, there were also Australian and Kenyan troopers as well as Italians, Germans, English, Irish, Scottish, citizens of most of the countries of Western Europe, and a handful of Belgian colons.

Although the United States is by far the largest English-speaking nation in the world, few Americans were in what Hoare christened 5 Commando. The United States was in the midst of the Vietnam War, and no American had to go looking for a place to fight. News about Hoare and his 5 Commando led to a kind of mercenary wannabe cult in the United States, however. A magazine, *Soldier of Fortune*, was established to glorify the "mercs," as "SOF" called them.

The beginning operations of 5 Commando were hardly glorious. The new recruits arrived in dribs and drabs. Equipment, even rifles and ammunition, was slow in coming from the government. Pay was even slower. The government pressed Hoare to move quickly although comparatively few of his men had any military experience. The first move was Operation Watch Chain, which began with Hoare slugging the Belgian malcontent and ended with the raiders being driven off by a large number of Simbas using machine guns.[7]

Hoare resolved to make no more moves until his troops were organized, equipped, and trained. He traveled to Leopoldville and demanded that his men be paid and given equipment and signed contracts. The contracts were for a term of six months' service. Then he organized 5 Commando. First he got rid of the misfits. A large number of men who had joined his outfit did not think there would be any fighting. When they learned that there would be, along with casualties and deaths, they left. Hoare then got rid of the drunks, drug users, and lazy bums. When he finished, his force of some 500 was reduced to 300. He divided 5 Commando into units of forty men, each with two officers and three sergeants. These smaller units would be designated 51 Commando, 52 Commando, 53 Commando, and so on. Training consisted of a minimum of close-order drill and a maximum of target practice and squad tactics.

The Simbas were practically knocking on the gates of Leopoldville when Hoare got a panicked call from headquarters. He picked forty of his best-trained and best-equipped men, named them 51 Commando, and sent them to the capital under 2nd Lt. Gary Wilson. Wilson was given a company of ANC in addition to his mercenary commando. Wilson led his mercenaries and Congolese soldiers against the town of Lisala, held by a thousand Simbas with machine guns and bazookas. He drove them out of the town, leaving 160 dead Simbas in the streets. One of his men was slightly wounded. The battle destroyed the myth of the Simbas' invincibility and showed that ANC troops could fight if properly led.

Hoare's commando continued to grow and get more equipment. The mercs had rifles, machine guns, bazookas, mortars, and armored cars. They were frequently able to get support from the Congolese Air Force, which was also growing. Most of the planes were piloted by Cuban exiles, who had participated in the Bay of Pigs affair and had been recruited by the CIA. And the mercenaries continued to rout the Simbas with lopsided victories. Hoare developed a new strategy and new tactics for conditions in the Congo. His strategy was based on the fact that, as he said:

> The Congo is so big that the enemy can only hold certain key positions and his line of communication cannot be guarded along its entire length. One of the main principles, therefore of this type of warfare is to recognize which points the enemy will defend and to get to them quickly.[8]

Hoare's tactics, too, were based on speed. He seldom tried to "soften" the enemy with preliminary bombardment. Instead, his columns, led by armored cars, would dash at the enemy at full speed and try to take them by surprise. Hoare admitted these tactics worried him, but they worked.

With the Simbas being beaten regularly, they tried to play their ace in the hole—the hostages. They had confined hundreds of white civilians and church people of both colors and threatened to slaughter them if the government forces did not stop advancing. The largest number of hostages were in Stanleyville, the rebel capital. Hoare's 5 Commando, striking from three directions, led the drive on Stanleyville. As 5 Commando was fighting its way on the ground, another operation was under way that involved forces from the United States and Belgium; U.S. Air Force planes dropped Belgian paratroopers into Stanleyville to rescue the hostages. A Simba chief, General Nicholas Olenga, had ordered that all Americans be arrested, tried, and "judged without mercy," which was the same as ordering their execution.[9] Olenga had just suffered a defeat during which American planes had carried an ANC battalion to the scene and CIA planes had provided close support for the ANC troops.

There had been a lot of negotiating and second-guessing in both American and Belgian leadership circles, but fortunately the Belgian Parachute Commandos landed in Stanleyville before the Simbas could kill most of the hostages.[10] The paratroops did not free all of the hostages, as Hoare learned when 5 Commando finished mopping up Stanleyville and continued on to outlying towns. By questioning prisoners and townspeople, the mercs discovered places where the Simbas had hidden their hostages. At the town of Bunia, for example, 53 Commando freed several hundred Congolese nuns at one place and seventy Belgian priests and nuns at another place. On New Year's Eve, 54 Commando wiped out a contingent of Simbas and freed a hundred white hostages. The Belgian paratroopers had dropped on the town of Paulis and freed hostages, but Hoare reported that his 52 Commando later liberated some 800 whites from the Paulis area. Hoare's men got to most of them before their captors could kill them, but most of the live hostages had been starved and tortured, both adults and children, and the women had been raped. One twelve-year-old girl had been raped repeatedly and lost her mind as a result.

The six-month contract of the mercenaries was about to run out. Fewer than ten of the original 5 Commando elected to sign up for another six months. Hoare himself was ready to quit. Col. Frederick Vandewalle, a Belgian who was the Congo security chief, was returning to Belgium, and Hoare had decided that his replacement team was filled with lightweights lacking both leadership and common sense. He was tired of struggling with the Belgian-Congolese bureaucracy. Joseph Mobutu talked him into signing a new contract. This time he would have his own pay section, two doctors, and his own hospital, and he would be a lieutenant colonel. The rebels still held most of the province of Orientale, and they were receiving Communist-bloc arms from Sudan, Uganda, and Tanzania. Hoare's mercenaries were needed to block access from Sudan and Uganda.

With the new 5 Commando, Hoare managed, with the help of Col. Leonard Mulamba of the ANC, to enlist a corps of native auxiliaries. The new recruits, nicknamed 5 Commando's Black Watch, provided intelligence the mercenaries could have gotten in no other way, and they persuaded villagers along the way to cooperate with the white soldiers. Hoare's troops blocked the flow of Communist arms from the desert lands of Sudan and from across Lake Albert from Uganda. Some Simbas had been using Sudan as a refuge between raids across the border. The mercs put a stop to that by pursuing them into Sudan and destroying their base. The troops of 5 Commando continued racing through Orientale Province and releasing those hostages still alive. When Hoare returned to Stanleyville this time, he and his commando had traveled more than a thousand kilometers through Orientale Province and his contract was again running out. He took a plane to Leopoldville to let Mobutu know that he did not plan to renew the contract. Once again the general begged him to stay on, even offering to build him a house so his wife and child could be with him in the Congo. And he again raised the spectre of Communism. The Communists, he said, had established a bridgehead on the shore of Lake Tanganyika, and they had brought in foreign Communists to advise them and stiffen their fighting forces. He was referring to Che Guevara and his Cuban expeditionary force.

What turned out to be Hoare's last battle began like the first in the Congo war. He and his men sailed up Lake Tanganyika and landed on the shore near rebel positions. But this time, instead of three motorboats, they had a small navy—a gunboat, a tugboat, two barges loaded with jeeps and armored cars, and six PT boats. Instead of 30 men, there were 200.

The enemy was different, too. Hoare recalled that they were not like any enemies they had met before when they landed at the lake port of Baraka:

> They wore equipment, employed normal field tactics, and answered to whistle signals. They were obviously being led by trained officers. We intercepted wireless messages in Spanish. . . . It seemed clear that the defense of Baraka was being organized by the Cubans.[11]

The defense of Baraka was so effective that Hoare asked for 300 more men to come from the ANC before moving on to the next objective. As Hoare waited for the reinforcements, the rebel forces continued to attack. "Dawn and dusk, regular as clockwork, they put in their formal attacks, which were notable for their lack of noise and shouting."[12]

The fifth day, the attack was different. A mob of men yelling "Mai Mulele!" dashed down the road in a solid mass. The mercenaries held their fire until the rebels were almost upon them, and then they cut loose. The rebels, astonished that the bullets had not turned to water, stampeded away.

The Cubans had gone.

And 5 Commando, with 400 ANC soldiers, went after them. Hoare's men and two battalions of ANC troops were crushing the last rebel pocket in the Congo when President Kasavubu dismissed Prime Minister Tshombe, as the antirebel PM had become too politically powerful. Kasavubu told the OAU he was dismissing the white mercenaries, but he quickly heard from General Mobutu and explained that he meant only mercenaries who were not attached to the ANC. The Cubans went back to Tanzania and thence to Cuba.

As part of the ANC, 5 Commando stayed in the Congo for a while, but Hoare went home. At one point he was invited to join the rebellion in

Biafra, but declined. John Peters, one of Hoare's most trusted subordinates and now commander of 5 Commando, told his old chief he had been asked to join in a revolt against Mobutu, who had overthrown the Congo government and become a dictator. Hoare advised him to honor his contract, because that was the only honorable choice. He later learned that he had been "credited" with spoiling a revolt that had been planned by Bob Denard and "Black Jacques" Schramme. He had no idea that his fellow mercenary chieftains and comrades in arms were planning a rebellion.

Conditions in the Congo went from bad to worse. Mobutu became one of the most successfully corrupt dictators in history.[13] He invited Mulele, living across the river in Brazzaville, capital of what had been the French Congo, to return to his homeland. Mulele returned and was guest of honor at a great celebration. Immediately after the celebration he was arrested and tortured to death in a particularly gruesome manner. Tshombe, in exile in Spain again, took a private jet to Mallorca, but the plane was hijacked and landed in Algeria. The Algerians were going to send him to the Congo, where he was to be marched in chains to the statue of Leopold II, and be beheaded. But first, Houari Boumedienne, who had made himself dictator of Algeria, demanded that Mobutu fire his Israeli advisers. Mobutu refused, so the Algerians threw Tshombe in jail, where he died two years later. Hoare believed that the kidnapping was too sophisticated for an African government and that the CIA must have been involved. But the kidnapping is almost a carbon copy of what the French did to Ahmed Ben Bella (see Chapter 17). It seems more likely that the Algerians just learned from experience.

In 1978, Hoare was inveigled into a harebrained scheme to overthrow the government of the Seychelles Islands. The exiled ex-president of the Seychelles—an island nation in the middle of the Indian Ocean—discussed a coup d'état with South African and American officials. The Americans were worried about the security of their new military base on Diego Garcia Island. The South Africans approached Hoare, who agreed to lead fifty-three mercenaries (several of them members of the South African special forces) to the island. They posed as members of a beer-drinking fraternity, "The Ancient Order of Frothblowers," but they had AK-47s in their luggage. A customs inspector spotted one of the guns. There was a firefight, and forty-five of the "Frothblowers" hijacked a plane back to South Africa, where they were arrested and served short prison terms.

This incident showed that the day of the freewheeling freelance mercenary was over. There still are mercenaries, but they are multimillion dollar corporations. Most of them profess to provide only support services, guard duty, and the like. Blackwater, a large American firm, is doing that in Iraq, although its president, Erik Prince, has offered to provide a full military unit to further the interests of the United States. Another company, MPRI, founded by a group of high-ranking American military officers, offers military advice. It provided extremely effective service for Croatia (see Chapter 13).[14]

Corporate mercenaries also provide a host of new problems that did not exist with freebooters like Hoare and Denard. Are they combatants if they are not actually firing at an enemy? How much control do field commanders have over them? The outsourcing of military work is requiring legal changes in the United States, some of which have been made, and more of which will come.[15]

CHAPTER 20

Two Traps, One Bait: Khe Sanh, 1968

The two antagonists watched each other warily as each planned to trap the other. The traps were quite different, but the bait was the same, a lonely outpost in the mountains. The result of their planning would change life in Southeast Asia and on the other side of the world.

Gen. William Childs Westmoreland, the American commander, was a spit-and-polish West Pointer who looked like every West Pointer's idea of what a general should look like. Scion of a wealthy South Carolina family, he was handsome, utterly self-confident, and gave the impression of knowing all the answers to unasked questions. He had what military professionals call "command presence." Even as a boy he had a passion for advancement that got him the Distinguished Eagle Scout award and the Silver Buffalo from the Boy Scouts of America. During World War II, he commanded an artillery battalion of the 82nd Airborne Division before becoming chief of staff of the 9th Division. After the war, he returned to the airborne when Gen. James A. Gavin asked him to command the 504th Parachute Infantry Regiment. In the Korean War, he commanded the 187th Regimental Combat Team. In 1956, at age forty-two, he became the youngest major general in the army.

In June of 1964, Westmoreland became commander of all U.S. forces in South Vietnam. He was tired of the protracted war against jungle guerrillas who appeared, struck, and disappeared. Before Westmoreland, the army had tried the "strategic hamlet" approach, modeled after British strategy in Malaya. The Malayan insurgency was conducted by ethnic Chinese, a despised minority, and the strategic hamlet program consisted of fortifying Malayan villages to protect the villagers from the Chinese, who raided them for food and supplies. But in Vietnam, the insurgents were Vietnamese. The strategic hamlet program there involved fortifying villages against other Vietnamese, most of whom had been born and raised in those villages. In the Mekong Delta, because farms were scattered over the landscape, it involved moving peasants from their own land, where they believed the spirits of their ancestors were living.[1] This did little to "win the hearts and minds of the people."

195

On assuming command, Westmoreland took more direct action. He ordered two large-scale sweeps through the countryside, acting on advice given him by retired general of the army Douglas MacArthur, who said "scorched earth" tactics might be the only way to win.[2]

This was a new type of "scorched earth," which was originally the Russian strategy in World War II of retreating before the Germans but leaving them nothing but "scorched earth." The first sweep, Operation Cedar Falls, involved moving 6,000 peasants out of their villages, destroying the villages, and herding the peasants into what amounted to the kind of concentration camps previously used in Cuba, South Africa, the Philippines, and Algeria. Cedar Falls netted few guerrillas or guerrilla equipment. But capturing enemies and enemy equipment was only one of two objectives. The main objective was "pacification."

"Having undergone long foreign occupations, Chinese, French, Japanese, the people are strongly xenophobic," Westmoreland said. Sometimes, he explained, "the only way to establish control is to remove the people and destroy the village."[3]

The second sweep, Operation Junction City, was like the first, but it also uncovered a treasure trove of guerrilla weapons, ammunition, records, loudspeaker systems, and even two printing presses. The guerrillas, who called themselves the National Liberation Front but whom their enemies called Viet Cong (Vietnamese slang for Vietnamese Communists) mostly fled and disappeared into the jungle.

Westmoreland longed for a big, classic battle in which he could use the overwhelming firepower of the U.S. forces. American operations were restricted to South Vietnam, but Westmoreland hoped to persuade Washington to change that policy. A full-scale invasion of North Vietnam, he believed, would quickly end this war. The United States was becoming increasingly involved in Laos, and that prompted another Westmoreland idea—an invasion of Laos, which would cut North Vietnam's "Ho Chi Minh Trail" and also cut Ho's people off from Laotian rice.

And so Westmoreland built up U.S. strength in the I Corps area, the northernmost of the four U.S. Army corps areas in South Vietnam. He personally inspected the area near the demilitarized zone (DMZ) that separated North and South Vietnam, and he selected a base area that could serve as a jumping-off place for either an invasion of North Vietnam or of Laos. It was near a village called Khe Sanh. The garrison would come from the Marine Corps, which provided a large part of the troops in the I Corps area.

It seemed that the North Vietnam Army (NVA) was also becoming interested in the DMZ area. In April 1967 the NVA began attacking American positions in the hills around Khe Sanh. The enemy in these "Hill Fights" was different from the guerrillas Americans had fought farther south. These

Gen. William Westmoreland in civilian clothes. Westmoreland commanded
American forces in Vietnam during the siege of Khe Sanh and the Tet Offensive.
He mistook Khe Sanh as the main Communist objective when it was really the cities
of South Vietnam. The Tet Offensive failed, but it destroyed Westmoreland's
credibility and enormously strengthened the peace movement in the United States.
LIBRARY OF CONGRESS

were NVA regulars, masters of camouflage, who dug deep field fortifications
and made them almost invisible. They had artillery, mortars, and .50-caliber
machine guns as well as small arms, and they used them expertly.

Westmoreland was delighted with this development. It looked as if the
North Vietnamese commander, Senior Gen. Vo Nguyen Giap, was planning
to make Khe Sanh another Dien Bien Phu (see Chapter 16). But this time
the result would be completely different. French airpower was weak in
Indochina, but the U.S. planes and helicopters could rain an absolutely
unprecedented amount of death and destruction on either North or South
Vietnam. Khe Sanh was supported by long-range 175mm guns at a separate
base. The American helicopter fleet gave the U.S. troops more mobility than
any other army in the world. Thousands of reinforcements could hit any
attackers from the rear. If the NVA tried to swarm over Khe Sanh as it had at

Dien Bien Phu, it would bloodily lose the decisive battle of this war. West-moreland saw Khe Sanh as the bait for a trap that would destroy the NVA.

Vo Nguyen Giap was indeed interested in Khe Sanh, but he did not see it as a new Dien Bien Phu. He knew a great deal about American firepower (as well as many other things involving the American military), and he did not plan to sacrifice his army.

Although he had never gone to a military academy like Westmoreland, the usually rumpled Giap was a thoughtful, well-educated man who had long demonstrated his strategic and tactical skills in the war against the French. He claimed to be of peasant stock, but no other type of family was really respectable in Communist North Vietnam. Actually, his father was a low-ranking mandarin, a scholar, and Giap took after his father. He attended the University of Hanoi, where he helped found the Vietnamese Communist Party. In 1939, France outlawed the Communist Party. Giap fled to China and begged his wife to go underground for her own safety and that of their baby daughter. It was not until 1945 that Giap learned what had happened to them.

"Thai [Giap's wife] was caught [by the French] because she didn't have time to find someone to care for the baby. She died in prison," an old com-rade told him. Giap heard that she had committed suicide because the French tortures had driven her insane. But U.S. intelligence sources reported that the French had hung her by her thumbs and beaten her to death.[4]

At the university, Giap had studied history and later became a history teacher. He was particularly interested in his country's military history. Viet-nam had seen many invaders—the Chinese, the French, the Japanese among them, and it had often been occupied. At one period, the Chinese, Vietnam's most frequent antagonist, occupied the country for a thousand years.[5] But the Vietnamese always got rid of the occupiers in the end. Giap was convinced that long, protracted hostilities were the Vietnamese way of war. The Vietnamese way of war was also guerrilla war. In the third century BC, a Chinese general complained, "The Viets are extremely difficult to defeat. They do not come out to fight, but hide in their familiar mountains and use the jungle like a weapon."[6] Giap also studied the writings of Viet-nam's ancient enemy, the Chinese. Around 500 BC, Sun Tzu had written: "All warfare is based on deception."[7] Giap agreed.

If Giap's troops made it look as if they were about to try repeating Dien Bien Phu, it was a good bet that that was NOT what they planned.

Westmoreland, however, was convinced that Khe Sanh would be the site of a great, decisive battle. There was a good deal of wishful thinking in that belief. But the American general had what looked like solid evidence for an enemy troop buildup around Khe Sanh. The area outside the combat base had been seeded by Air Force sensors. These gadgets located heat sources, recorded vibrations in the ground, and even measured vapor from sweat or urine in the air, and then broadcast the results to a secret Air Force detachment that would analyze the information and alert artillery and infantry units. This information could not give an exact figure for the number of enemies hidden in the jungle, of course, but it did indicate that there were a lot of people out there in the woods.[8] In addition to information from the sensors, aerial photos showed that the North Vietnamese were digging approach trenches toward the marines' lines—the same tactic they had used at Dien Bien Phu.

Digging was a sore point for Westmoreland. He thought the marines were not digging enough. He also wanted control of the marines' airplanes. That idea was furiously resisted by Gen. Robert Cushman, commander of the marines in I Corps. Cushman had reasons. The Marine Corps was not merely, in the immortal words of Air Force Gen. Curtis LeMay, "A small fucked-up army talking Navy language." It was a force specializing in amphibious landings and small-unit actions. Marine units had less artillery than comparable Army units, because they could receive fire support from navy ships. When they were too far from water to get help from the Navy, they had to rely on their planes and helicopters. Marine fliers all trained as infantrymen; they understood the problems of air support of ground troops literally from the ground up. And when marines called for an air strike by Marine air forces, there was no delay.

Digging was another matter.

"Digging is not the Marine way," said General Cushman.[9] That statement would have amazed the marines in the mountains of eastern Korea sixteen years earlier. They dug field fortifications and dug them well. No North Koreans, soldiers as tough and well-trained as any in North Vietnam, ever got past those lines. At Khe Sanh, according to *Esquire*'s Michael Herr, the marines seemed to think there was something shameful about fighting from holes. They didn't seriously begin digging until the shelling began. As a result, their field fortifications were an even sorrier mess than those at Dien Bien Phu.[10]

On January 20, 1968, a North Vietnamese officer waving a white flag appeared in front of the American lines. He introduced himself as 1st Lt. La Thon Tonc. He said he had served in the NVA for fourteen years, but he had been passed over for promotion in favor of a less experienced and less qualified officer. He had had enough, he said, and he was leaving the army. He also had information. His information jibed so well with what the Americans knew about the enemy positions they couldn't help believing him.

He told them the 304th, 308th, 320th, and 341st North Vietnam Army divisions and two regiments of the 325th Division had crossed the DMZ and were in position to attack. The attack would begin the next morning at precisely 12:30 A.M. The attackers would crush Khe Sanh and sweep over Quang Tri and Tua Tien provinces like a tidal wave and capture Hue.

If anybody doubted that a soldier who had served his cause loyally for fourteen years would desert to the enemy over a missed promotion, those doubts ended at 12:30 A.M. The enemy attack began with a tremendous artillery and rocket barrage, and NVA troops breached the barbed wire with Bangalore torpedoes and poured through the gaps. The marines drove them back, but the fight continued. One rocket struck the bunker containing the Americans' ammunition, and fifteen tons of it exploded, flattening tents and overturning helicopters. Fires raged at the ammunition dump and on many of the bunkers. To repel rats, the marines had soaked the sandbags on their bunkers with fuel oil. The oil burned. Another shell struck 1,000 pounds of plastic explosive, resulting in another tremendous blast.

Marine aircraft strafed areas where enemies were believed to be hiding. Marine artillery vainly tried to silence the enemy guns, but the NVA shelling gradually tapered off. "We were never able to silence the heavy artillery and rockets that could bear on the Khe Sanh Combat Base," a marine gunner said later.[11] At the end of January 21, the combat base was a shambles; fighting and the explosions had used up 98 percent of the marines' ammunition, but they still held the base.

Apparently nobody analyzed the really bad news. The predicted North Vietnamese "tidal wave" consisted of only about a thousand men. After they hit the ammunition dump, the attackers should have known that the marines would soon have nothing to fight with. But they did not press the attack.

Westmoreland believed the January 21 attack was merely a probe. He instituted Plan Niagara to counter the expected big attack. Aircraft—fighter-bombers, helicopters, and even the giant B-52 strategic bombers—would drown the North Vietnamese in a waterfall of ordnance. Almost every day a pea-soup fog covered the Khe Sanh area, but the NVA continued attacking, and the American aircraft delivered Niagara. Just how effective Niagara was is doubtful. Several captured NVA officers later said that "foreign agents" had tipped off their commanders when and where the B-52s were going to bomb, and the thick fog made it impossible to verify results on the ground. Marine patrols pushing out from the base were invariably ambushed, so long-range patrolling was stopped. Supplies were delivered to Khe Sanh by air, as they had been at Dien Bien Phu. And at the times the fog lifted, aerial observers could see North Vietnamese approach trenches snaking toward the combat base. Westmoreland moved more troops into the north. Ready to help the 6,000 marines in Khe Sanh were 40,000 more troops. When the NVA launched its big push, Westy would destroy it.

Holding Khe Sanh was absolutely vital, military spokesmen said. Briefing officers said Khe Sanh was a roadblock on enemy infiltration routes and the northern anchor of the western flank.[12] They did not explain how Khe Sanh happened to be surrounded if it were blocking enemy routes. Some of the enemy obviously had not been blocked, because they were behind the "roadblock." General Earle Wheeler, chairman of the Joint Chiefs of Staff, according to *Time* magazine, "believe[d] that the loss of the outpost would allow the Communists to roll from the mountains of Laos right down to the South China Sea."[13] The interesting thing about this quote is that Wheeler made it a month after Giap had sent 84,000 men down from the north and hit all the coastal cities of South Vietnam.

On January 31, 1968, Giap struck. But he didn't strike Khe Sanh. Taking advantage of the informal truce that had always been observed for Tet (New Year's), Giap hit Saigon and every other major city in South Vietnam with both Viet Cong guerrillas and North Vietnamese regulars. The Viet Cong did the bulk of the fighting, with the regulars acting as a backup.

Westmoreland's reaction to Tet was that the offensive was really a feint to distract the United States from Khe Sanh. Then he sent more troops north to keep an eye on Khe Sanh.

The Communists achieved startling surprise with the Tet Offensive, but they often assigned companies to tasks that would take battalions, and they made serious intelligence blunders. For example, the Viet Cong 6th Battalion was supposed to capture the South Vietnamese armor school and use its tanks and armored personnel carriers to attack Tan Son Nhut Airport and the U.S. headquarters in Saigon. But all the armored vehicles had been moved out of the school two months earlier. The Tet Offensive was beaten back, but the Communists held Hue for twenty-five days, during which most of the city was destroyed.

Communist losses were undoubtedly high, but not as high as American officers claimed. One officer told UN ambassador Arthur Goldberg that 45,000 enemies had been killed in the Tet Offensive. Goldberg asked how many enemies participated, and the officer said between 160,000 and 175,000. Goldberg asked about the killed-to-wounded ratio. It was three and a half to one, the officer said.

"That's impossible!" said Goldberg.[14]

Arithmetic was apparently not the officer's specialty. Three and a half times 45,000 is 157,500, which, added to 45,000 dead is 202,500. And that is 27,500 more than the highest estimate of enemy participants.

Westmoreland claimed a victory. But in guerrilla war or any other kind of war, victory does not depend on which side killed the most enemies. It depends on which side accomplishes its objective. Giap knew that he had nothing like the manpower, wealth, or weaponry of the United States. He wanted to discourage the American from continuing the war. He accomplished that with a great boost from the U.S. military. The U.S. Army had stressed the need to hold Khe Sanh because it blocked potential invaders from the north. Then, while U.S. troops tenaciously held Khe Sanh, invaders from the north ravaged the cities of South Vietnam. The U.S. military instantly developed a serious credibility problem.

Worse was to come.

Westmoreland and the rest of the army brass continued to insist that Khe Sanh must still be held. But there were signs that Giap and his troops were losing interest in Khe Sanh. Some of the divisions that had been threatening Khe Sanh had taken part in the Tet Offensive. The daily bombardment fell off to between 100 and 500 shells on the two square-mile combat base. In World War II, the Japanese hit the much smaller Corregidor with 16,000 shells in 24 hours, and in the Korean War, Sandbag Castle, a complex of bunkers and tunnels about ten yards long and five yards wide, received 800 shells in one night—and that was far from a record in Korea. But at Khe Sanh, the Americans just couldn't knock out the NVA guns and rockets, fired from caverns in the mountains, or mortars sited in deep pits and camouflaged perfectly. And the shells struck at all hours of the day and night.

Eventually, even Westmoreland, fervently hoping for that great decisive battle for Khe Sanh, came to understand that it was not going to happen.

That presented a problem. Khe Sanh and the impending decisive battle had received so much publicity the marines could not just walk away. The "siege" had to be broken. That was one more blow to the marines. They had been forced to defend an outpost, something that was not their specialty and which they did not want to do. Then they had been criticized for the way they defended it. Then they eventually lost control of their air arm. And finally, they had to be "rescued" from an enemy that was almost not there.

Westmoreland ordered Operation Pegasus by the 1st Air Cavalry Division—troopers who rode helicopters instead of horses. As correspondent Robert Pisor put it, "The commander of the 1st Air Cav, Lieutenant General John J. Tolson, knew it was a charade. He had read the intelligence reports and did not expect to find any North Vietnamese at Khe Sanh."[15]

He didn't. "But this was a military operation for cameras and politicians—not for war."[16]

The 1st Air Cav executed a letter-perfect air-ground tactical operation, and of course it didn't have any opposition to speak of. But there was a story. Douglas Robinson of the *New York Times* told it. Surprisingly few weapons—almost all small arms—were found. That supposed 20,000-man siege force left very few bodies. And those approach trenches like those at Dien Bien Phu?

Some of the zigzag trenches come within a few feet of the barbed wire on the edge of the mined no man's land that separated the marines from their attackers by about 30 yards.

However, the trenches are only fourteen to twenty inches deep and wide enough for just one man at a time to crawl toward the Marine positions.[17]

How many North Vietnamese had been killed during the siege? Bernard C. Nalty in *Air Power and the Fight for Khe Sanh*, the official Air Force history of the battle, writes:

The enemy's losses around Khe Sanh cannot, of course, be confirmed since no actual body count was possible. General Westmoreland's Systems Analysis Office prepared four mathematical models from which its technicians concluded that the total enemy killed and wounded numbered between 49 and 65 percent of the force that began the siege—between 9,800 and 13,000 men. The generally cited estimate, 10,000, is half the number of North Vietnamese troops believed committed at the outset of the operation.[18]

The American public suddenly became tired of fortresses that anchored flanks in a flankless war, computerized body counts without bodies, and a general who had fallen for the biggest military ruse since the Trojan horse. When Westmoreland asked for more than 200,000 additional troops, he was called back to Washington and kicked upstairs to be chairman of the Joint Chiefs. President Lyndon Johnson announced that he would not run for another term. Robert Kennedy, who now opposed the war, was the front-runner for the Democratic nomination until he was assassinated. Hubert Humphrey, nominated by the Democrats, could not overcome his association with the war, and Richard Nixon ran as the peace candidate. After much hemming and hawing while seeking "peace with honor," Nixon agreed to leave Vietnam.

CHAPTER 21

"Giving the Soviet Union Its Vietnam War": The Afghan-Soviet War, 1979–1989

Many people believe that when the Soviet Union sent troops into Afghanistan U.S. President Ronald Reagan first authorized the CIA to aid the Afghan resistance. Actually President Jimmy Carter had ordered the CIA to provide covert aid to the Afghan insurgents, and he ordered it six months *before* the Soviet invasion. Reagan continued that aid. Reagan, however, was never one for keeping covert anything that could bring him votes.

It seems that Carter's role in the affair was much greater than merely providing covert aid to the Afghans. According to Zbigniew Brzezinski, Carter's national security adviser, by aiding Afghan insurgents before the Russian invasion he and Carter tried to *provoke* the Soviets to invade Afghanistan:

> We didn't push the Russians to intervene, but we knowingly increased the probability that they would. . . . The day that the Soviets officially crossed the border, I wrote to President Carter, "We now have the opportunity of giving the Soviet Union its Vietnam War."[1]

As the Afghan war has always been considered one of the major reasons for the Soviet collapse, Carter may be considered one of the few who won the Cold War.

Like most things concerning Afghanistan, the real story of U.S. involvement in the Afghan-Soviet War is extremely complicated. It's important to understand the war, though, because it helped cause earth-shaking developments, from the demise of the Soviet Union and the end of the Cold War to the sudden rise of fanatical Islamists in the Middle East and the sudden growth and change in the international heroin trade.

Afghanistan and the Soviet Union had been close since 1919, when the Soviets sent the Afghans gold, guns, and planes to help fight off the British.

Since 1924, Afghan Army officers received military training in the Soviet Union. In 1956, the two countries signed an agreement giving the Soviet minister of defense responsibility for training *all* Afghan officers. In 1972, the U.S.S.R. sent 100 military advisers to Afghanistan to train Afghan troops on their home ground. Six years later, the number of advisers increased to 400. During this time, a Communist party, the PDPA, grew in strength. In December 1978, Afghanistan and the Soviet Union signed a treaty providing that Soviet troops would deploy in Afghanistan if the Afghan government requested them.

For most of its history, Afghanistan was a monarchy. The last king, Muhammad Zahir Shah, was overthrown in 1973 by his cousin, Muhammad Daoud Khan, who made himself president and accepted financial aid from both the United States and the Soviet Union. In 1975, Jemaat-e-Islami, a fundamentalist Islamic group, rebelled against Daoud, who was attempting to modernize the country in what they considered un-Islamic ways. The rebellion failed, and the rebels fled to Pakistan. Among them were Gulbuddin Hekmatyar and Ahmed Shah Massoud, two men who would later play key roles in the wars ahead. Pakistan was particularly interested in Afghanistan because of British colonial wheeling and dealing in 1893. In that year, the British induced the Amir of Afghanistan to sign a treaty establishing the border between his country and India. It's a strange-looking border on a map. Afghanistan has a long, narrow rattail of land extending along the crest of the Hindu Kush Mountains to the border of China. That was to prevent what was then Russian Central Asia from having any direct contact with India. But the border is much stranger than the map shows. It cut through the lands of the Pashtun tribes, dividing families between Afghanistan and India. It also gave almost all of the Baluchi people, close relatives of the Pashtuns, to India.

The Afghans, especially Pashtun Afghans, have never recognized this border, known as the Durand Line (because it was drawn by Sir Mortimer Durand). Amir Abdul Rahman Khan, who signed the treaty, Afghans say, signed only the English version of it, and he did not understand English. He did not sign the translations in either Dari or Pashto, languages he did understand.[2] With the end of the British Raj, Pakistan was created from the western, predominantly Muslim, part of India. Pakistan inherited the area within the Durand Line.

One Afghan who certainly did not recognize the Durand Line was Muhammad Daoud Khan, the president of Afghanistan. Daoud talked openly of uniting all the Pashtuns and the Baluchis, too, in a "Pashtunistan." That would reduce Pakistan to less than half its current area. Consequently, Pakistan welcomed any Afghans rebelling against Daoud.

Three years after the Islamist rebellion, Daoud was deposed and killed in a bloody coup instigated by the PDPA party. Muhammad Taraki, secretary general of the PDPA, strongly supported by the Soviet Union, established himself as leader of the Democratic Republic of Afghanistan.

If Daoud's un-Islamic ways angered traditionalists, Taraki's drove them to frenzy. Men could not wear beards; women could not appear in burqas. Taraki claimed he was only going to "clean Islam . . . of the ballast of dirt and bad traditions, superstition and erroneous belief."[3] But anyone who disagreed with him was shot, hanged, or buried alive.

Mutinies broke out in the Afghan army, and Hekmatyar, Massoud, and the other *mujahideen* (holy warriors) again took up arms against the infidel Communists. It was at this point that Carter began sending aid to the mujahideen. A growing rebellion in a Communist country would surely tempt the Soviet Union to intervene. The Americans found that oil-rich Sa'udi Arabia was also eager to help the holy warriors in their fight against the godless Communists. The Sa'udis agreed to match American aid to the insurgents dollar for dollar.

Distribution is always a problem with clandestine weapons shipments, especially in a country like Afghanistan, which is entirely landlocked. Further, the CIA, unlike the Sa'udi intelligence, had few contacts in Afghanistan. So the CIA worked out a deal with its Pakistani counterpart, Inter-Service Intelligence (the ISI). The ISI had a lot of contacts with the mujahideen, who had once sought asylum in Pakistan. One problem for the United States was the Pakistani dictator, Zia ul-Haq. Zia had a terrible record on human rights, even hanging his predecessor Zulfikar Ali Bhutto, on a trumped-up charge of murder. Even worse, shortly before the Soviet invasion, Pakistani students sacked and burned the U.S. embassy, while Zia did nothing to restore order. He didn't even appear at the smoking ruins of the embassy until he believed—erroneously—that all of the staff were dead. He was definitely not the American government's favorite Pakistani.

Zia drove a hard bargain with the Americans. Their arms and other supplies could only land at Karachi if sent by ship or at the military airport at Islamabad if by airplane. From there the ISI and the Pakistani army would take over. CIA agents would not be allowed to cross the border into Afghanistan or to visit the mujahideen training camps in Pakistan.

Zia was an enthusiastic Islamist who encouraged the building of madrassas (Islamic schools) all along the Afghan border. Most of the teachers at those schools were either Sa'udi Arabian Wahhabis or men strongly influenced by Sa'udi Arabian Wahhabis. (See Chapter 10.) In dealing with Afghan mujahideen, Zia favored Islamic extremists, chief among them, Gubbudin Hekmatyar. So did the ISI officers, who were mostly Pathans (the Pakistani nickname for Pashtun tribes that straddled the Pakistan-Afghan border).[4] That did not worry the CIA. The Americans, in fact, helped to proselytize radical Islam by printing Qur'ans in various Turkic and Iranian languages and smuggling them across the borders of Soviet "republics" in Central Asia.

Hekmatyar, Zia's favorite mujahideen, was a fanatical Islamic fundamentalist. As a student, he had organized a gang that would throw acid in the faces of any girl students who did not wear a veil in public. With leaders like Hekmatyar, the jihad in Afghanistan became a magnet for fundamentalists from all over *Dar es Islam,* especially Sa'udi Arabia, Egypt, and Algeria. A notable foreign participant was a very rich Sa'udi Arabian named Osama bin Laden.

Hekmatyar was also one of the largest opium growers in Afghanistan. Hekmatyar and his fellow opium plantation owners presented the opium trade as a patriotic duty. It raised the money needed to buy weapons and ammunition. "We must grow and sell opium to fight our holy war against the Russian nonbelievers," said the brother of Mullah Nasim Akhunzda, a leading resistance fighter and the only other man with more fields of opium and more heroin factories than Hekmatyar.[5] Opium had never been an important part of the Afghan economy before the war: the country had no outlet to the sea. But when the fighting started, Pakistani officials furnished transportation to the outside world. Pakistani general Fazle Haq, commander of the Northwest Frontier Province, made several *billion* dollars transporting dope.[6] American Drug Enforcement Administration agents fumed over this situation, but because the CIA was involved with the mujahideen, the drug trade was under de facto CIA protection. Moving dope wasn't the only source of wealth for Pakistani army and ISI officers. Many of them also sold some of the weapons they were supposed to be supplying to the mujahideen.[7]

Meanwhile, the mujahideen were conducting guerrilla warfare and Afghan soldiers were deserting. Before long, half of the army had joined the holy warriors. Then Hafizullah Amin, another high-ranking Communist, deposed and killed Taraki. Both Amin and Taraki had been on the KGB payroll, but after he seized power, Amin turned out to be an annoying subordinate to Moscow. The KGB, to discredit him, started a rumor that he was an American mole. When Amin began meeting American officials (who considered him a dangerous tyrant), the Russians thought their false rumor was really true. They invaded Afghanistan, killed Amin, and replaced him with Babrak Karmal.

The invasion raised fears that the Soviets were aiming for Middle Eastern oil. Soon after it began, Jimmy Carter announced the creation of the Rapid Deployment Force and committed the United States to defend Sa'udi Arabia and the Persian Gulf states. The Sa'udis and Americans began building massive and elaborate bases in Arabia. These bases proved valuable in the Gulf War, and they also aroused the anger of Osama bin Laden, who considered the permanent presence of infidels on the "sacred soil" of Arabia to be a sacrilege.

The mujahideen were controlling more than half the country when the Soviet 40th Army moved in with artillery, tanks, fighter-bombers, and helicopters. The Russians rapidly pushed the Afghan guerrillas out of heavily settled areas and into the mountains.

Edward Luttwak, billed as "the most brilliant and controversial defense analyst and military historian writing today," was typical of outside observers.[8] After he completed a study commissioned by the Pentagon, Luttwak reported that supporting the mujahideen was a lost cause. The guerrillas could never prevail.[9]

But this was a people's war, and the guerrilla fighters weren't the only combatants. Partly because of that, the war was also notable for its atrocities. The Soviet planes carpet bombed any towns that showed resistance, and the mujahideen tortured prisoners to death, often skinning them alive.[10] Russian civilians were terrified of the Afghan fighters. Gennady Bocharov, a Russian correspondent, a month after the invasion was cowering in his hotel room with a group of diplomats and the Soviet commandant of Kabul while Afghan mobs filled the streets shouting, *Marg, marg, marg bar Shurawi!*" ("Death, death, death to the Soviets").

"Each of us knew that the fanatics take their time about killing you," he wrote. "We knew that the first thing they do is pierce your forearms with their knives. Then they hack off your ears, your fingers, your genitals, put out your eyes."[11] Bocharov was eventually rescued by a company of paratroopers. Athough outside observers expected an easy conquest by the Soviets, Bocharov, the diplomats, and the officers knew better.

In the beginning, the mujahideen got mostly Lee Enfield rifles, which being the former British service rifles were common in both Afghanistan and Pakistan.[12] The Lee Enfield has been derided as "a World War I era rifle." It was, but so were almost all of the rifles used in World War II. The U.S. M-1 (Garand) was a glaring exception. The Lee Enfield is both more powerful and more accurate at long range than the AK-47. A good rifleman can fire thirty aimed shots a minute with it, and good riflemen were common among the belligerent Afghan hill tribes. Many firearms authorities call the Lee Enfield the best hand-operated battle rifle ever built.[13] One principle the CIA followed early in the war was to give the Afghans nothing that could be traced to the United States, even though Ronald Reagan was making no attempt to keep American aid to the mujahideen secret. Former Soviet weapons were favorite gifts to the mujahideen. The CIA bought AK-47s, RPGs (antitank grenade launchers), Russian light and heavy machine guns, and other weapons on the open market and got others from the Chinese and Egyptians.

In no place was Afghan resistance more troublesome than the Panjshir Valley. The valley was the fiefdom of Ahmed Shah Massoud, a mujahideen warlord of Tajik, rather than Pashtun, descent. The valley was close to Kabul, the Afghan capital, and the airfields and camps where Soviet planes, helicopters, and troops were based. It was also close to the Salang Highway, the main supply route for Soviet troops in Afghanistan. As a military commander, Massoud was far and away the most talented of the mujahideen leaders. Soviet troops repeatedly invaded the valley with infantry, tanks, and helicopters, first bombing everything in sight. Each time, Massoud led his people out of their homes and into the caves that abounded in the mountains. The fighting men would then fire down on the Soviets from their mountains until the Russians retreated. Some of the mujahideen positions were so high in the mountains the guerrillas were able to fire *down* at the helicopters. This was a serious problem for the hedgehopping Russian helicopter pilots, because Soviet gunships like the Hind were armored on the bottom to protect against ground fire. They had no armor on the sides and top.

Massoud was able to hold his own even though he got virtually no aid from the ISI. He was a pious Muslim but not a fanatic and, unlike the Pashto-speaking Pathans in the ISI, he was a Tajik. Pashtuns and Tajiks spoke similar Iranian languages, but they hated each other. The Russians sent Spetsnaz troops to Afghanistan. Spetsnaz were Soviet special forces troops trained in mountain warfare. The Spetsnaz were almost as good as the native mujahideen at scrambling around mountains. The new troops and armored helicopters gave Massoud's Tajiks a very hard time. He needed more weapons, but helping Massoud was far down on the ISI list of priorities. And all CIA aid had to come through the ISI. Further, General Zia was afraid that if he gave too much help to the mujahideen, the Russians would invade Pakistan.

That left Massoud in a very dangerous situation. So he negotiated a nonaggression pact with the Soviet military: if they stayed out of the Panjshir Valley, he would refrain from raiding them in other places.

Gust Avrakotos, acting chief of the CIA's Afghanistan operation, came to the rescue. Avrakotos was close to many British MI6 agents, who had no arrangements with Zia and went anywhere they wanted to go in Afghanistan. They agreed to take weapons and other supplies to Massoud, and the Tajik leader reentered the war. The British not only delivered CIA weapons, they gave Massoud some of their own. Because American aid was supposed to be absolutely covert, the CIA would not give the Afghans anything that could be traced to the United States. That's why they concentrated on old British weapons, which could have been in Afghan houses for years, and Russian-designed weapons, most of which came from Russia's Communist rival, China. The British were not restricted to such extreme secrecy. With the new weapons, Massoud, a brilliant tactician, thrived. And there were plenty of new weapons—artillery rockets, antitank rockets, surface-to-air missiles, and 120mm mortars (a Communist weapon superior to any American mortar). The CIA was able to buy these weapons because it had received a huge increase in appropriations thanks to a most unlikely figure.

He was a tall, boisterous, alcoholic, skirt-chasing, drug-using congressman from Texas named Charles Wilson, widely known in the nation's capital as "Good-Time" Charlie. He came from Texas's 2nd Congressional District, the heart of the Bible Belt, where the only thing people hate more than a sinner is a hypocrite. Charlie wasn't a hypocrite. He practically advertised his sins.

Two sides of a propaganda leaflet dropped on Afghanistan. One side shows happy Afghan children and food labeled "USA" being unloaded and says, "America has provided over $170 million in aid to Afghanistan." The other side, showing a ruined building, a wounded man, and a woman being executed, says, "This is what the Taliban has done." LIBRARY OF CONGRESS

But he also fought for the poor and the oppressed. He battled for regulation of utilities, Medicaid, tax exemptions for the elderly, the Equal Rights Amendment, and a minimum wage bill. In an area of east Texas where the poor were the great majority, those battles made him popular. About his only major conservative position was protection of gun ownership. That didn't hurt him, either.

In 1973, then-state representative Wilson ran for Congress in a special election to replace a congressman who had been caught taking a bribe. Wilson didn't lose his charm by going to Washington. He was the only gentile in the Congressional Jewish Caucus and the only white in the Congressional Black Caucus. He didn't hunt around for the levers of power. He gravitated to them. He made friends with the right people, like House Speaker Tip O'Neil, John Murtha, chairman of the Defense Subcommittee; and Clarence D. "Doc" Long, chairman of the House Appropriations Subcommittee on government operations. Long, though little known to the public, was one of the most powerful men in the country.

Good-Time Charlie loved to junket, and he usually traveled—at government expense, of course—with a succession of striking young women, many of them former beauty queens. On his travels, he managed to charm, and be charmed by, a crowd of foreign leaders, a few of them rather repugnant dictators.

One of his girlfriends, Joanne Herring, was different from the crowd of former Miss Humble Oils and Miss Northern Hemispheres. Herring was a gorgeous Houston socialite who also had a lot of connections, ranging from European nobility to General Zia ul-Haq. She was not exactly the liberal Wilson's political soul mate. She belonged to the Minutewomen, the Minuteman auxiliary, and was involved with several groups on the lunatic right. About the only political idea Herring and Wilson had in common was deep hatred for Communism. Herring introduced Wilson to Zia ul-Haq, who proceeded to charm the charmer. Good-Time Charlie managed to visit Pakistani frontier posts where Afghan mujahideen were training and gathering supplies. He actually crossed into Afghanistan and heard about the problems the holy warriors faced, especially the Russian helicopters. He told Zia and the Afghans he would get them more weapons and supplies.

And he did. As a member of the government appropriations subcommittee, he was able to double the appropriation for the CIA. Then he doubled that amount. The appropriations kept growing. Wilson's zeal to help the mujahideen counter the Russian helicopters led to a monomaniacal crusade to get the CIA to buy the Swiss Oerlikon 20mm antiaircraft gun. The Afghans had been using Russian DShK 38/46 12.7mm machine guns, whose performance was practically identical to the U.S. .50 M2 Browning. The

Russian gun couldn't penetrate the Hind helicopter's floor armor. The Oerlikon could, but so could a lot of other weapons.

Why Wilson was so fixated on the Oerlikon is something of a mystery, but it may have been because after he graduated from the U.S. Naval Academy, Charlie Wilson was a gunnery officer on a destroyer. The U.S. Navy had been using Oerlikons since World War II. The Oerlikon was an excellent shipboard defense against dive bombers and torpedo bombers, but it was heavy and delicate. It was not an excellent weapon for guerrillas constantly moving over rugged, dusty mountains. The CIA was able to hold off Wilson and his Oerlikons until it found a guerrilla war expert who argued that there was no "silver bullet."

What the mujahideen needed, said Michael Vickers, was a mix of weapons. Vickers had joined the Army Special Forces to learn about guerrilla warfare. He became an expert in unarmed combat, trained with the British SAS and the U.S. Navy Seals. He learned to maneuver a parachute, gliding as many as thirty miles to land on a target. When he decided he had learned as much as he could in the Special Forces, he joined the CIA. And as a very low-ranking agent, the equivalent of an army captain, he proceeded to design the weapons mix for the mujahideen campaign.

Vickers and Gust Avrokotos traveled the world purchasing weapons for the Afghan rebels, spending the money Wilson's maneuvers had gained for the CIA. Vickers said the Oerlikon was unnecessary. A Russian machine gun, the 14.5mm (about .57 caliber) KPV, could penetrate the Hind's armor, and it was both lighter and more rugged than the Oerlikon. Even better than machine guns, though, were shoulder-fired surface-to-air missiles. The Russian SA-7 homed in on heat. Planes and helicopters were ideal targets. Aircraft could toss out flares to confuse the missile's guidance system if they knew they were facing SA-7s. But the British Blowpipe did not rely on heat-seeking guidance. The firer merely held the aircraft in his sights to keep the missile on course. Best missile of all, said Vickers, was the American Stinger, but the CIA was still not allowed to give the Afghans any American weapon.

By 1985, the war had been going on for six years, had cost the Soviet Union billions upon billions, and the new Soviet premier, Mikhail Gorbachev, was getting tired of it. He put two new generals, Mikhail Zaitzev and Valentine Varennikov, in charge and ordered them to finish the war within two years. Zaitzev would be the field commander, reporting to Varennikov.

The same year, the United States began to change its policy concerning Afghanistan. William Casey, director of central intelligence, developed a new plan in what was called National Security Decision Directive 166. It amounted to a major escalation of U.S. efforts in Afghanistan. Gone was the useless effort to hide what everyone knew—that the United States was helping the Afghan rebels. The new program would include the export of U.S.

military technology to the Afghanistan insurgents and training for the mujahideen in bomb-making, assassination, and other terrorist techniques, as well as intensive training in modern military techniques. (Previously, the mujahideen got only about a week of training in how to use their weapons.) Mike Vickers, still one of the low men on the CIA totem pole, selected 150,000 from the 400,000 mujahideen, armed them with the best weapons and had them trained as a modern, high-tech guerrilla force. The guerrillas would be aided by such developments as satellite photography and burst communications (radio messages concentrated electronically and then transmitted in an almost instantaneous burst to thwart interception). The rest of the mujahideen would keep their weapons and be a militia. And the Americans would no longer be restricted to what was permitted by General Zia-ul-Haq.

Although the CIA would keep a major share of control of U.S. efforts in Afghanistan, the program would be supervised by a panel of agencies. Representatives to the interagency council would be selected by the White House's National Security Council. The Pakistani ISI was still a major source of weapons to the mujahideen, but the Afghan warlords began making their own contacts in the United States, Sa'udi Arabia, and Europe.

But during this period, the Russians were also busy. They replaced Babrak Karmal with Muhammad Najibullah, the ruthless and sadistic chief of the Afghan secret police. Spetsnaz troops in high-tech communications vehicles patrolled Afghanistan's borders looking for mujahideen caravans transporting supplies. When they spotted a caravan, they would run ahead to take up an ambush position and call for their new Mi-24D helicopters. The Russian copters would fly over the Pakistan border and approach the caravan from behind. They would then mow down everything they could see, after which the Spetsnaz ambush would finish off the remainder. Spetsnaz troops also grew beards and disguised themselves a mujahideen. Some would join the guerrillas as spies; others would attack the genuine mujahideen to create dissension in rebel ranks.

The guerrillas also had some successes. In one case, they captured an intact Mi-24D and shipped the craft to the United States to let American helicopter makers learn the latest Russian secrets. They also wreaked havoc in Russian-controlled areas with their new terrorist tools, booby trap bombs, poison, and long-range .50-caliber sniping rifles. They appeared outside Kabul and indiscriminately fired into the city with heavy mortars and artillery rockets. Gorbachev was becoming extremely impatient with his generals.

But in Washington and Islamabad, officials did not see much to celebrate. They feared that the Soviets were on the verge of invading Pakistan. But on September 26, 1986, a mujahideen named Ghaffar aimed a new anti-aircraft weapon at a Russian helicopter. It misfired, and the rocket hit the ground a few hundred yards away. Ghaffar fired again. The helicopter exploded. He and his companions fired more rockets. Two more Soviet choppers blew up.

The United States had finally decided to release its Stingers. The Stinger at that time was the most advanced shoulder-fired antiaircraft rocket in the world—miles ahead of either the Soviet SA-7 or the British Blowpipe. It had an infrared guidance system that could not be foiled by any current Soviet countermeasures. Mike Vickers was right—there was no silver bullet. But the Stinger came as close to one as anything could.

Less than two months after Ghaffar shot down that helicopter, Marshal Sergei Akhromeyev, chief of staff of the Soviet armed forces, told Mikhail Gorbachev that the 40th Army could not stop the supplies pouring into Afghanistan. There was no realistic military solution to the Afghanistan problem.

Gorbachev frowned. "People ask: 'What are we doing there? Will we be there endlessly? Or should we end this war?'" Gorbachev was bothered by the war he had inherited. Early in 1986, he had referred to it as a "bleeding wound." Now, he told the Politburo, "The strategic goal is to end the war in one, maximum two years, and withdraw the troops. We have set a clear goal. Help speed up the process so we have a friendly, neutral country, and get out of there."[14] It would be another year before Americans learned of the decision. That was because Gorbachev wanted his puppet, Najibullah, to pursue a policy of "national reconciliation," but he was making little progress, because the Americans, not knowing the Soviets planned to withdraw, were heavily supporting Najibullah's enemies. In September 1987, Soviet Foreign Minister Eduard Shevardnadze told U.S. Secretary of State George Shultz about the decision. Gorbachev hoped the United States would help by cutting off aid to the Afghan rebels, but Reagan told him at a summit meeting that that would be impossible.

The Soviets left anyway and left the United States with a new set of problems.

Contrary to expectations in the CIA, the Najibullah regime did not fall when the Soviets left. The various warlords in the mujahideen ranks fought each other as much as they fought Najibullah. Each was so eager to seize power when the Communist was ousted, they neglected to oust him. The Americans, disgusted with this civil war, and watching the Soviet Union disintegrate, in 1991 agreed with Russia to a mutual cessation of all aid to the Afghans. But the civil war raged on. Najibullah steadily grew weaker, and the armies of Gulbuddin Hekmatyar and Ahmed Shah Massoud approached Kabul. Each saw himself as the conqueror of the Communists: there was no cooperation. Osama bin Laden, once a disciple of Hekmatyar, was now a leader of the Arab volunteers, which had become a third factor in the civil war. He tried to mediate between the Pashtun and Tajik leaders, but to no avail. Massoud's troops fell on Hekmatyar's and drove them out of Kabul. And the war raged on. Then a brand-new force appeared.

They called themselves "Taliban" ("Students") because they were products of the madrassas Zia had established. The ISI shifted its support from the somewhat erratic Hekmatyar to the Taliban, its own creation. The Taliban gradually conquered the warlords, and the Afghan people welcomed them as peacekeepers. As they approached Kabul, Hekmatyar and Massoud allied themselves against the common enemy. Bin Laden made another move. He reportedly spent $3 million of his own money to pay off mujahideen chiefs who stood between the Taliban and Kabul.[15]

Massoud led his troops against the Taliban and was defeated, while the chiefs bribed by bin Laden looked on. Massoud withdrew to the Panjshir Valley, and Taliban troops entered Kabul and executed the imprisoned Najibullah. The Taliban proceeded to enforce Sharia (Islamic law) with a strictness that would have gladdened the heart of Muhammad ibn Abd al Wahab himself. The Taliban temporarily solved the dope problem the way the Chinese Communists earlier had solved their opium problem: they killed both opium producers and addicts.

Massoud organized what became the Northern Alliance, composed of mostly non-Pashtun tribesmen like the Iranian Tajiks and the Turkish Uzbeks. The Northern Alliance held territory in the northern part of Afghanistan. Hekmatyar broke with Massoud and became an independent, violent Islamist, ferociously anti-American. Bin Laden used his money to organize al Qaeda ("the Base"), an organization dedicated to destroying Western influence in Muslim lands and otherthrowing what bin Laden considered corrupt Muslim rulers. It was an international organization, based on the foreign fighters who had flocked to Afghanistan to fight the infidels. While in Afghanistan, many of them had been trained in the techniques of terrorism by the CIA (via the ISI).

When bin Laden was driven out of first Sa'udi Arabia, then Sudan, he came to Afghanistan, where his old friends, the Taliban, welcomed him. That, of course, resulted in the U.S. invasion of Afghanistan. Initially successful, the invasion was followed by more problems:

1. The Americans failed to capture bin Laden, who is still, probably, plotting more terrorist schemes.
2. Agents of al Qaeda assassinated Ahmed Shah Massoud, the only man who could rein in the warlords of the Northern Alliance.
3. The warlords carved up Afghanistan into a collection of robber baronies and resumed the production of opium and heroin, making Afghanistan the world's largest, by far, source of opiates.

4. The weakness of the central Afghan government and the lack of foreign troops allowed the Taliban to make a comeback in southern
   Afghanistan. And this time, Taliban power had no effect on the drug
   trade. The "holy warriors" decided that instead of eliminating opium
   and heroin, it was better to tax the producers.
5. Militant Islamism continued to grow in Pakistan, and the dictator,
   Pervez Musharraf, who had been able to keep them in check, lost
   control of this country with nuclear weapons.

The Afghan war eliminated the Soviet Union, but it gave a tremendous
boost to Islamic terrorism all over the world—in Algeria, Britain, Chechnya,
Indonesia, the Philippines, Spain, and the United States, among other
places. One lesson it should teach us is to look beyond the immediate
situation. The old adage, "The enemy of my enemy is my friend," is not
always true.

Epilogue: What Does History Show?

All guerrilla wars are different, of course, but if you look at enough, some features recur in successful wars, and other features recur in unsuccessful ones. Here are a few:

THE FISH AND THE WATER

Mao Zedong said it, but the principle was true thousands of years before Mao was born. Guerrillas have always depended on the surrounding population the way fish depend on the water they swim in. Guerrillas who lack the trust of the population occasionally win, but usually only when their opponents are similarly deprived. Mike Hoare's white mercenaries are a good example. Guevara's Cubans, although all but Che were black, were just as foreign to the Congolese. In China, where soldiers customarily robbed the peasants, Mao made sure all his troops were courteous, fair, and even generous to the people they lived among. Fred Funston talked tough at home, but in the Philippines, "his actual conduct was characterized by lenient surrender terms, rewards for collaboration and personal friendship." He went out of his way to cultivate community leaders—like the one who persuaded Aguinaldo's courier to surrender. The North Koreans in the Inch'on area showed what happens when troops don't win the "hearts and minds." An American and two South Koreans turned the whole population against their occupiers.

MOTIVATION

Successful guerrillas feel a real need to win. King Hussein's men were no match for ibn Sa'ud's because the former knew they were fighting for Hussein while the latter thought they were fighting for God. Motivation is one of the main things that made the Afghans such a formidable foe. Better weapons and training helped, too, but the Russians knew they were in for tough going before Charlie Wilson's money kicked in. In contrast look at Iraq, where troops, after training for years, still weren't reliable. (In the Korean War, troops who had only a few weeks of basic training pushed the Chinese and North Koreans across the 38th Parallel.) Most Iraqis joined the army because it was a steady job, while their enemies were motivated by

217

religion, nationalism, or both. The Irish rebels of the twenties were motivated by nationalism, but after achieving a measure of independence,
decided that full independence was not worth the agony of continued civil
war.

DISCIPLINE

It's a mistake to think of guerrillas as undisciplined mobs. Successful guerrillas may not have polished boots or know the manual of arms, but they
have discipline. They follow orders, whether they are as "military" looking as
von Lettow-Vorbeck's Schutztruppen or as ragged as Abd el-Krim's Riffian
Berbers.

LIBERATORS MUST BE CAREFUL

An outside power may help a beleaguered people and leave them grateful
for generations. Or they may find themselves bitterly hated. French help
during the American Revolution was greatly appreciated. On the other
hand, Pershing's pursuit of Villa brought the United States and Mexico to
the   brink
of war. It depends largely on the approach of the liberator. The fact that
eighteenth-century France was an absolute monarchy and twentieth-century
America was a thriving democracy meant absolutely nothing. The king of
France did not attempt to dictate policy. Woodrow Wilson did. Ed Lansdale
in the Philippines demonstrated some of the most effective ways to provide
outside help. He got Filipino officials to come up with ideas he wanted them
to express.

NOTHING SUCCEEDS LIKE SUCCESS

T. E. Lawrence found that victories, even minor ones, brought in more volunteers. A long string of minor victories is usually even better than a single
big one. A string of victories gives a unit the aura of invincibility.

PROPAGANDA IS IMPORTANT

Especially in this age of instant communication. Irish propaganda aimed at
world opinion, and especially English opinion, was the most important factor in the Irish struggle for independence.

TERROR IS NOT A GOOD STRATEGY

In the first place, it rarely terrorizes. Against all prewar expectations, the
mass bombings of civilians in World War II did not terrorize the British, the
Germans, or the Japanese. Even the two nuclear bombs merely gave the
Japanese emperor a face-saving excuse to surrender. In guerrilla war, terror
usually provokes counterterror, and the habit of indiscriminate killing takes

on a life of its own. Algeria is a good example. The war with France was over long ago, but Algeria is still coping with terrorists.

CONCENTRATION CAMPS RARELY WORK

Depriving the "fish" of their "water" by locking up the water sounds like a good idea, but it's seldom successful. An occupying power has a hard time cutting guerrillas off from ALL food, weapons, and ammunition. They are usually able to smuggle some in from the outside and often able to steal more from the enemy. On the negative side, concentration camps are public relations disasters.

Notes

CHAPTER 1

1. Jameson had been impressed with the performance of the water-cooled Maxim machine gun against charging Matabeles. He equipped his column with Maxims and assured the troops that with this superweapon they would be invincible. But he forgot to take along water to fill the guns' water jackets, and the Maxims quickly became useless. John Ellis, *The Social History of the Machine Gun* (New York: Random House, 1993), 91.

2. One of these weapons, a 155mm gun, nicknamed "Long Tom," was actually the direct ancestor of the U.S. 155mm gun, the famous "Long Tom" of World War II.

3. The Africans who were the victims of this weapon called it the "pom-pom" because of the noise it made. The name stuck and was applied to the automatic antiaircraft cannons used in World War II. W. H. B. Smith, *Small Arms of the World* (Harrisburg, PA: Stackpole, 1960), 101.

4. Bruce I. Gudmundsson, *Stormtroop Tactics* (Westport, CT: Praeger, 1995), 20.

5. Ibid., 1.

6. Col. R. Meinertzhagen, *Army Diary, 1899–1920* (Edinburgh: Oliver and Boyd, 1960), 15.

7. Thomas Pakenham, *The Boer War* (New York: Random House, 1979), 143.

8. Ibid., 419.

9. Ibid., 418.

10. Richard Harding Davis, *Notes of a War Correspondent* (New York: Scribner's, 1910), 141–42.

11. The British used an elongated shell suitable for use in rifled cannons that was a development of the spherical shot shell invented by Lt. Henry Shrapnel.

12. Byron Farwell, *Queen Victoria's Little Wars* (New York: Norton, 1972), 340.

13. Kitchener recaptured Khartoum, which had been taken by the Mahdi, after the battle of Omdurman. Omdurman consisted basically of British and Egyptian troops forming squares and mowing down hordes of spear- and sword-wielding Sudanese with repeating rifles and machine guns. One witness said, "It was not a battle, but an execution." John Ellis, *Social History of the Machine Gun,* 86. Kitchener did not exactly display tactical genius.

14. Pakenham, *Boer War,* 363.

15. Farwell, *Little Wars,* 352.

16. Pakenham, *Boer War,* 423.

17. Ibid., 520.

18. Thomas Pakenham, *The Scramble for Africa* (New York: Random House, 1991), 578.

CHAPTER 2

1. David Haward Bain, *Sitting in Darkness: Americans in the Philippines* (Boston: Houghton Mifflin, 1984), 90.
2. Ibid., 57; G. J. A. O'Toole, *The Spanish War: An American Epic, 1898* (New York: Norton, 1984), 96.
3. Bain, *Sitting in Darkness*, 57.
4. Ibid., 72.
5. William Weir, "The Guns of the Philippine Wars . . . As Much Myth as Fact," in *Gun Digest* (1992), 6.
6. The first American soldiers in the Philippines were volunteers, like Funston's. Volunteers were armed with the .45-70 caliber Springfield rifle, a single-shot rifle firing a black powder cartridge. Regulars, and later volunteers, got the .30–40 caliber Krag, a repeater using smokeless cartridges. It was a good rifle, but not as good as the Mauser.
7. *Bolo* is Philippine Spanish for a large knife, usually shorter than the Cuban machete but used for the same kind of jobs. It is sometimes confused with *bolas,* a Patagonian missile weapon consisting of three stone balls connected with thongs, which is thrown by hand.
8. O'Toole, *Spanish War,* 91.
9. Bain, *Sitting in Darkness*, 77.
10. O'Toole, *Spanish War,* 388; Bain, *Sitting in Darkness,* 184–85.
11. Bain, *Sitting in Darkness,* 185; Veltisezar Bautista, *The Philippine-American War (1899–1902),* excerpted from *The Philipino Americans: From 1763 to the Present: Their History, Culture, and Traditions,* 2nd ed. (accessed January 18, 2007). http://www.filipino-americans.colfilamwar.html
12. Brian McAllister Linn, *The U.S. Army and Counterinsurgency in the Philippine War, 1899–1902* (Chapel Hill, NC: University of North Carolina Press, 1989), 76.
13. Bain, *Sitting in Darkness,* 98.
14. Ibid., 210.
15. Frederick Funston, "The Capture of Emilio Aguinaldo: A Personal Account of the Exploit Which Ended the War in the Philippines," *Everybody's Magazine,* March 1901.
16. Ibid.
17. O'Toole, *Spanish War,* 394.
18. Ibid., 395.
19. Ibid.
20. Julian S. Hatcher, *Textbook of Pistols and Revolvers* (Plantersville, SC: Small Arms Technical Publishing Company, 1935), 413–14.
21. George Cameron Stone, *A Glossary of the Construction, Decoration and Use of Arms and Armor* (New York: Jack Bussel, 1934), 67.
22. The late Joseph E. Smith, chief of the Army's Combat Systems Division in a letter to the author. Smith's father was a soldier in Moroland.
23. Jolo got its name from a Spanish misunderstanding of Sulu.
24. Leonard Wood was Theodore Roosevelt's personal physician when TR was assistant secretary of the navy. He and Roosevelt organized the Rough Riders, and Wood stayed in the army after the Spanish-American War.

CHAPTER 3

1. Herbert Molloy Mason, Jr., *The Great Pursuit* (New York: Random House, 1970), 27–28, quoting Anita Brenner and George Leighton, *The Wind That Swept Mexico* (New York: Harper, 1943).
2. Jim Tuck, "Usurper: The Dark Shadow of Victoriano Huerta," www.mexconnect.com/mex_/history_/jtuck/jtvhuerta.html (accessed January 30, 2007). Huerta was addicted to brandy; Villa, a teetotaler, to women.
3. Burke Wilkinson, *The Zeal of the Convert: The Life of Erskine Childers* (Sag Harbor, NY: Second Chance Press, 1985), 165.
4. Under Huerta, eighty-four congressmen were imprisoned and a number of them murdered. At least thirty-five political opponents were murdered during his seventeen months in office. Josh Burnham, "Victoriano Huerta: Excellent General or Terrible Tyrant?" http://historicaltextarchive.com/sections.php?op=viewarticle&artid=549 (accessed January 30, 2007). Martin Donell Kohout, "Victoriano Huerta," http://www.tsha.utexas.edu/handbook/online/articles/HH/fhu81.html (accessed January 30, 2007).
5. Huerta promised Madero and his vice president, José Pino Suárez, to spare their lives if they would resign. They did, and the minister of foreign affairs, Pedro Lascurain, automatically became president. He then appointed Huerta minister of foreign affairs. Then Lascurain resigned and Huerta became president.
6. Mason, *Great Pursuit*, 35–36.
7. Ibid., 36.
8. Kohout, "Victoriano Huerta".
9. Mason, *Great Pursuit*, 37
10. Ibid., 43.
11. Luke S. Weir, the author's father.
12. Funston, a former volunteer with rebel forces in Cuba, won a Medal of Honor in the Philippines and later, in the most daring coup in that, or any other, guerrilla struggle, captured Emilio Aguinaldo, the *insurrecto* president of the Philippines.
13. Jay Monaghan, ed., *The Book of the American West* (New York: Bonanza, 1963), 419.
14. Mason, *Great Pursuit*, 51.
15. Ibid., 39–40.
16. He later came to the United States, where he was arrested for conspiring to violate U.S. neutrality. He died of cirrhosis of the liver while in custody.
17. During the meeting, Villa told Scott that only two weeks earlier he had been approached by a Japanese naval officer who asked what Mexico would do if Japan attacked the United States. "I told him that if Japan makes war on the United States, she would find that all the resources of Mexico would be used against her," Villa said (Mason, *Great Pursuit*, 59). The incident shows that the rivalry between the navies of the two Pacific powers was of much greater duration that most landlubbers and almost all Europeans understand.
18. "Troop" in the cavalry was the unit called "company" in the infantry.
19. Julian S. Hatcher, *Hatcher's Notebook* (Pittsburgh, PA: Telegraph Press, 1962), 93.
20. Mason, *Great Pursuit*, 78. But Pershing's most important action in the Philippines—defeating the Sultan of Sulu at the battle of Bagsak Mountain, didn't occur until 1913—seven years after the promotion.

21. William Weir, *The Encyclopedia of African American Military History* (Amherst, NY: Prometheus Books, 2004), 268. Pershing got the nickname Black Jack because of his service with the 10th. But in spite of his admiration and affection for the black soldiers during the Spanish American War, during World War I, he authored a secret memo to French officers advising them not to fraternize with the black American soldiers serving in French units. Ibid., 231–32.

22. Patton, according to legend, tried to lighten the trigger pull on his automatic, but he lightened it too much. One day, he stamped his foot and the gun went off, wounding him in the leg (Edward C. Ezell, *Handguns of the World* [New York: Barnes & Noble, 1993], 636). That, supposedly, is why he always favored revolvers, especially the Colt Single Action Army, which was the regulation sidearm in 1873. Patton represented the United States in the 1912 Olympics on the modern pentathlon team, in which competitors vie in pistol shooting, as well as fencing, riding, running, and swimming. So he must have understood the rules of gun safety. Why he was carrying a cocked automatic with the safety off—the only way it could possibly have fired—the legend does not say. At any rate, the report of the future general's shooting in Mexico, witnessed by other soldiers, is far more credible than MacArthur's tale of potting seven mounted Villistas with his tiny derringer while riding a railroad handcar.

23. Mason, *Great Pursuit*, 97.

24. Ibid., 199.

25. By German aerial observers in 1915.

26. But Washington wouldn't take the sword either. Cornwallis had sent out O'Hara to surrender because his ego was badly bruised. Washington refused to accept the sword of a subordinate, so he sent O'Hara to Gen. Benjamin Lincoln, the American second in command.

CHAPTER 4

1. Peter Hathaway Capstick, *Warrior* (New York: St. Martin's, 1998), 61.

2. Richard Meinertzhagen. *Army Diary (1899–1926)* (Edinburgh: Oliver and Boyd, 1960), 10.

3. Edwin P. Hoyt, *Guerrilla: Colonel von Lettow-Vorbeck and Germany's East African* (Empire, NY: Macmillan, 1981), 31; Meinertzhagen, *Army Diary*, 84.

4. Hoyt, *Guerrilla*, 39; Meinertzhagen, *Army Diary*, 89.

5. Meinertzhagen, *Army Diary*, 93; Capstick, *Warrior*, 188.

6. Hoyt, *Guerrilla*, 118.

7. John Ellis, *The Social History of the Machine Gun* (New York: Random House, 1975), 116.

8. W. H. B. Smith, *Small Arms of the World: A Basic Manual of Military Small Arms* (Harrisburg, PA: Stackpole, 1960), 301, 453.

9. Hoyt, *Guerrilla*, 88.

10. Meinertzhagen, *Army Diary*, 165.

11. John T. Greenwood, ed., *Milestones of Aviation* (New York: Crescent Books, 1991), 29.

12. John Toland, *Ships in the Sky: The Story of the Great Dirigibles* (New York: Holt, 1957), 56.

13. Hoyt, *Guerrilla*, 5.

CHAPTER 5

1. T. E. Lawrence, *Seven Pillars of Wisdom* (New York: Dell, 1962), 195.

2. Ibid.
3. Ibid., 196.
4. T. E. Lawrence, *Revolt in the Desert* (London: Jonathan Cape, 1927), 97.
5. Ibid., 280.
6. Lawrence, *Seven Pillars*, 196.

CHAPTER 6

1. W. Bruce Lincoln, *Red Victory: A History of the Russian Civil War* (New York: Simon & Schuster, 1989), 32, quoting a secret telegram sent January 14, 1917, by M. Paleologue to the French Ministry of Foreign Affairs.
2. John Keegan, *The Second World War* (New York: Knopf, 1999), 309–71.
3. Ibid., 335.
4. Lincoln, *Red Victory*, 40.
5. Ibid.
6. Keegan, *Second World War*, 389, quoting E. Mawdsley, *The Russian Civil War*, 27.
7. Lincoln, *Red Victory*, 239.
8. Ibid.

CHAPTER 7

1. J. F. C. Fuller, *A Military History of the Western World*, vol. 3 (New York: Da Capo, 1957), 334.
2. Ibid., 340.

CHAPTER 8

1. The IRB Oath: "The Supreme Council of the Irish Republican Brotherhood is hereby declared in fact, as well as by right, the sole government of the Irish Republic. Its enactments shall be the laws of the Irish Republic until Ireland secures absolute National Independence, and a permanent Republican Government is established. The President of the Irish Republican Brotherhood is in fact as well as by right President of the Irish Republic." Tim Pat Coogan, *Eamon de Valera: The Man Who Was Ireland* (New York: Barnes & Noble, 1999), 43–44. This oath was to cause trouble in Ireland for years.
2. Max Caulfield, *The Easter Rebellion: Dublin 1916* (Boulder, CO: Roberts Rinehart, 1995), 291–93.
3. Ernie O'Malley, *On Another Man's Wounds* (Dublin: Anvil, 1979), 40.
4. Calton Younger, *Ireland's Civil War* (New York: Harper Collins, 1986), 108.
5. Andrew Boyle, *The Riddle of Erskine Childers* (London: Hutchinson, 1977), 265.
6. Tom Barry, *Guerrilla Days in Ireland* (Boulder, CO: Roberts Rinehart, 1995), 50.
7. Ernie O'Malley, *The Singing Flame* (Dublin: Anvil, 1997), 12.
8. Frank O'Connor, *The Big Fellow: Michael Collins and the Irish Revolution* (Dublin: Clonmore & Reynolds, 1965), 145–46.
9. Frank O'Connor, *An Only Child* (New York: Knopf, 1961), 211.
10. Ibid., 233; Burke Wilkinson, *The Zeal of the Convert: The Life of Erskine Childers* (Sag Harbor, NY: Second Chance Press, 1985), 217.
11. Boyle, *Riddle of Childers*, 288.
12. O'Connor, *The Big Fellow*, 145–46; Wilkinson, *Zeal of Convert*, 201.
13. O'Connor, *An Only Child*, 232.

CHAPTER 9

1. Douglas Porch, *The Conquest of Morocco* (New York: Farrar, Straus and Giroux, 1982), 9.
2. Ibid.
3. Perdicaris had a Greek father and an American mother. Roosevelt, of course, assumed that he was an American citizen. But his mother had owned property in South Carolina that was in danger of being confiscated by the Confederate government during the Civil War. In 1863, Perdicaris had gone to Greece to acquire Greek citizenship and so block the confiscation. In so doing, he also forfeited his American citizenship.
4. Biographies: Abd el-Krim, http://www.Balagan.org.uk/war/iberia1909/personalities.htm (accessed February 22, 2007).
5. 1911–1927 Rif War/Second Moroccan War: Chronology, 3, http://www.balagan.org.uk/war/iberia/1909/index.htm (accessed February 22, 2007).
6. These figures are from Wikipedia, "The Battle of Annual," http://www.en.wikipedia.org/wiki/Disaster_of_Annual (accessed February 22, 2007). Antony Beevor in *The Battle for Spain: The Spanish Civil War 1936–1939* (New York: Penguin, 2006), 16, says 10,000 Spanish were killed and 4,000 taken prisoner. He adds, "A week later, another major position was lost, another 7,000 soldiers were massacred and all the officers were led away in chains." Presumably, that refers to Monte Arruit. What is indisputable is that for the Spanish, the Anual campaign was a disaster.
7. In *Beau Geste* the bodies of dead soldiers were used instead of straw-filled uniforms.

CHAPTER 10

1. Although during the recent fighting in the Balkans, a Bosnian Muslim was quoted as saying, "Muhammad said you shouldn't drink wine, but he didn't say anything about slivovitz."

CHAPTER 11

1. Chiang attended the Paoting Military Academy in northern China, but to further his military education, he enrolled in the Japanese Military Academy and served in the Japanese Army from 1907 to 1911. He left Japan when the Chinese Revolution began and returned to lead a revolt in his native province. During the revolt against Yuan Shi-k'ai, who tried to make himself emperor, he was defeated and hid out in Shanghai. He joined the Green Gang, one of the world's oldest criminal organizations, which once specialized in financial manipulation and is now involved in drug trafficking. (On the Green Gang, see Alfred W. McCoy, *The Politics of Heroin* (Brooklyn, NY: Lawrence Hill, 1991), 14–15.) He was arrested several times, once for armed robbery, but became a trusted aide of Sun Yat-sen. As a leader of Sun's military arm, he solidified Sun's control of the southern provinces. See Trevor N. Dupuy, *The Harper Encyclopedia of Military Biography* (Edison, NJ: Castle Books, 1992), 159–60.
2. Mao Tse-tung, *On Guerrilla Warfare* (New York: Frederick A. Praeger, 1962), 93.
3. Ibid., 92.
4. Ibid., 110.
5. Ibid., 111.
6. Ibid., 97.

7. Ibid., 103.
8. Sun Tzu, *The Art of War* (New York: Oxford University Press, 1971), 66.
9. Mao, *Guerrilla Warfare*, 113.
10. The strategy did not work in the Korean War, because the Koreans hated the Chinese. A lone Chinese could find either South or North Korea a dangerous place. Early in the war, a Chinese liaison officer, Col. Wong Lichan, narrowly escaped being executed as a spy by the North Koreans. See Russell Spurr, *Enter the Dragon* (New York: Newmarket Press, 1988), 92–103.

CHAPTER 12

1. Christopher Sykes, *Orde Wingate* (London: Collins, 1959), 136.
2. Leonard Mosley, *Gideon Goes to War: The Story of Major General Orde C. Wingate* (New York: Scribner's, 1955), 48.
3. Ibid., 57.
4. Ibid., 58.
5. Hugh Foot, *A Start in Freedom* (New York: Harper & Row, 1964), 52.
6. Mosley, *Gideon Goes to War*, 63–64.
7. He wrote, "Orde Charles Wingate, D.S.O. is a good soldier, but so far as Palestine is concerned, he is a security risk. He cannot be trusted. He puts the interests of the Jews before those of his own country. He should not be allowed in Palestine again." (Ibid., 95.)
8. Ibid., 109.
9. Sykes, *Orde Wingate*, 248–49; Trevor Royle, *Orde Wingate, Irregular Soldier* (London: Weidenfeld & Nicolson, 1995), 182–83.
10. Ibid., 291; Mosley, *Gideon Goes to War*, 127–29.
11. Royle, *Wingate: Irregular Soldier*, 187.
12. A Zionist doctor, Ben Zion Koumine, got him an interview with Lord Horder, honorary physician to the king. Chaim Weizmann gave Lord Horder his personal guarantee of Wingate's sanity. So did his cousin, Sir Reginald Wingate.
13. Derek Tulloch. *Wingate in Peace and War* (London: Macdonald, 1972), 265.

CHAPTER 13

1. John Keegan, *The Second World War* (New York: Penguin, 1990), 154.
2. Not submachine guns, or *maschinenepistolen,* as the Germans call them. They were modifications of the old Mauser C 96 pistols (the Model 1932) capable of full automatic fire.
3. See http://www.historylearningsite.co.uk/resistance_movement_in_yugoslavi. htm (accessed March 20, 2007).
4. David Mountfield, *The Partisans* (London: Hamlyn, 1979), 128.
5. Ibid., 140.
6. Ibid.
7. P. W. Singer, *Corporate Warriors* (Ithaca, NY: Cornell University Press, 2003), 127.

CHAPTER 14

1. Bevin Alexander, *Korea: The First War We Lost* (New York: Hippocrene Books, 1996), 148.
2. Eugene Franklin Clark, *The Secrets of Inchon* (New York: Berkley Books, 2002), 6.

3. The author remembers a South Korean during this war who, whenever he heard "Japan" or "Japanese," would say, "Forty (expletive deleted) years!" and spit.

4. In most navies, "captain" is a job as well as a rank. Any officer commanding a ship, even an ensign or a lieutenant (junior grade) is captain of that ship and is addressed as such. A captain is also a rank (wearing four stripes in the U.S. Navy) just below an admiral. A naval captain is theoretically equivalent to an army colonel but, as a result of centuries of naval tradition, usually has more power and prestige than most colonels. In the U.S. Navy, all officers up to commander are addressed as "Mister."

5. Clark, *Secrets of Inchon*, 27.

6. Ibid., 90.

7. Ibid., 115.

8. Ibid., 116.

9. Ibid., 164.

10. William Manchester, *American Caesar: Douglas MacArthur, 1880–1964* (New York: Dell, 1978), 316.

CHAPTER 15

1. William Manchester, *American Caesar: Douglas MacArthur, 1880–1964* (New York: Dell, 1978), 188. The pre–World War II Philippines had a commonwealth constitution, with a president and two-house congress. The commonwealth had its own money and its own army, the Philippine Constabulary. Until the nation became independent July 4, 1946, the government was overseen by an American high commissioner.

2. Edward Geary Lansdale, *In the Midst of Wars: An American's Mission to Southeast Asia* (New York: Harper & Row, 1972), 10.

3. Cecil B. Curry, *Edward Lansdale: The Unquiet American* (Boston: Houghton Mifflin, 1988), 27.

4. Ibid., 28–29.

5. Ibid., 39.

6. Ibid., 40. After his first wife died, Lansdale married Pat Kelly.

7. Ibid., 43–44.

8. Ibid., 44.

9. Ibid., 71.

10. Ibid., 45.

11. Lansdale, *Midst of Wars*, 83.

12. Curry, *Edward Lansdale*, 44-45.

13. Ibid., 87.

14. For more on Lansdale's work in Vietnam, see William Weir, *Soldiers in the Shadows* (Franklin Lakes, NJ: New Page, 2002), 220–29.

CHAPTER 16

1. Bernard B. Fall, *Hell in a Very Small Place* (Philadelphia: Lippincott, 1967), 47.

2. Ibid., 35–36.

3. Ibid., 40.

4. Phillip Davidson, *Vietnam at War* (New York: Oxford University Press, 1988), 189.

5. Fall, *Hell in a Small Place*, 88.

6. Ibid., 101.

7. It has been reported that Lt. Col. Pierre Langlais and a group of paratroop officers confronted Castries and told him that while he was nominally in com-

mand, Langlais was taking over. This has been confirmed by others, including Langlais. The story seems somewhat exaggerated, however. Langlais and Castries remained friendly and continued to play cards with each other whenever they had time. And Castries, not Langlais, ordered the counterattack on the Viet Minh AA guns. That was well after the alleged coup. Still later, Langlais ordered Bigeard to retreat from outpost Eliane. Bigeard refused, indicating that Langlais's word was not necessarily law. And if there was a change in command, it didn't change the results.

8. Davidson (*Vietnam at War*, 261), says TOT was a French innovation. The author personally witnessed TOT being used in Korea in 1952.
9. French Defense Ministry Archives.
10. Fall, *Hell in a Small Place*, 438.

CHAPTER 17

1. Colons were not only French. They came from just about anywhere in southern Europe. People of Spanish, Italian, and Maltese descent were especially plentiful. There is some mystery as to why they were called pieds noirs—black feet. There are several stories, but none is very probable.
2. Alistair Horne, *A Savage War of Peace* (New York: New York Review of Books, 2006), 27.
3. Ibid., 28.
4. Ibid., 101–2.
5. Ibid., 221.
6. Ibid., 110.
7. Ibid., 122.
8. Ibid., 184.
9. Actually, relations between the Communists and the FLN were never good. The Algerian Communist Party, mostly colons, was a major participant in the 1945 ratonnnade following the Setif uprising. Later, the Communists tried to take over the FLN, which resulted in a couple of massacres of Communists by the Algerian nationalists.
10. For more information on Trinquier, a specialist in unconventional warfare, promoter of the heroin trade, Congo mercenary, and advocate of suppressing civil liberties to fight insurrection, see *The Politics of Heroin* by Alfred W. McCoy (Chicago: Lawrence Hill Books, 1991) and his own *Modern Warfare* (Westport, CT: Praeger, 2006).
11. Teitgen was opposed to the use of torture. He tried to resign, but was begged to stay at his post. Thinking he might do something to mitigate the barbarity, he stayed for a while and made some improvements, but finally could not take it any longer and left government service.
12. Horne, *Savage War*, 282.
13. Ibid., 287.
14. Ibid., 340.
15. Ibid., 344–45.
16. They were also involved in a gang war of sorts with other Algerian groups in France, the so-called café wars.
17. In his *Battle of Algiers*, Pontecorvo presents this as a purely spontaneous outbreak for no apparent cause. There is no mention of the pied noir riots on the previous two days or the attempt to have Muslims join an anti–de Gaulle protest. In fact, there is no mention of de Gaulle or his visit at all, and there is

no mention of the months of organizing the FLN had put in. The second "riot" shown was not a protest but a celebration. The United Nations had just decided that Algeria should have self-determination. Neither mob action had much effect on the Algerians' struggle for independence. The film is, of course, a brilliant work of propaganda.

18. Horne, *Savage War,* 455.

19. Ibid., 457.

20. The Secret Army Organization was founded by an ex-paratrooper and an ex-legionnaire when the plotting for the Generals' Putsch was just beginning. It included the most extreme elements among the soldiers and the pieds noirs. A number of copycat organizations sprang up among the pieds noirs, all of them killing almost indiscriminately in a vain attempt to derail peace negotiations. They were aided in this effort by the FLN, which began murdering colons as well as Arabs and Berbers suspected of being soft on France.

21. Horne, *Savage War,* 538.

CHAPTER 18

1. Ernesto Guevara de la Serna, *The Motorcycle Diaries* (London: Verso, 1994).

2. Ernesto Guevara de la Serna, *Back on the Road: A Journey through Latin America* published in Spanish as *Otra Vez* (New York: Grove Press, 2001).

3. Ibid.

4. The United Fruit Company was one of the principal landowners in Guatemala. It began complaining to the U.S. government that Arbenz was a Communist proxy. John Foster Dulles, secretary of state, and his brother, Allen, director of the CIA, had ties to United Fruit through their former law firm. Walter Bedell Smith, undersecretary of state and a retired general close to President Dwight D. Eisenhower, had once sought a management position at United Fruit. All three were United Fruit stockholders. United Fruit had been lobbying the CIA to oust Arbenz's predecessor, Juan Arvalo, who had begun land reform, but it got no action until Eisenhower became president.

5. Jon Lee Anderson, *Che Guevara: A Revolutionary Life* (New York: Grove Press, 1997), 271–72.

6. Ramon Eduardo Ruiz, *Cuba: The Making of a Revolution* (New York: W. W. Norton, 1968), 15.

7. Ernesto Guevara de la Serna, *Guerrilla Warfare* (Lincoln, NE: University of Nebraska Press, 1985), 47.

8. See http://en.wikipedia.org/wiki/Cuban_Revolution (accessed July 31, 2007), 3.

9. Anderson, *Che Guevara,* 360.

10. Even after Castro proclaimed his own Communism, Moscow was annoyed with him for bypassing the regular Cuban Communist Party. And it was looking for allies who would side with the Soviets against the Chinese. Similarly, Beijing was looking for allies against Moscow. Castro sided with neither. Little Algeria asked for nothing and remained grateful for the large quantity of American weapons, which Castro captured from Batista and then smuggled in to the FLN during its war for independence.

11. Ernesto Guevara de la Serna, *The African Dream,* introduction by Richard Gott, (New York: Grove Press, 2001), xii–xiii.

12. Ibid., xxiii.

13. The tangled history of the Congo in the 1960s is covered in more detail in Chapter 19.
14. Antonio Maceo, one of the leading Cuban generals in the 1890s revolt against Spain, was black.
15. In spite of rumors to the contrary, Castro and Guevara remained close. When he went to the Congo, Guevara had written to Castro giving up his Cuban citizenship and all his honors. He was devoting his life, he said, to creating a Third World alliance of poor nations in South America, Africa, and Asia against U.S. imperialism.
16. *The World Almanac and Book of Facts* (Stamford, CT: Griffin, 1999), 768.
17. Peter Kornbluh, National Security Electronic Briefing Book No. 5. The Death of Che Guevara: Declassified. CIA, Intelligence Information Cable, October 17, 1967. http://www.gwu.edu/~nsarchiv/NSAEBB/NSAEBB5/index.html (accessed August 2, 2007).

CHAPTER 19
1. Colonel Mike Hoare, *Mercenary* (New York: Bantam, 1979), 39–40.
2. *Heart of Darkness: The Tragedy of the Congo, 1960–67,* http://worldatwar.net/chandelle/v2/v2n3/congo.html (accessed August 15, 2007).
3. Trinquier's enterprise was stymied by Tshombe's Belgian advisors, who saw it (probably correctly) as a French scheme to supplant Belgium's influence in Katanga. Trinquier went home and became a wine grower, but most of the men who went to the Congo with him stayed as part of Katanga's *Compagnie Internationale.*
4. The uranium that went into World War II's atomic bombs came from Katanga.
5. Katanga's union with the rest of the Congo went back no further than King Leopold and his agent, Henry Morton Stanley. In the mid-nineteenth century, a chief named Msiri traded copper, ivory, and slaves for guns and gunpowder and used them to found the kingdom called Garanganza, from which the name Katanga is derived. Msiri was killed in 1891 by a Belgian expedition led by William Grant Stairs, a lieutenant of Stanley. Even after its integration with the Congo, Katanga retained a large measure of autonomy until 1933.
6. Anthony Mockler, *The New Mercenaries* (New York: Paragon House, 1987), 47.
7. The Simbas got arms and ammunition as well as other supplies from the European Communist countries and also from Uganda, Tanzania, Algeria, and Egypt.
8. Hoare, *Mercenary,* 84.
9. Maj. Thomas P. Odom, *Dragon Operations: Hostage Rescues in the Congo* (Fort Leavenworth, KS: U.S Army Command and General Staff College), 83.
10. For a detailed description of this parachute operation—actually two operations, *Dragon Rouge* in Stanleyville and *Dragon Noir* in Paulis—see Major Odom's Leavenworth paper.
11. Hoare, *Mercenary,* 302.
12. Ibid.
13. Mobutu ruled the Congo for thirty-two years. In 1984, while his impoverished country's infrastructure was crumbling and inflation raged, he had stashed away an estimated $5 billion in Swiss banks. He was overthrown May 16, 1997, and died of cancer while exiled in Morocco on September 7, 1997.

14. P. W. Singer's *Corporate Warriors* (Ithaca, NY: Cornell University Press, 2003) and Robert Young Pelton's *Licensed to Kill* (New York: Crown, 2006) provide good overviews of this new breed of mercenaries.
15. Lt. Col. Alison Weir, J.D., *Contractors on the Battlefield: A Legal Primer* (Maxwell AFB, Alabama: Air University, 2004), 70-71.

CHAPTER 20

1. Frances FitzGerald, *Fire in the Lake: The Vietnamese and the Americans in Vietnam* (New York: Vintage, 1973), 165–67.
2. Robert Pisor, *The End of the Line: The Siege of Khe Sanh* (New York: Ballentine, 1982), 42.
3. Ibid.
4. Cecil B. Currey, "An Officer and a Gentleman." In *Nobody Gets off the Bus: The Viet Nam Generation Big Book*, vol. 5, nos. 1–4, March 1994. http://www3.iath. Virginia.edu/sixties/HTM_docs/Texts/Scholarly/Currey_Giap.html (accessed August 26, 2007).
5. "Viet Nam" in Chinese means "South Viets." Who were the North Viets? Today, we call them Cantonese. The North Viets had been absorbed into the empire of China.
6. Pisor, *End of the Line*, 126.
7. Sun Tzu, *The Art of War,* translated by Samuel B. Griffith (New York: Oxford University Press, 1963), 66.
8. The vibrations picked up by seismic sensors, for example, depended on how much and what kind of activity hidden enemies were engaged in. The sweat analyzers' readings also varied with human activity and the temperature; the urine analyzers on sanitation discipline.
9. Michael Herr, *Dispatches* (New York: Knopf, 1977), 105.
10. Ibid., 105–6.
11. Pisor, *End of the Line*, 98.
12. *New York Times,* January 26, 1968.
13. *Time*, March 1, 1968.
14. Pisor, *End of the Line*, 238.
15. Ibid., 218.
16. Ibid.
17. *New York Times*, April 10, 1968.
18. Bernard C. Nalty, *Air Power and the Fight for Khe Sanh* (Washington: Office of Air Force History, 1973), 103.

CHAPTER 21

1. Interview with Zbigniew Brzezinski in *Le Nouvel Observateur,* January 15–21, 1998.
2. Mir Azaad Khan Baloch, *End of Durand Line,* afghanland.com/history/ durrand.html (accessed September 15, 2007). W. P. S. Sidhu, "Why the Durand Line Is Important" *Indian Express* (Bombay), November 16, 1999.
3. Christopher Andrew and Vasili Mitrokhin, *The World Was Going Our Way: The KGB and the Battle for the Third World* (New York: Basic Books, 2005), 389.
4. It's also the old name (in English) for Pashtuns, as readers of Rudyard Kipling's stories know.
5. Alfred McCoy, *The Politics of Heroin: CIA Complicity in the Global Drug Trade* (Brooklyn, NY: Lawrence Hill Books, 1991), 458. *New York Times,* June 18, 1986.

Nasim Akhunzda and Gulbuddin Hekmatyar later fought a war when Hekmatyar tried to seize some of the mullah's land and a heroin factory. Hekmatyar
lost, but Akhunzda died.

6. McCoy, *Politics of Heroin*, 456. U.S. State Department Bureau of Narcotics Matters, *International Narcotics Control Strategy Report*, 1990, 290–91.

7. Brian Cloughley, "Charlie Wilson and Pakistan," *Counterpunch*, August 14, 2003,
http://www.counterpunch.org/cloughley08142003.html; Steve Coll, *Ghost Wars*
(New York: Penguin, 2004), 67.

8. George Crile, *Charlie Wilson's War* (New York: Atlantic Monthly Press, 2003), 210.

9. This was just a few years after another superpower, using far more troops and
heavy weapons in another primitive land, was forced to leave Vietnam. One
wonders how all these "experts" gained their reputations for expertise.

10. In 1985, a group of right-wingers, including Richard Perle and Oliver North,
came up with a plan to win the war. The rebels would set up loudspeakers and
induce the Russian troops to desert with such exhortations as "Lay down your
arms, there is passage to the West and to freedom." It was based on the notion
that all Russians felt that they were enslaved and yearning to taste Western freedom. CIA agents tried to explain that the Russians were terrified of what would
happen to them if they ended up in the hands of the guerrillas. Perle and company insisted that the CIA find and send to the States the many Russian defectors they believed were in Afghanistan. The agency paid the rebels $50,000 for
any prisoners—not just defectors—they had. There were no defectors, but they
got two who had been captured in battle. Both had been tortured and raped so
much they were mental basket cases. See Crile, *Charlie Wilson's War*, 331–33.

11. Ibid., 17.

12. In both Pakistan's Northwest Frontier and Afghanistan's mountains, small
workshops had been turning out excellent copies of the British Lee Enfield for
years. That was another reason for the early emphasis on Lee Enfields.

13. For example, Peter G. Kokalis of *Shotgun News*. What makes the AK-47 more
desirable than the Lee Enfield is that it is selective fire, that is, it is capable of
both semiautomatic and automatic fire. In semiautomatic mode, it fires one
shot each time the trigger is pulled. There is no need to manually cock and
reload. In automatic mode, it fires automatically as long as the trigger is held
back. The cartridge is of relatively low power to facilitate automatic fire. Automatic fire is desirable for such tasks as spraying brush in which enemy troops
are believed to be hiding and firing at night when sights are not visible. There
is also a legend among ordnance men that most troops can't hit anything with
a single bullet at ranges much greater than 100 yards.

14. Coll, *Ghost Wars*, 158.

15. Ibid., 332.

Index

Page number in italics indicates illustrations.

Stackpole Military History Series

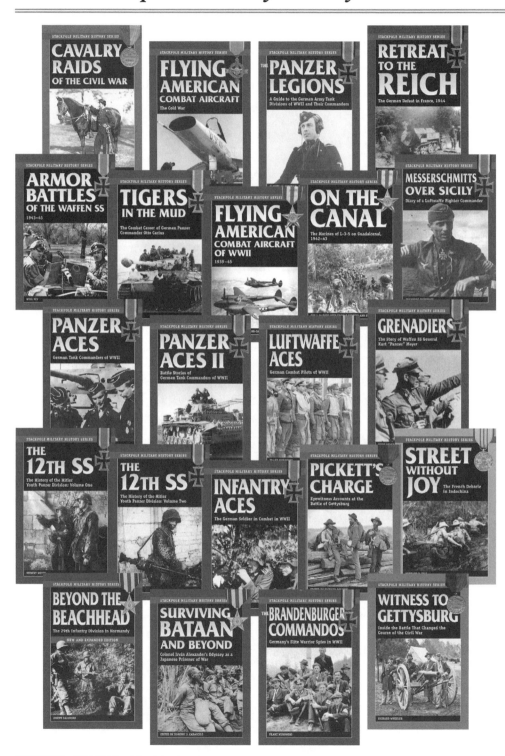

Real battles. Real soldiers. Real stories.

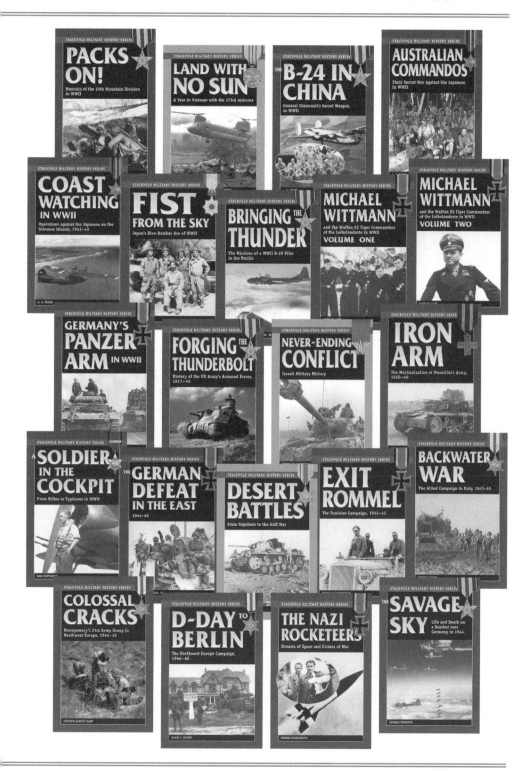

Stackpole Military History Series

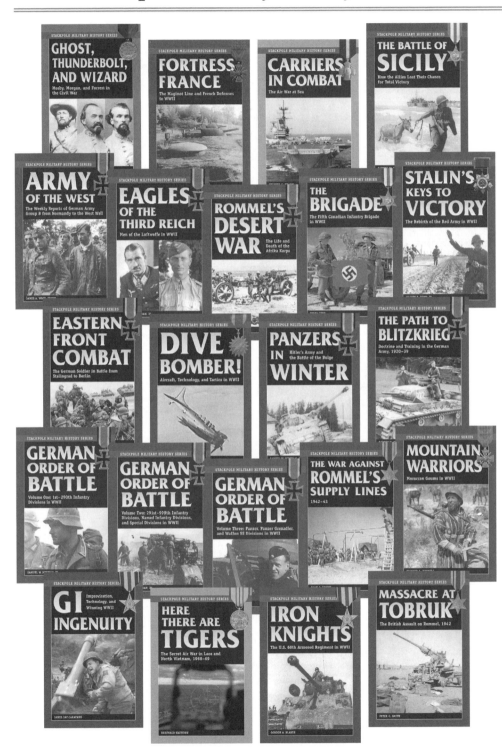

Real battles. Real soldiers. Real stories.

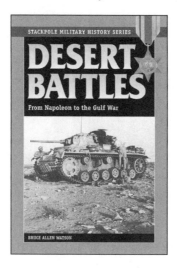

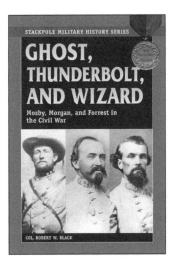

Stackpole Military History Series

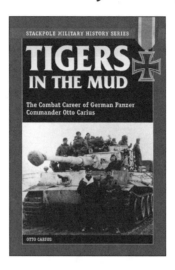

TIGERS IN THE MUD
THE COMBAT CAREER OF GERMAN PANZER
COMMANDER OTTO CARIUS

Otto Carius,
translated by Robert J. Edwards

World War II began with a metallic roar as the
German Blitzkrieg raced across Europe, spearheaded
by the most dreadful weapon of the twentieth century:
the Panzer. Tank commander Otto Carius thrusts the
reader into the thick of battle, replete with the
blood, smoke, mud, and gunpowder so common
to the elite German fighting units.

$19.95 • Paperback • 6 x 9 • 368 pages
51 photos • 48 illustrations • 3 maps

WWW.STACKPOLEBOOKS.COM
1-800-732-3669

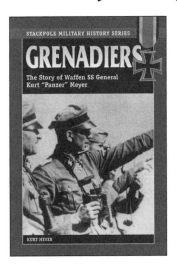

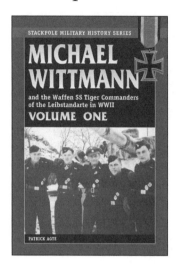 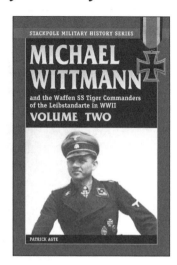

Stackpole Military History Series

THE BRANDENBURGER COMMANDOS

GERMANY'S ELITE WARRIOR SPIES IN WORLD WAR II

Franz Kurowski

Before the German blitzkrieg stormed across Europe in 1939–40, a group of elite soldiers prepared the way by seizing bridges and other strategic targets ahead of the attack. In the following years, these warrior-spies, known as the Brandenburgers, operated behind enemy lines around the globe, from Russia and Yugoslavia to Egypt, Iraq, and India, often bending the rules of war while completing their daring covert missions.

$19.95 • Paperback • 6 x 9 • 384 pages • 114 b/w photos

Stackpole Military History Series

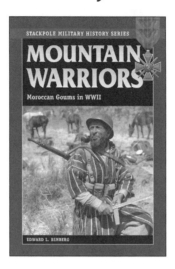

MOUNTAIN WARRIORS
MOROCCAN GOUMS IN WORLD WAR II
Edward L. Bimberg

Labeled "savage Africans" for their untamed ferocity, the Moroccan Goums served as irregular mountain troops for the Allies during World War II. Beginning with the Tunisia campaign in 1942, these tribal warriors frightened their opponents with their traditional garb, long knives, and merciless attacks. An impressed Gen. George Patton requested the Goums' service in Sicily, and they went on to fight in the final battle for Monte Cassino in May 1944 and later liberated Marseille in France. After helping to clear the Colmar Pocket, the Goums breached the Siegfried Line and ended the war in Germany, having secured their reputation as unorthodox but effective soldiers.

$16.95 • Paperback • 6 x 9 • 224 pages • 6 b/w photos

WWW.STACKPOLEBOOKS.COM
1-800-732-3669

Stackpole Military History Series

INFANTRY ACES
THE GERMAN SOLDIER IN COMBAT IN WORLD WAR II
Franz Kurowski

This is an authentic account of German infantry
aces—one paratrooper, two members of the Waffen-SS,
and five Wehrmacht soldiers—who were thrust into
the maelstrom of death and destruction that was World
War II. Enduring countless horrors on the icy Eastern
Front, in the deserts of Africa, and on other bloody
fields, these rank-and-file soldiers took on enemy
units alone, battled giant tanks, stormed hills,
and rescued wounded comrades.

$19.95 • Paperback • 6 x 9 • 512 pages
43 b/w photos, 11 maps

Stackpole Military History Series

BEYOND THE BEACHHEAD
THE 29TH INFANTRY DIVISION IN NORMANDY
Joseph Balkoski

Previously untested in battle, the American 29th
Infantry Division stormed Omaha Beach on D-Day and
began a summer of bloody combat in the hedgerows
of Normandy. Against a tenacious German foe, the
division fought fiercely for every inch of ground and,
at great cost, liberated the town of St. Lô. This new
and expanded edition of Joseph Balkoski's classic
follows the 29th through the final stages of the
campaign and the brutal struggle for the town of Vire.

$19.95 • Paperback • 6 x 9 • 352 pages
36 b/w photos, 30 maps

Stackpole Military History Series

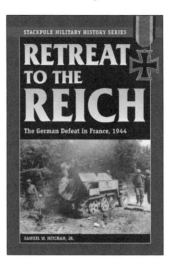

RETREAT TO THE REICH
THE GERMAN DEFEAT IN FRANCE, 1944
Samuel W. Mitcham, Jr.

The Allied landings on D-Day, June 6, 1944, marked the beginning of the German defeat in the West in World War II. From the experiences of soldiers in the field to decision-making at high command, military historian Samuel Mitcham vividly recaptures the desperation of the Wehrmacht as it collapsed amidst the brutal hedgerow fighting in Normandy, losing its four-year grip on France as it was forced to retreat back to the German border. While German forces managed to temporarily halt the Allied juggernaut there, this brief success only delayed the fate that had been sealed with the defeat in France.

$17.95 • Paperback • 6 x 9 • 304 pages • 26 photos, 12 maps

WWW.STACKPOLEBOOKS.COM
1-800-732-3669

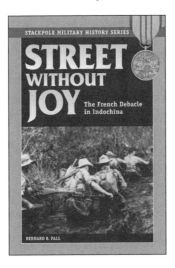

Stackpole Military History Series

PACKS ON!
MEMOIRS OF THE 10TH MOUNTAIN DIVISION
IN WORLD WAR II

A. B. Feuer

Foreword by Bob Dole

From February to May 1945, the 10th Mountain
Division battled the veteran German troops of Albert
Kesselring in the Alpine mountains, valleys, and rivers
of northern Italy. The boys of the 10th fought, skied,
and climbed their way to victory—and into history as
one of the most legendary units of all time.

$14.95 • Paperback • 6 x 9 • 176 pages
33 b/w photos, 10 maps

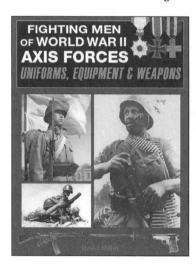
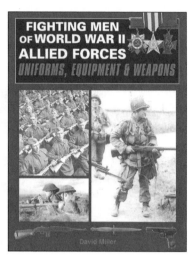